Memoir of a

SWISS
CHEF

Memoir of a
SWISS
CHEF

*and how he got to Grass Valley
to open his own restaurant*

KARL RESCH

Karl and Lily standing in the Empire House dining room.

Karl and Lily are dedicating the Swiss House memoir to all of our loyal and dedicated customer and friends we had the pleasure to serve over 30 years. Our concept was fine international cuisine and was based on the old classical concept which gave us the difference between our competitors. A lot of our guests came to celebrate special occasion. We had white table cloth napkins, candle lights for a classical set up. As a chef and owner I was doing all the cooking to order and the meat was cut also to order so that quality and consistency was maintained. Our guests were always aware of our high quality and consistency. Lily made sure the dining room and bar had the best attention to have a good dining experience. We ware successful over 30 years and still today I meet customer at the supermarket saying that they miss the Swiss House restaurant. My memoir is also an inspiration for many young upcoming culinary talent and it will give them an inside of what it will take to be successful in the food business.

In appreciation for over 30 year support I thank you.

Karl Resch,
Retired chef de cuisine.

CONTENTS

Chapter 1   The Way It All Began   1

Chapter 2   When I Was Fifteen   20

Chapter 3   Lets Get Serious   32

Chapter 4   Keep In Touch With Mr. Huber   41

Chapter 5   Testing Your Will   52

Chapter 6   Changing Tradition & Moving To Hong Kong   60

Chapter 7   The Haole In Hawaii   71

Chapter 8   Don't Be Afraid To Wash Dishes   75

Chapter 9   My Urge To Travel   83

Chapter 10   Learning And Then Practice   92

Chapter 11   Working In Hong Kong   141

Chapter 12   Twice Around The Globe   173

Chapter 13   The Brass Bell Story   198

Chapter 14   Lily's One Hundred Percent Support   216

Chapter 15   Reminiscing Over My Career   227

Chapter 16   Cooking Demonstration   274

Chapter 17   Homemade Sausages   323

Recipe Index   331

IMAGES

Karl and Lily standing in the Empire House dining room   v

Chef's portrait   x

Swiss House restaurant front view   39

Ham display for the food show in Washington D.C.   51

Ham display for the food show in Boston Rose truffle drawing   51

Seafood display for the food show in DC   51

Seahorse sculpture for buffet display   51

Finishing details on my show piece before it was sent to Frankfurt, Germany   55

Promotion for the Ilikai hotel on Oahu   59

Ice carving demo at the Hyatt Regency in Dearborn Michigan   62

The go away Lion sculpture at the Royal Lahaina in Maui   67

Food display arrangement for the Sheraton Waikiki hotel promotion   69

My first tallow sculpture at the London Hilton   70

Showpiece for the Chaine des rotisseure Goument dinner   73

Chaine des Rotisseure dinner display   74

My very first hotel promotion at the Ilikai in 1967   74

Tallow eagle sculpture food show, Washington Hilton DC   82

Flying horse sculpture London Hilton   140

Truffle drawing on ham for buffet display Caribe Hilton Puerto Rico   215

Cold roasted turkey display at the Hong Kong Plaza Hotel   273

Cold ham display Sunday brunch, Plaza Hotel Hong Kong   273

Ham buffet display, Sheraton Boston Hotel   322

My last day in the kitchen at the Swiss house   330

The reason I wrote my memoirs was to share the experiences I created during a lifetime and my strong desire to get into the culinary field. When I was a youngster growing up in Switzerland, it was a prestige to be a chef de cuisine and a pastry chef. To build a career, I moved from place to place across Switzerland, working in the best hotels and with top-notch chefs. I then worked in many foreign countries and many places in the United States, including London; Puerto Rico; Rochester, New York; Washington, DC; New Orleans; Boston; Hawaii; Hong Kong; Canada; and finally ended up in Grass Valley, California.

Chef's portrait.

CHAPTER 1

THE WAY IT ALL BEGAN

I grew up in a small town called Mannedorf in Switzerland, near Zurich. I was born in 1939 just before the Second World War broke out.

We were three kids: Alvin was born in 1938, Karl in 1939, and Fritz the youngest one in 1941. I was born two months premature and as a twin, but my brother Kurt passed away at birth. I also was in an incubator and on life support for seven weeks.

Martial law was implemented during the war, and things were rationed. Food stamps were issued for such things as coffee, chocolate, and all kinds of luxury items. You were able to get those items only once a month, and rations were based on the number people in the family.

Lawns were turned into gardens, and everybody had a little garden to grow their own food, which was also used to barter with your neighbor. Life was simple as everybody tried to survive. Some had vegetables, and others had fruits or even meat from pigs, cattle, and chickens.

I remember my father had purchased a farmhouse that had a barn and a large parcel of land. He became a real farmer besides running his plumbing, heating, and sheet metal business.

During that time, he also raised chicken, rabbits, pigs, and even cows. He hired a farmhand named Jost, who came from Germany. Jost took care of all the animals. He milked the cows, made sure he fed them, provided them water, and walked them every day so that they did not become unruly.

Jost lived with us. He was always teasing my little brother, Fritz, when he did not finish his hash browns for breakfast.

During the war, the local butcher made house calls. Usually in October, he would come by to butcher a pig. Sausages were made, even salami and blood sausages. A lot of meat was preserved, and the bacon was smoked. Every item from the pig was utilized. The back fat was rendered, the pork fat was then used for cooking, and the remaining items from the back-fat rendering were turned into crispy kernels, which were fed to the birds in the winter months.

We made our own cider from the apples grown on the farm, and we as kids helped pick up the fallen apples. This was usually late in the fall, mid-October to early November. At that time of year, early in the morning the grass was still wet and had dew on it, and it was chilly! Every now and then you needed to warm up your hands so that you could handle the apples.

Father had his own press, and he made the cider in the barn and then stored it in the cellar of the farmhouse. He kept the cider in a large wooden barrel that had a spigot on it for easy pouring.

There were all kinds of food kept in the cellar because it was cold there. Some of it was dug into sand in wooden crates. There were carrots, root celery, and potatoes. The cabbages were wrapped in newspaper to keep them fresh. The roots were still intact, and they were wrapped and stuck upside down in the sand. It was easy to find the cabbages this way. Fruits such as apples and pears were laid out on wooden racks and closely watched to minimize waste and keep an eye on the ripening process.

Mother made her own sauerkraut, and she pickled pork shanks, pig ears, and many other pork parts that you could serve with the sauerkraut later. She also made her own jelly, preserves, and raspberry syrup. The dried fruits were kept in the attic in cloth bags. This went on till the war was over in 1945.

In 1947 we had a bad drought. Water was scarce, but the barn had its own well with a fountain, and the amount of water coming out of the tap was just like a spring but nice and cold.

The government commandeered automobiles from private owners during the war and used them for military transportation. Gasoline was hard to come by during this time. I remember the garbage truck ran on a steam engine, which used steam from a wood fire to make it run.

Only emergency vehicles could use gas. Streetlights had to be dimmed with a blue light bulb so that it was hard to detect. This was for security purposes, and the borders were tightly guarded. The Swiss Army had a general named Henry Guisant and was on high alert.

The kitchen in the farmhouse was heated with wood, and the cooking was done on top of the farm-style stove. To use smaller pots, you had some sort of iron rings you could adjust to make the smaller pots fit. It was messy! After cooking, all the pots turned black from the wood fire.

The way the whole heating system was set up, we had a large Dutch tile oven that was fired by wood. This also heated the living room. There was a passage where the food was passed through from the kitchen into the living room and kept warm. To keep ourselves warm during the winter, we sat on a bench that was built into the right side of the tile oven.

At the beginning we had no central heating, and in the winter at times we had ice flowers on the windows because it was so cold. We kept our feet warm in bed on pillowcases filled with cherry stones. The stones were kept after Mother made jam out of the meaty part of the fruits. The stones then were washed, dried, and kept in small pillowcases. In the same space where the food was kept warm and when dinner was over, then the so-called Stein sack took their place.

There was a large orchard around the farmhouse with all kinds of fruit trees, including apple, pear, plum, prune, cherry, and apricot. In the garden, lots of vegetables were planted, such as carrots, celery, potatoes, cabbage, and tomatoes. There were a lot of berries, too, including strawberries, raspberries, gooseberries, and blackberries.

The grass was cut during the summer using a scythe. There was no mechanical mower. The grass was easier to cut while it was still wet. For the steel blade of the scythe to retain its sharp edge, Father had a sharpening stone. Early in the morning before the grass was cut, you could hear him sharpening the scythe with a hammer over a specially formed piece of steel mounted on top of a sandstone, on which he sat to do the sharpening. This exercise was called *tangela*, and the sound of it surely woke you up. Some of the grass was fed to the animals, and the rest turned into hay and then stored in the barn for the winter.

Once a week, usually on Saturday evenings, it was bathing time for the kids. Mother heated water in a large copper kettle with a wood fire in the wash kitchen located in the basement of the farmhouse. Then she poured the boiling-hot water into a freestanding steel bathtub and added some cold water to lower the temperature.

Since we all were small, the three of us fit right into the tub. Then came the trauma when one of us would get soap in his eyes.

We were all soaped up, then rinsed and wrapped in a warm towel. Then off we went upstairs to the warm living room for supper and then went upstairs to bed. There were two bedrooms (*Schlafzimmer*) for us boys. The two younger ones slept in the bigger room, and our older brother had his own room. We had wooden shutters and single glass windows.

We all had separate beds. The bed frames were made of wood

and had headboards. The mattresses were filled with horsehair. The sheets were made of linen. The pillows were stuffed with chicken feathers and covered with a pillowcase. The comforters were made the same way as the pillows but was large enough to cover the whole bed, and it kept us nice and warm.

At the beginning, we had no heating, and sometimes Mother placed a space heater in the bedroom to take the chill out of it. The heaters were about a foot and a half in diameter, like a large pizza.

The house had electricity but no hot water except in the bathroom, which had a gas heater mounted to the wall. Every time you wanted hot water, you had to light it. For the rest of the house, you constantly had to heat water on the wooden stove.

The laundry was done by hand on a washboard. There was a large sink divided into two compartments in the wash kitchen so that the laundry could be thoroughly rinsed before it was hung outside on a clothesline to dry. When it was cold in the winter, the bedsheets sometimes became frozen on the line. Mother heated the water for the laundry in the same fashion as for us to take a bath.

On that day we usually had a large cheese and apple tart (called *waja*) and coffee for lunch, which was ordered from the bakeshop. Mother made all the ingredients except the dough and then sent to the bakeshop. The bakery laid out the pans with dough and then used the proper type of filling to complete the tarts.

My mother had her hands full with all three of us, and besides that she did the cooking, worked in the garden, and helped Father in his office.

A lot of our clothes were handmade. Mother knit sweaters for us. They were all the same color, but she put a monogram on each one so we could tell which one was for each one of us. Socks and hats were a neutral color. She was really talented and got her training from her own mother.

At that time, cell phones, computers, and even televisions were not yet invented. We had a radio, and there was a daily newspaper called the *Zürichsee-Zeitung*. Purchases were made in cash in those days, because there were no credit cards.

We as kids occupied ourselves with simple things, like building tree houses, playing soccer, flying kites, making soapbox cars and paper planes, fishing on Lake Zurich, and riding bikes we constructed from parts found in people's attics and from mechanics who were fixing bikes.

We all had shoes with wooden soles. At that time, it was the in thing. Toys we had were also made out of wood—small trains, hand-carved farm-related animals like cows and horses, and things of that nature. Quite often we used our neighbor's toys to satisfy our shortcomings.

Gifts for Christmas usually were of a practical nature, sometimes ski boots, jackets, or things we had outgrown that needed to be replaced. The Christmas tree was decorated with real wax candles, apples, and some chocolate ornaments.

We became able to occupy our spare time by learning to work with our hands. After the war was over and father got his car back, a lot of improvements were made. Out with the wood stove—a gas oven was installed, and central heating came to be.

Father's car was a Mercedes. On Sundays when Father was done washing the car and Sunday school was out, we were then treated to a ride around Lake Zurich. At times we stopped at a restaurant for pastries and hot cocoa. Among the three kids we fought over a window seat. Most of the time it was senseless. On some occasions one of us would get carsick.

As a youngster I often hung out on Lake Zurich, watching people fishing and dreaming one day of having my own fishing pole, but money was hard to come by. We had a retired architect named Mr. Hausamann living across the street. He had bamboo growing in his backyard. I decided to ask him for a nice stick so that I could make myself a fishing pole.

I made primitive hooks out of wire and then attached them with electrical tape where the line would run through. I hammered two small nails at the thick end so that I could wind the fishing line around it to prevent the line from tangling up.

For a floater, I used a cork from a wine bottle. The sinker was a metal bolt I found in Father's workshop, and I got a small hook from a local utility store. At that time, I was already quite determined, and if I set my mind on something, I would complete it regardless of the circumstances.

A few months later there was a fishing derby for kids in town, and I decided to enter it. I caught 120 small fishes called *leugel* in about two and a half hours. I remember that I was using small maggots for bait. With my primitive gear, I won second prize—a nice fishing pole. The fishes I gave away to an Italian family living next door, because I once was forced to eat fish and the small bones made me gag, and ever since then I became leery of eating fish.

For a new way to catch small fish, my friends and I took clear white glass bottles and a tight cork, then we got some carbite from my father's workshop. Carbite is a stone that will produce gas when it is put into water. We cut the carbite into small pieces so that it would fit into the neck of a bottle. We added some water to the bottle, resealed it with the cork, placed it in the middle of a small swarm of fish, and waited till the bottle exploded. This way we had an easy catch.

It did not last too long, because we were apprehended. We knew it was illegal, and that was the end of it.

It was funny among the guys. If one did not find a crazy thing to do, another one surely did. I guess boys are boys, and it is part of growing up. We never had a dull moment.

We all had chores to do after school, and as soon as we came home, we changed into overalls. First Mother gave us apples and a sliced farmer-style bread, and every now and then apples were substituted with a piece of Swiss chocolate. Then we did our home-work, and after homework we got our assignment for our chores. Often it was in father's workshop, cleaning rusty steel pipes. Or we would pick weeds in the garden or sweep around the house.

I remember every Wednesday during school we had only a half day of school and the afternoon was free. Usually, a bunch of my classmates came by to play soccer, but sure enough my old man always found something for me to do before I could play. One day he told me to dig up a large parcel in the garden, and when I looked at it, I knew that it would take the whole afternoon to complete it.

Maybe he wanted to punish me for something—who knows? The doorbell was ringing and five of my schoolmates were asking me if I was ready to go play. I told them what my dilemma was and that I first had to finish my job. I was the only one who had a soccer ball—my godfather had given me the ball for Christmas. And my friends depended on me to play soccer.

They asked me how many shovels and spades I had. I checked in the barn and found just enough for all of them to help me. It took us about three-quarters of an hour, and off we went. Once again, I found a way to get thing done just, like Houdini.

The town where I grew up near Lake Zurich was called Manne-dorf, which had a population of eight thousand people. The schoolhouses were located in the middle of the town and were laid out around a large playground with a gym for indoor games and gymnastics. The arrangement for the school was first kinder-garten, which took one year, then elementary school, which was first through third grade and took three years or six semesters. Then there were three years of primary school and three years of secondary school.

Each grade had its own separate curriculum and a different teacher. The classes had girls and boys combined, and each class had twenty-five students and one teacher. The subjects were reading, writing, arithmetic, language, art, and gymnastics. The girls had their own female instructor for gymnastics.

We wrote on a tablet made out of some sort of thin black stone. It looked like a small blackboard with a wooden frame. We used chalk to write on it, and the eraser was a small sponge.

A lot of information was written by the teachers on a blackboard, and we had composition books. There were textbooks for math and the other subjects. The books were handed out by the school, and by the time you completed third grade, they were returned to the teacher.

As you moved on to fourth to sixth grade, you had three different grades in the same classroom and about twenty-five students. New teachers came in, and the basic curriculum became more sophisticated. New subjects were added—math had fractions, and all the subjects were geared toward higher learning. My new primary teacher in fourth to sixth grades was Mr. Godfried Brugger.

The distance from home to school was about three-quarters of a mile, and we walked it four times a day, four and a half times a week. On Wednesdays it was only two times a day because we had half a day of school. In the winter we often had up to three feet of snow, and many times we went to school on skis.

During the winter months, there was a hot milk service provided by the school until the third grade. It was consumed during the long break and was paid for by the children's parents. I was a really skinny kid in elementary school.

The first teacher I had was a woman named Miss Gwalter. This was in first to third grade, and I was a thorn in her eyes. She did despise me. Often when she thought I was not properly behaving, she pulled me by my ears and told me to stand in a corner facing the wall for an hour. That punishment did not work too well, because it just irritated me even more.

My mother realized that my ears were starting to look really out of place because of the constant pulling by my teacher. I told her what was happening, and she went to see the teacher and told her to cut it out.

Yes, I was not always on my best behavior as a kid in class, and I guess the chemistry between me and my teachers was lacking. The substitute teacher was also a woman, Mrs. Kneuenbueler. She filled in when my regular teacher was attending a seminar for a week or so.

Sometimes she tried to discipline me with a brand-new ruler that had sharp edges. Mrs. Kneuenbueler hit me over my hands with the ruler, which broke my skin badly. A secondary class student from another class told me to aggravate the cuts by pouring salt over them. So I put salt over my hands, and my torn skin became irritated and the wounds started to get really swollen.

When I returned to school after my lunch break, I showed my hands to her. She was scared, and from that time on, hitting for me was out. I surely did fix her kettle.

During that time, in the second grade, we had a student in class named Philip Eckert. His uncle was Dr. Albert Schweitzer, and he visited our class. My stepmother, Hedwig Meier (her maiden name), told us that at one time she worked for Dr. Schweitzer in Lambaréné, Africa.

In grades 4 to 6, instruction between the different grades was rotated based on the grade you were in, and certain subjects were combined. These included geography, music, handwriting, science, and even botanical field trips to the forest to identify trees and plants. Throughout your time in school, your curriculums were in all subjects, including math, chemistry, bookkeeping, language, geometry, and gymnastic.

Art classes had many different subjects. We did a lot of drawing and painting of scenery and flower bouquets, using pastels and watercolors. We also worked with clay. We made animal figurines out of clay, which were then sent to be treated with heat in a special oven. In art class we also learned how to sing.

We also had a contest for building hot air balloons, which we were able to let fly. Unfortunately, if there was just a little bit of wind, you could say goodbye to your balloon; sorry, it went up in flames!

In art class we also made fancy Christmas decorations out of colored foil. It was educational and very rewarding. Most of the knowledge we gained would last a lifetime.

My teacher Mr. Brugger was a person who was great at dealing with boys. Yes, we had some fights among each other, and he knew how to deal with them effectively.

I remember at one time I stole a small cigar from my father's office desk and took it to school. On that day, we had a field trip. During the trip to the forest, I decide to light up the small cigar. The teacher became aware of it, so I quickly threw the cigar away.

After the class was dismissed, I went home. The next day school started at 7:00 a.m., and after the entire student body was seated, Mr. Brugger called out my name and told me to come in front of the class. He opened his desk drawer, took out a big black cigar, gave me matches, and told me to smoke it. He thought that I would throw up, so halfway through he told me to stop. I surely got the message.

Mr. Brugger also had the school supply store for three more schools, and he put me in charge of filling the needed requests. When he had to go find something in the back room and could not find it, he called on me. I was also in charge of putting newly arrived material away, such as books, pencils, erasers, and chalk. Mr. Brugger also disciplined the unruly students in the back room, and it was sometimes over his knee.

I remember very well when my mother passed away in 1949 at the age of forty-one. She had diverticulitis, and during an operation, a blood clot went into her lung and took her life. I was ten years old. Mr. Brugger gave me enormous support so that I could cope with my situation.

In the fourth grade, Mr. Brugger organized a bike tour of eight chosen kids to tour the French part of Switzerland. We stayed in tents, mostly on private property where the teacher got permission to do so. We did the cooking over open fire like the Boy Scouts. The trip built a special bond among all of us.

On several occasions we had other teachers to teach different subjects, even chemistry and religion. One time I had to write the word *geography* on the blackboard, and I misspelled it three times. As a punishment I was told to write it one hundred times as part of my homework.

In the last three years of school, you moved on. Foreign languages such as French and English were taught. Woodworking and sheet metal work were also taught, but these were your choice and were not obligatory. I chose woodwork. The last piece of woodwork I made was a six-foot wooden stepladder. The class gave you a good idea what a trade would look like.

By that time, at the age of sixteen, most of the students had already chosen their careers. Some went on to higher education or trade school. I chose trade school.

During the winter of 1956, Lake Zurich was completely frozen over and you could walk across it in about an hour. Sometimes you could see a small car going across. We played ice hockey right after school was out in the afternoon. The skates we had needed to be mounted on your boots and then secured in place with a special key. Sometimes when you tightened it too hard, the whole heel of the shoe came off, and you could not skate on one foot. During that winter, I found a pair of skates. They were like hockey skates and were in one piece.

My buddies while I was going to school came from all kinds of backgrounds. Some of their parents were bankers, doctors, lawyers, farmers, teachers, and tradespeople. We all got along fairly well and stuck together based on our mutual interest in playing soccer or fishing.

I remember one of my closest friends was named Hans Detomas. On the way home from school, there was one boy who always picked on me. His name was Huldy Meier, and sometimes he dragged me to the ground. When Hans had had enough, he kicked out one of Huldy's front teeth. That was the last time I was ever bullied by Huldy. Hans became one of my best buddies. Unfortunately, his life ended when he was seventeen. He was heartbroken over a girl, and he took his own life.

The teachers paid close attention to each student, and there was no time for pranks. At that time no calculators or ballpoint pens were allowed—we wrote with pencils or feather pens.

A lot of physical exercise was stressed, and there were even trips to the forest to keep you healthy. Also, many trade-related subjects based on individual interests were taught.

Growing up at that time, we had no big shopping centers. Instead, there were many mom-and-pop stores, but in order to do your shopping, you had to visit several places to get everything on your list. This meant for your meat you went to the butcher shop, for bread to the bakery, for milk and cheese to the dairy store, and so on. Large shopping malls did not come to be until much later, when the economy started to pick up. I was the middle child in the family, and Mother sent me to pick up the things we needed for the day. She ordered these in advance.

Being the middle one in the family, I surely received the most punishments, because the older one could not have done the misdeed, and the little one was too young. So take a guess who did it. Sometimes I was sent to bed without food or did not get any attention and was completely neglected, as if I did not even exist, like a cold war. If you would say for an excuse that one of the other brothers did it, to my father that was an absolute no-no. You took the punishment regardless of who did it.

One time—it was December 6, 1948, on Saint Nicholas

Day—I was locked up in the cellar for several hours. It was pitch black. To this day I still have no idea what I was being punished for.

I went through many changes along the way, and as I got older, I was able to defend myself. I guarded my things of value that were given to me by my Godmother. I hid them from my older brother so he could not use them to show off.

Mother told me one time that I was the only one who kept my belongings very clean. This included shoes, sweaters, pants, and jackets.

I started helping out in the kitchen at an early age, washing dishes and doing little things just to help. I was fascinated with how food was put together. I just had a feeling for such a trade. While she was alive, my mother, Margret Sennhauser (her maiden name), even taught me how to bake a pound cake and make some simple dishes like nice crispy *rösti*, a sort of Swiss hash brown potatoes with bacon and onion.

Mother was the oldest of five kids and had a brother named Arnold. Their parents had a small restaurant called the Buch in Herrliberg, near Zurich. The restaurant was located in the middle of a vineyard overlooking Lake Zurich and was surrounded by mountains and a large forest.

My father at one time wanted to buy the restaurant, but it never materialized. Before my father passed away, he gave me a drawing of the Restaurant Buch made with just a pencil by my grandpa. I had it framed, and I will cherish it always. Now it is hanging in my office. Grandpa was a real artist.

The food concept they had at the restaurant was a lot of seafood caught in Lake Zurich, rösti Swiss (hash browns with a veal dish typical of the region), bratwurst, and many typical Swiss dishes, such as *Chas schnite*, which is cheese toast with ham and Swiss cheese sprinkled with some white wine and then baked in the oven and topped with a couple of fried eggs. They also served pork chops,

Wiener schnitzel, and wurst salad, which is made with knockwurst.

My mother attended an apprenticeship program to become a professional chef in Zurich at a restaurant called Fischerzumpft. It specialized in seafood. Later on, she worked at her parents' restaurant until she got married.

She was an excellent chef, and even though at the time it was difficult to get the proper ingredients, especially during the war, she had the know-how to come up with the proper substitutions. She had a handwritten cookbook where she kept all her secret recipes, such as black currant schnapps, and even how to cure meats. I tried to locate her cookbook, but I think one of our hired housekeepers got her hands on it before I could.

Eggs were scarce, and sometimes when you bought a cake or anything made with eggs, you only found some pieces of eggshells in it. Yellow coloring was used to make it look like there were eggs in it.

For special occasions, Mother showed off with special dishes such as *hasenpfeffer* (rabbit stew), osso buco (braised veal shanks), and *rahmschnitze*l (veal tenderloin medallions topped with mushroom brandy cream sauce). For our Easter feast, we always had her prepare a small roasted lamb.

I remember way back, I spent some time at her parents' restaurant. I was about four or five years old. I was away from home to take some load off of Mother. My two other brothers could not go away from home because they became homesick.

My grandparents had a Saint Bernard dog named Frisch. He was a jolly, overweight, happy dog. He hung around the restaurant looking for goodies. He was very friendly, and sometimes when I was sitting in the restaurant, he would come by and sit on my feet till I had no feeling left because my feet went to sleep. Frisch had his own routine. But he never missed his food, and since he was raised on restaurant food, his belly was nice and round. His was very gentle and never showed a mean streak.

I became Grandma's favorite kid. I felt that I was being nourished for the shortcomings of attention I missed at home. I was never homesick and was well taken care of by Grandma. She always slipped me special treats.

One of our neighbors in Mannedorf was a furniture maker who also fixed broken windows. His name was Karl Schaefer. I spent a lot of time at his place to learn how to work with power tools. He also had the pleasure of fixing windows that I broke with tennis balls. If my parents ever had to look for me, I was usually hanging out in his place.

Communities were closely knit. Most of the people knew each other, and respect for each other was never in doubt. Mrs. Fischer, our next-door neighbor, had a small garden she could overlook from her apartment, and she grew strawberries in the garden. One day I felt hungry and decided to use her nice, delicious berries for a meal. I cleared out half of the strawberries and snuck back into the house.

During supper, the doorbell rang. Mrs. Fischer stood there with a bowl of strawberries topped with whipped cream and said to my mother to give it to Karl. There was no other mention of my misdeed.

Mrs. Fischer knew my situation. I was always on the lookout for fruit in the neighborhood. But we were taught from the get-go to be polite.

My father, Alvin Resch Sr., had a small business for installing heating, plumbing for bathrooms and kitchens, and sheet metal work.

We were three kids with all kinds of fantasies about our lives. Usually on Sundays during supper, my dad would ask the three of us what we would like to be to earn a living. We had all kinds of dreams—fireman, police officer, and even farmer. When I was about six years old, I knew already that I wanted to become a professional pastry chef and then also a professional chef. That meant I would need to do two different apprentice programs.

One time my parents went into the city of Zurich to watch a

movie. Mannedorf had only a small theater, and the choices were limited. I then took the chance to make hard caramel. I used all the sugar and cream I could find in the kitchen. The result was quite good, but afterward, when mother went looking for sugar or cream, she was out of luck. She gave me a scolding, but my desire was overwhelming. I surely was determined to practice.

Usually on Saturday afternoons, I picked up an almond paste–filled fish made with puff dough at the bakeshop. It was for Sunday's dessert. I could peek into the bakery, and sometimes the owner, Mr. Meier, gave me a small piece of pastry to taste. It was always a treat.

Bread had to be picked up daily, which I did around 4:00 p.m., after school. The bread was kept in the back hallway on a rack. The baker's wife, who worked in the store, had to go back into the hallway to get it, and it normally took a few seconds.

I was looking at the display cases where all kinds of goodies were facing me.

I could not resist. One day it was raining, and I was wearing a long raincoat that had two deep pockets inside. I decided to slip a large piece of Swiss chocolate inside my pocket. I knew it was shoplifting.

The baker's wife must have seen it and later on reported it to my mother. I surely got a licking. Mother paid for the chocolate, and I had to apologize for stealing it. It was embarrassing.

Usually at home, I was not taken seriously by my father. It took many years for me to overcome this type of downgrade. Nothing I ever did was right. He often said to me you are bluffing or lying. It was upsetting and made me insecure, and at one time I told my father that when I was old enough and could stand on my own two feet, I would leave and never come back. He responded by saying, "*Ja, ja.*"

My older brother, Alvin, followed in my father footsteps. So did my little brother, Fritz. When I was ten years old, in 1949, my mother passed away. I became the chef cook and bottle washer for a while, until my father hired a housekeeper.

My father remarried about two years later, in 1951, and it took some time to get used to our newly adopted stepmother. She was very supportive, and I got along with her great. Then they had two more siblings, Max and Katharina. I felt that Max was the substitute for my passed-on twin brother, Kurt. Max was also the name of Father's brother. He was killed in a motorcycle accident while he was visiting his mothers graveyard over the Easter holiday. Father seldom mentioned his death and kept his feelings to himself. It must have been hard on him.

We had relatives on my fathers side near Luzern. They owned the Hotel Seehof Restaurant and Bar in Gersau, near Lucerne. It is a summer resort place nestled in between the majestic mountains, right on the lake. I wanted to go there as an intern during my summer school vacation and basically just snoop around to see whether what I had in my mind could materialize. So when I was thirteen, my father and stepmother drove me to the place where it all began.

The little experience I had from home served me very well. The experience surely confirmed my interest, and I even made some money by picking up hotel guests at the ship landing. They came by steamboat from all around Lake Lucerne, which is called Vierwaldstättersee in Switzerland. They were on a schedule, and before the ships were about to arrive, you heard the sound of a horn.

The distance from the hotel was about five hundred yards. I met the guests with a cart, and I was wearing some sort of a captain's hat with Hotel Seehof written on it to identify myself. I had to put a folded newspaper inside the hat so that it would not fall over my ears.

I picked up their suitcases and then delivered them to their rooms. When the guests retired for the day, they left their shoes out in front of their quarters. I had to pick their shoes up, polish them, and then return them back outside the correct rooms. This was a common practice in the hotel field at that time, and it is a tradition in Switzerland.

They also had a garden restaurant across the street right on the lake with a cake shop. I stocked all kinds of bottled beverages there, including beer and Coke. I also replaced the tablecloths on the glass-top tables and straightened out the pebble stones. Sometimes I found coins in the pebbles.

Then I helped in the kitchen, doing things like chopping parsley and cooking French fries. I helped out in the pastry shop, too, glazing pastries with apricot glaze and placing the pastries into paper cups. They were then sold in the cake shop. I also cleaned up after the pastry chef. Eating habits in the kitchen were very inconsistent, and you ate whenever you could.

The owner was the chef, and she had a couple of Italian helpers to assist her. She also had several helpers to clean the rooms and take care of the hotel guests.

CHAPTER 2

WHEN I WAS FIFTEEN

I was rooming with the pastry chef, and he liked his booze. One time he did not show for work the next day, and I had to go to the next town, Brunnen, to pick up pastries from another bakeshop to fill the need for that day. The round trip took about an hour and a half by bicycle, and the street was accented with heavy traffic.

On Sundays Mrs. Kamanzint, the owner of the Hotel Seehof, sent me to church. But instead, I went fishing on the lake with a stick of wood. I wound a short fishing line around the stick and added a hook, a sinker, and a floater. The whole thing was some kind of a gadget. When the church bells began ringing, I knew the service was over, and I returned to the restaurant. Mrs. Kamanzint asked me what the pastor was preaching. I just told her a story I remembered from Sunday school. She believed me.

Her husband, Dagobert, ran the dining room as a waiter and bartender. He had a couple of waitresses under his supervision. The hotel had seventy-five guest rooms and could seat about one hundred people in the dining room. The hotel was mainly seasonal; in the winter it would get cold, and mostly the locals hung out in the bar.

I also was running some errands, such as paying bills and picking up produce. When the three weeks were over, my parents came to pick me up. They wanted to know how everything went, and my answer was positive.

I made good tips and was proud of it. For the first time, I had pocket money and did not have to get it the dishonest way. My little experience during the summer did assure my future dream.

When I was fifteen, the time came and my father found a place for me to start my apprentice program as a *konditor* (pastry cook) in Winterthur, near Zurich.

My father sold a piece of his own land to the father of my future boss, where he built his retirement home. While my father installed the heating in the house, he found out that the man's son took over his business, the Konditorei Rusch, in Winterthur. It was a so-called konditorei tearoom that served pastries, cakes, tea, coffee, ice cream, small hot dishes like patty shells filled with a fine ragout of veal and mushrooms in a cream sauce, and different styles of omelets. That was the way my apprenticeship came about.

This type of apprenticeship is a nationally controlled program by the government in Switzerland. You are required to sign a three-year contract, and the place has to have a master pastry chef in order to teach an apprentice the trade. The program is very detailed, with high standards, and teaches every aspect of the trade. It will qualify you, at the end of three years, as a pastry journeyman.

Every apprentice goes through the same program, and there is no deviation. The program sets the standards for pastry chefs in Switzerland. We are talking about to become a certified professional pastry chef, not just some experimental baker. Swiss-trained chefs and pastry chefs are well recognized all over the world and are well thought of.

You are trained also as a chocolatier to make chocolate candies. In order to be of value to the trade, you have to work as an employee in the best place you can find after your apprentice program, until you have the experience and knowledge maybe one day to open your own business. Before doing so, you also have to be certified as a master pastry chef.

Very often the program will take you to different countries and hotels as a pâtissier to become exceptional. You learn to make pulled sugar works, marzipan roses, petit fours, and all kinds of wedding cakes. It is important you choose your notch wisely at the beginning and make sure it is what you really want.

I finished school when I was sixteen and was old enough to enter the program; the minimum age was sixteen. This was in 1956. My father had to pay four hundred Swiss francs (about one hundred dollars) and sign a three-year contract. There was also eight weeks' probation. It was a very strict, no-nonsense, disciplined program. You had to study your trade-related books daily, and a lot of practice went into decorating cakes.

Work started at 7:00 a.m., and we had twenty minutes for *früh-stück* (breakfast), then back to work. At noon we had another break for twenty minutes for lunch, then right back to work. Around 5:00 p.m. the day was usually over, but not for the apprentices. I had to go back and clean up and do whatever else needed to be done. By 7:00 p.m. my day was usually over.

Super was served around 5:00 p.m. six days a week. There was no break after dinner. I started with washing pots, pans, and all other utensils needed in the pastry shop.

I also delivered orders, come rain or shine. I remember one time I had to make a delivery. It was raining very hard, and I had a delivery of bakery-type bar food—pretzels, beer *stengels*, cheese straws, and small hard rolls in a basket. When the front wheel of my bike got caught in a streetcar rail, I lost my balance and fell flat on my face.

I was lucky there was a police officer nearby. He helped me pick up all the goodies. I told him to report it to my boss, and he called with his phone. When I returned to the bakeshop, I was not punished.

It was just an old bike with an advertising plate with "Konditorei Rusch" written on it.

There was no time to become rebellious then as a teenager. Once a week you got a dollar from your boss as a gesture of goodwill.

On your day off, late on Saturday every second week, you could visit your family and could take home a nice tort from the pastry shop. You also had to take home your laundry and soiled uniforms. It took an hour by train for me to arrive in Mannedorf.

There were three apprentices: Rolf, Andres, and myself. One was in the first year, one in the second year, and one in the third. As soon as one entered the last six months of the program, the boss would hire a new apprentice.

We always had three apprentices and had some sort of a challenge between the three of us. No one wanted to be a loser, and we always tried to outdo each other. The boss was very picky, and all the work was closely checked to make sure you would be able to produce professional products and would be confident in every section of the program. We covered each other's back. If one of us were in charge of doing the baking, we would remind each other of what was in the oven so that it would not burn.

Once a week you went to trade school in your white coat. You had to walk about a mile to get there. The school building had multi-trade education in different classes, even beer brewing. It was government run, and my boss was one of the instructors for pastry apprentices. The school taught all the technical aspects and a lot of decorating, and let's say a little bit of artistic skills. You were taught in every facet of the trade and practiced the art of cake decorating. Writing on a cake is very difficult, and only practice will make you confident. Several times a week in your own place of learning, you practiced on a makeshift cake made out of wood, decorating it for all occasions, including wedding, birthdays, Christmas, Mother's Day, and so on.

Frequent tests were given every three months at school to see how you were progressing, especially with decorating. For competitions for special occasions, you had to decorate a cake for a specific holiday, such as Mother's Day or Easter. It was your choice which holiday. The cake had to be eye-catching and have clean colors, and it had to be all natural, nothing artificial. Prizes were given for the best work as an incentive. It was also based on whether you were in the first, second, or third year of your apprenticeship.

The tests also included theoretical questions about the trade, such as how to put recipes together and combine the ingredients in the proper proportion so that you would get the correct results. If the teacher found some shortcomings, you would not pass. For correct answers, you were rewarded with things such as a pastry knife, dough scraper, and small things mainly used in the pastry shop. This was done by the teacher to make sure you understood what you were taught.

Many times in school, none of the apprentices had the proper answer. Since my boss was in charge, as soon as I entered the konditorei, I got an earful telling me that he was embarrassed and I should have the answer regardless of the subject.

Usually on Saturdays, the pastry shop was closed at 2:00 p.m. and needed to be completely scrubbed down. The floor was a mess from all the flour and sugar dust and had to be washed thoroughly.

There was also a curfew. You were not allowed to go out of the house after 9:00 p.m. until you were in the last year of learning. If you wanted to go to a late movie, you had to ask for permission, which was rarely granted.

There was a new ice rink in Winterthur. During my second year as an apprentice, I signed up to play junior ice hockey during the winter months. You had to bring your own gear and had to be there by 7:30 p.m. The transportation was by bus, which ran every hour on the hour.

One time I missed the bus. I knew that if I was late, I would miss out on the practice. I was thinking, how would I get there? The next bus didn't run for another hour. Then I then saw a bike leaning against a building near the bus station. I got on it and off I went. And after the practice, I returned the bike.

As the off season came, Mr. Rusch gave me an ultimatum. I either had to concentrate on my job or play ice hockey. And that was the end of that story.

Mr. Rusch had a son named Arnold who was about my age. He liked to play soccer in the bakeshop when it rained. One day he asked me to join him, and the soccer ball slammed into the long-handled pizza peel. The peel split, but it was not really noticeable till next day, when we had to place the hard rolls on it to bake. We slid the rolls into the oven, but all of them got stuck together. In other words, the peel was useless Mr. Rusch could not just blame me, because his son was the instigator. The boss had a spare peel, thank God.

Sometimes we had late orders on Saturdays, and while we were doing the cleaning, we sometimes also had to bake things such as almond fish made with sweet dough. We did not really concentrate on the baking, so sometimes the item burned up and could not be sold. It happened on one occasion that we burned it up three times, and the boss got really ticked off.

There were also three qualified professional pastry chefs at the konditorei. Their hours were from 7:00 a.m. to 3:00 p.m., and most of the time you worked under one of them. They gave you a lot of instructions and showed you exactly what the items you were working on should look like. They also shared and some tricks of the trade. When you were introduced to a new recipe and wanted to be sure you got the proper yield (amount) of pieces that were called for, you just added a handful of each ingredient. This way you would not be short in servings. In other words, cheating.

One pastry chef came from Vienna. His name was Felix

Finkenzeller. His work was always outstanding. When he left the place, he gave me some of his professional tools.

We apprentices teased each other a lot, but it was constructive. It helped the morale in the tightly wound environment. We were teenagers, and it was almost like boot camp.

The first six months, you learned how to make French pastries. Europe is well known for fine small pastries called pâtisserie, and there is an enormous variety of them, such as Linzer *schnitten* (Linzer torte), Japanese, Sappho, meringues, Napoleon, and many more. You do not see that too often in the United States except in fancy restaurant or hotels. There is quite an extensive variety, and they have to be made by hand—no mass production—to high standards. They must have a clean presentation and be very consistent in size. Every piece of French pastry weighed about an ounce and a half, and the price of a single piece of pastry was twenty-five cents in 1956. Some were made with butter cream, some with pastry cream, and others with jelly.

In order to prevent the apprentices from picking at any kind of pastries during work, on the first day of learning to make pastries, the boss gave you an assortment of ten freshly made pastries to eat so that you were healed of future temptation. After you became somewhat familiar with making the standard pastries, you were told to create one of your own idea. There were several pastry shops nearby, and quite often I went to see what our competition was doing. That gave me some ideas for my own creation. A professional pastry cook had to turn out 350 pieces of pastries a day in order to earn his pay.

The program changed every six months till the whole cycle was complete. One section was dedicated strictly to learning how to bake all kind of things and how to be very consistent. This included croissants, small breads, sponge cakes, and Danish.

There was a large double-decker electrical Speicher oven that stored the heat overnight. You first had to bake the items that needed the most heat, such as small breads, croissants, Danish, and hard rolls. Then as the heat got weaker, you attended to items that would need less heat and would otherwise burn up—for example, *Gugelhopf* (sponge cake). You also learned how to use a wooden peel with a very long handle, and often you needed to lift one pan over another to rotate the space in the oven because at times you had more than one item in the oven and needed less time to bake things such as hard rolls and Danish—and remember, you were dealing with a large, hot oven.

You were responsible for all the items that you baked, and in between you assisted your supervisor in whatever he was doing. You had to make sure you did not burn anything. Most everything was ordered in advance and was accounted for. If you burned anything, sometimes you had to pay for it, and came out of the 400 Swiss francs you had to pay at the beginning of your program. I never had to pay for burned items, as it seldom happened.

You were instructed in the fundamental things before you could assemble products. One section was working with chocolate. You had to learn how to properly temper the chocolate. If it was too warm, it would not settle and then it would turn gray. To make fancy pralines, you poured tempered chocolate into molds to produce an Easter bunny for the Easter holiday or Santa Claus for Christmas. Swiss chocolate is world famous.

Later on, you had to work on hard candies, sugar candies, and caramels. Then came all the different dough: puff dough, yeast dough, sugar dough, pâte brisée, and egg bread. Everything was handmade, including Christmas stollen and gingerbread dough. It was quite complex. You were taught how to work with all kinds of small breads, like French bread, hard rolls, and croissants.

On slow days you had the pleasure of peeling fifty pounds of almonds. This way the boss could save the extra cost of buying the almonds already peeled. And for making marzipan, you needed the almonds soft—in other words, right after they were peeled and washed.

The apprentices were utilized to the max during the learning process. Sometimes you learned a new item that the program called for, and all of a sudden it would not turn out right. It can be very frustrating when this happens. It takes a lot of practice, and you need to concentrate, especially putting a new recipe together, to make sure you are paying attention to what you are doing. Only that will tell you where you went wrong. And since there is a timetable for everything to pass your final exam, it was important while you practiced to always challenge yourself on time wisely.

If you miss a particular item in your recipe, everything goes haywire. I remember one time I missed the yeast in the hard roll dough because I wanted to reduce the time it took to make it, so it was a disaster. The last six months of the three years, you rehearsed everything you learned during that time and started to get ready for your own final exam. You fine-tuned everything you learned to pass the exam. The exam was based on all the requirements by the government and was standardized. A complete outline of what you would be tested on, called a *Bachzetel*, was handed to you the morning of the testing.

You started your test at 7:00 a.m. The first thing was tempering, or warming your chocolate with a double boiler water bath. You cannot work with a hard block of chocolate. It had to be kept somewhat soft so that when the time came you were able to do your chocolate work.

Next you had to get your yeast dough ready. You were tested on doughnuts, puff dough, ice cream, butter cream, chocolate candies, hard candies, nougat, caramel, chocolate Easter bunnies, marzipan, even macaroons. You had to make sure you kept your eyes on the time during the test, because yeast dough needs time to proof.

In early December during the second year of my program, I

remember a situation where I was practicing doing something out of the ordinary to show my boss that I had an interest in the trade. All kinds of special items were made for Christmas. At that time I had a subscription to a trade magazine from Germany called *Konditorei und Café*. It had a very unusual marzipan figure in it that looked like a small Santa Claus. One night when the boss and his wife were out of town, I decided to copy the idea. I made twenty-four pieces, all of them Santa Claus. It was late when I finished making them, around 11:00 p.m. I went up to my room, and I heard the entrance door open just as I was about ready to fall to sleep.

The next morning the boss was ready to get the central heating going (a coal fire) for the whole house. He went down to the basement where I had left my creatures, and when he saw them, all hell broke loose. He disgustingly took my creations up and put them up for sale in the cake shop. Lo and behold, within two hours all of them were sold. Then I did not feel so bad, because I thought that I was showing interest in this line of business.

For your exam you had a specific amount of time to complete all the mandatory items, and if you were not able to complete everything, you could get a low grade or even fail. You were also judged on presentation and cleanliness. Your recipe book was judged, as well as your drawings of decorations for tortes.

I was skinny then and weighed about 115 pounds. My boss fixed me a pitcher of hot Ovomaltine to make sure I had the stamina and energy to get through eight hours under heavy stress.

After the physical exam, around 3:00 p.m., you were grilled on the technical knowledge for about two hours. Then your work was displayed and graded.

As a showpiece I made a very large Easter egg out of chocolate, using a large mold. Then I stood it up and made it into an Easter bunny house, well decorated with marzipan bunnies. On my exam day, my parents came from Mannedorf to witness my test and were surprised to see what one has to know to become a real pastry chef. I passed with flying colors. My father gave me 100 Swiss francs (twenty-five dollars) to go with the two other finalists for a drink.

There were three apprentices from different pastry shops to take the final exam the same day. When I started my apprenticeship program in 1956, we had ten in the class, and at the end just three made it.

Before I was ready for my own test, I was taken to watch three exams from other apprentices, even in other pastry shops out of town. My boss was one of the people who judged final exams, even for master pastry chefs. He took me along just to stand there and observe what was to come, so that I would be well aware of what to expect. Mr. Rusch made sure I was able to see the whole process of each test and told me to watch carefully so that I would benefit from it.

We had a konditor named Anton Pfeifer who was also certified as a chef. I sometimes tried to find out what he thought of being a chef, and said that there is too much stress in the kitchen.

Long before I started in the pastry shop, I also knew that I was going to learn to become a chef. This was a secret between my parents and myself. I could not tell my boss about it beforehand; otherwise, he would not have accepted me for the apprenticeship program.

The day after my exam, Mr. Rusch wanted me to go to work for Honold, one of the best konditorei in the city of Zurich. I declined and told him that I would be entering another apprentice program at the five-star Hotel Quellenhof in Bad Ragaz, in the canton of St. Gallen, to become a professional chef. He was very upset. I agreed to work for him in the pastry shop till the summer season started in Bad Ragaz.

The apprentice program in the kitchen was in seasonal hotels and normally involved more than one restaurant; therefore, it was conducted in different kitchens and hotels throughout its term, which normally takes three years. In my case it was a year and a half because I already had my certification as pastry cook, which is a part of the program. I was sixteen when I started at the pastry shop, and by age nineteen I had my certification as konditor. This was in 1959. My chef's apprentice program was done in two different seasonal hotels. The program is also government controlled and is the same throughout the country.

The pay was ten dollars a month. Cooking is not just a hobby, it is the real thing.

On my day off I went to the local butcher shop besides the practicing I had at the hotel to get extra practice boning meat and get to know all the cuts of meats. What a difference compared to the pastry shop! It was like day and night. It was very clean and well organized. We had breaks there; at the pastry shop I never had a break except for lunch and dinner. We ate well, and the laundry was done. We had room and board, and I was housed with the assistant pastry chef, Alois Strailer. He had a Vespa motor scooter, and he often took me for short trips to the nearby towns. One of them was Chur, about thirty kilometers from Bad Ragaz.

CHAPTER 3

LETS GET SERIOUS

Hotel Quellenhof had its own power plant, and everything was electrical. The hotel also had a casino and a golf course. Bad Ragaz is near Maienfeld, where the movie *Heidi* was filmed. It is also the gateway to all the classical winter resorts, such as Arosa, Davos, and St. Moritz.

The Quellenhof had a hot mineral spring coming out of the ground of the mountain, and the water was collected while still hot and used in a couple of covered swimming pools. Private cabins were available for extra therapy and masseuses. The kitchen crew had the privilege to take advantage of using the mineral water treatment, which was a bonus. It was in a different building.

Bad Ragaz is well known for a place of curing illnesses and is a resort town. The town had several other hotels with similar concepts. Hotel guests came from all over Europe to cure their arthritis and other related illnesses.

In the pastry shop, everything needed to go by recipes and weight. There was no guesswork. If you did not follow your recipe, the end product could not be used. The kitchen is completely different. It has recipes for some items, but a lot of things are based on personal preference and taste.

Mr. Useglio, the chef, was French, and the language in the kitchen was French. The French chefs take their language and the kitchen almost like a religion and are very proud. The classical French kitchen is based on a sound structure. It is practiced all around the world. It takes several years to become familiar with it.

The chef was from Marseille, and he introduced the fish soup bouillabaisse to me. Even when there was an order for an à la carte fish soup, I knew what to set up for it. By the end of the season I prepared it for the guests, but the chef always looked over my shoulder.

During my year and a half of apprenticeship and in between the seasons, I went to trade school in Davos at the Hotel Bündnerhof for seven weeks straight. It was a special program for apprentices working in seasonal hotels. It was all hands-on, and you were taught in the hotel kitchen at the Bündnerhof by professional teachers. They gave you all the required trade instructions to qualify for certification, as well your practice on the job where you did your apprentice program.

At the end of seven weeks in Davos of business school, you took an exam on all the subjects. During the apprentice program, you were taught bookkeeping, as well as all the basic terms and ways to construct menus. You learned all the meat cuts and what type of food was available during each season to cook with. You also learned the classical French terms and presentation.

You were taught how to prepare stocks and soups and how to cook all the meats, including fish and poultry, to the right temperature. You also learned how to make sausages.

You learned how to prepare fancy vegetables like artichokes and asparagus, ratatouille, and many more items. You got to know what kind of wine to serve with different meat, fish, or poultry. You learned to make ravioli, fresh noodles, and lasagnas. You were also taught how to butcher meat, lamb, beef, pork, veal, fish, poultry, and lobster.

Then you got to know the cold kitchen. This included the proper presentation of cold buffet items: different salads, salad dressings, and fancy hors d'oeuvres. You also learned to sculpture and carve ice.

The pastry section is a special place, and it is almost a different department. It takes special sills. You learned to make croissants, brioche (small hard rolls), Danish, and other typical breakfast items. Then you learned to make chocolate candies and desserts such as hot Grand Marnier soufflés, crème brûlée, baked Alaska, crêpes suzette, and flamed bananas, just to mention a few.

All of this was part of the apprentice program. And then to qualify, you needed to be able to prepare any type of food you were asked to cook on the day of your exam.

I remember one apprentice we had during school. When a teacher asked him how to store flour safely, he answered, "In a bag." The proper answer would have been, "In a cool, dry place."

The whole class of twenty students cracked up. You see, not everybody is Einstein.

Since I had the entire pastry requirement behind me, I was allowed some leisure time, and I often made Berliners for all the students. I did not attend all the classes related to pastries.

There was an assistant cook in Bad Ragaz who had to cook for the help, and the menu called for spaghetti with meat sauce. The chef wanted to see if the cook would fall for a trick—to cook extra pasta and then hang it over a cloth line to dry.

The chef told him were to hang the spaghetti, and it was a hoot to watch him trying to place the cooked, wet pasta on the cloth line. He was not a genius, but he surely was the talk of the town.

In the winter during my second season as an apprentice, I worked in Arosa at the Hotel Eden. The chef was also Mr. Useglio. I was able to fill in for the pastry chef on his day off, and I got the trust from the hotel garde manger (cold kitchen chef) to cut meat, prepare fish and poultry, and make special pâté for the cold appetizer. This used *forcemeat*, which is very finely blended meat that has to be kept cold so that it will not separate. The appetizer was first baked in dough and then filled with meat jelly. After it has cooled completely, it is cut into portions and served with Cumberland sauce. This is a sauce that is made by first caramelizing sugar, then adding orange juice, currant jelly, and fine julienne (small strips) of orange rind.

Galantine is a chicken that is completely boneless—just the skin. This is then filled with forcemeat of chicken meat truffle and pistachio nuts, then poached in chicken stock tied up with butcher string to keep its shape. It is then sliced and served cold. Today you do not see it too often on a menu, but it is a real classic and takes a lot of skill.

For entertainment we went skiing and ice-skating. At night we sometimes went dancing. During that winter season in Arosa, I caught a bad fever. I told the chef, but he thought that I was faking it. So I called on the house doctor, who took my temperature. It was extremely high, and the chef got a scolding from the doctor. I was out for one week.

As the junior in the kitchen brigade, I was chosen to make late bar orders (night chef). These orders sometimes called for steak tartare, smoked salmon, and *bündnerfleisch*, which is dried beef meat shaved very thin and served with rye bread and cornichons (small pickles). Those items are typically served in the Swiss mountain areas. Sometimes at 3:00 a.m. you were awakened by the bartender to cook. The hotel bar was open weird hours and stayed open very late, based on the number of people staying for entertainment and beverages.

After the winter season in Arosa ended, I went back to the Hotel Quellenhof in Bad Ragaz. During the summer season, I took the practical part of the examination. There were two chef de cuisines, or executive chefs, at the hotel who came to the Hotel Quellenhof to judge my exam for certification as chef. One had his own business and the other was employed in a first class hotel. They both watch me during the whole time and one was always on my side no cheating was allowed. Both watched my work for five hours, then I was again tested on the theoretical aspects for another two hours, including figuring out how much all the ingredients for a menu item would cost and then determining the price to charge customers.

The menu I had to cook came at random out of my menu book, where I had written all fancy menus collected during the three seasons for reference during the apprentice program. Next you had to write out your food requisition for everything you needed to cook your menu, then issue it from the storeroom. You had to be sure you got everything needed to prepare the item you had on your menu; for example, butter. It is like going to the supermarket and then realizing when you get home, "Oh, I forgot to get bread for dinner!" You could not miss anything, otherwise it would affect your grades.

You had to have a complete display of all the possible items necessary to do your task, including basic stocks, brown sauces, chopped shallots, wines, brandy, vegetables, mushrooms, cream, butter, salt, pepper, chopped parsley, and all sorts of fancy cut potatoes such as French fries, château potatoes, and many more. The potatoes were raw and kept in a separate silver container in cold water for display. This is called a setup, or in French *mise en place*.

I also made a sugar cube monument as a showpiece for the occasion. It was a replica of Kyburg, a castle in Switzerland.

You would not be able to make all the sauces the same day and then do your exam. So you were allowed to prepare the basics in advance the day before. During the exam, one of the experts was at your side constantly, so you could not cheat.

The menu consisted of appetizer, soup, salad, main course, vegetable, starch, and dessert. My appetizer was poached Dover sole fillets with mushrooms in a white wine sauce (also called *sauce au vin blanc*) grazed with hollandaise sauce. The soup was a chicken cream soup with slivers of almonds. The salad was hearts of Bibb lettuce with a walnut vinaigrette.

The main course was sautéed veal tenderloin medallion *forestiere*. It had different wild mushrooms such as chanterelle crêpes blended with a light brown sauce, called a demi-glacé. The vegetable was small artichoke bottoms filled with fresh sautéed baby spinach. The starch was fresh homemade noodles.

During the exam, I had to bone meat, including a whole leg of veal with the short loin, fish, and poultry, then portion it. I had to cook for ten people, and the food was served course by course. Serving it course by course gave me an opportunity to judge proper timing and allowed the examiners to give me proper credit for every dish I had to cook.

My dessert was a hot Grand Marnier soufflé with homemade chocolate sauce. It is very delicate to make. You had to take into consideration how long it will take to bake and make sure that it was baked properly, not raw inside and not fallen in. The timing had to be perfect. It had to be done by the time the main course was eaten.

I passed with high grades and got my certification 1961.

The next day I celebrated with the kitchen crew. I invited them to a nice restaurant and thanked them for all the passion they had shown in helping me to succeed.

During the summer season, there were hardly any days off, but Mr. Useglio, the chef de cuisine, granted me two days off to visit my family after my exam. During the season, we all went to a bowling alley one night a week to bowl. The camaraderie was great, and most of us worked together again in the upcoming season.

The pastry chef we had during the first season in Ragaz, Hans Huber, used to work in Cairo, Egypt. He liked to drink kirschwasser. When he had a few drinks too many, he started to sing in Arabic. He was an expert in making pulled sugar showpieces combined with chocolate candies.

After I completed my apprenticeships, I first worked at the Hotel

Waldhaus in Sils Maria, near St. Moritz. The hotel looked like a castle. I worked as an assistant to the chef garde manger in the cold kitchen. His name was Charlie Boss. The executive chef's name was Fritz Steiner. It was a short winter season.

You can see that I moved around quite a bit, but that is the way seasonal employment works. It is less boring than just spending years and years in the same place. Your horizons will be expanded because you always work with new chefs.

The kitchen crew at the Hotel Waldhaus consisted of well-accomplished chefs. They were all around forty-five years of age, and all the assistants were young. As assistant to the cold kitchen chef, I helped prepare the cold buffet for New Year's Eve. Most of the work was done at night. It is a tradition to have a fancy buffet display for the occasion. There were ice carvings and a butter sculpture. Everything was done fresh, even the meat glaze.

I remember it was just after New Year's Day, and a few guys of the kitchen crew decided to go out for a few drinks. By the time the place was ready to close, we were not feeling any pain. On the way back to the hotel, where we all had room and board, it was snowing heavily. There were a couple of telephone poles along the side of the road, and guess what? We decided to grab one of them, and we carried it up the hill and placed it in front of the hotel entrance and then left it there overnight.

The next morning, we were called to the manager's office. We knew we had some explaining to do and felt a kind of stupid. We were told to go and remove the pole and take it back to where it belonged, and next time to think first and not to be ridiculous. We apologized and were lucky not to be fired.

For recreation we went skiing and ice-skating. Seasonal work means you are always on the way and your coworkers became your family. The season was short and ended in the middle of January 1961. Most of the assistant cooks, including me, had to go to the

Swiss Army. It is an obligation for each Swiss male to do so by age twenty.

It will make a man out of boys. We were in a *kaserne* (barracks) in the city of Zurich for a few days, then we were moved around in the country for our military training. The basic training is tough, and you get to know how to deal with the elements, the weather, and all kinds of weaponry.

There are different branches. I was assigned to the infantry and mostly trained in the mountains. We dug our own igloo and housed in it over several nights. It surely will teach you discipline.

After I completed my obligation in the middle of April 1961, I returned to the Hotel Quellenhof in Bad Ragaz. Before I left there after my apprentice program, I was given a contract as an assistant sauce cook.

The season was already underway, and there was a new chef de cuisine in the kitchen from Switzerland, Mr. Fritz Huber. I introduced myself to the chef, and he asked me what my contract called

Swiss House restaurant front view.

for. I mentioned my position and then was asked how many seasons I had worked after my apprenticeship program. I told him one, and he looked at me and said, "Is that all?"

He mentioned that it usually takes more experience to claim this title and said that he would give me a chance, but if it did not work out, he would use me on another station in the kitchen. Training to become a real chef means that you work on all the stations related to the kitchen in hotels and restaurants.

CHAPTER 4

KEEP IN TOUCH WITH MR. HUBER

First you start as an apprentice, then you become an assistant cook. Then after you have worked in every phase, you next get the title as chef de partie, or station chef. Again you make the rounds, and you will become a sous-chef, the next position before you get the title chef de cuisine.

As I looked around in the kitchen, I saw a new apprentice. His name was Reto Flury. We had sat in the same school back at the hotel in Davos, and his father owned the Hotel Bündnerhof.

The kitchen brigade had fifteen chefs, and every station was well covered.

The person in charge of the sauce station, Mr. Max Rauch, was also at the hotel during my apprentice time. He had asked me prior to the summer season to be his assistant.

The new Swiss chef had a completely different style and absolutely no shortcuts. He came to Ragaz from Berlin, Germany, where he was working at the Hilton Hotel when his wife became ill, and he decided to go back to Switzerland and seek proper medical attention for her.

The season went well, and the hotel was occupied for the whole six months. At the end we had a convention for a steel company, which took over the entire hotel for one week. It was very well orchestrated.

When the season was over, all the hotel guests left. It took about a week to completely close the place, and during that time I did the cooking for the staff. The number of employees dwindled down quickly as all the guests left. Everything had to be properly cleaned and put away. It is a seasonal hotel and was closed during the winter.

By the end of the summer season, Mr. Huber asked me what I planned to do for the winter season. He offered me a position again as an assistant sauce cook in Davos at the Hotel Belvédère. He must have been satisfied with my performance. I sure gained confidence.

My first dish in the kitchen as apprentice at the Hotel Quellenhof was fixing *kartoffelpuffer*. This is a German potato pancake that is made with finely grated potatoes, pan-fried crispy and served with apple sauce. It was for the help, and cooking for the help gives you the practice you need before you are allowed to cook for guests. During my whole time as an apprentice, I never peeled an onion or potato. This is strictly constructive work. You needed to be able to learn everything properly, and you do not learn to cook by peeling onions.

I took a shorter time to complete the program. You also have to get to know all your stocks, soups, and sauces and all the basics and then turn them into different end products—for example, from brown sauce to peppercorn sauce, fish stock into fish sauce, chicken stock into chicken sauce, fresh tomatoes into tomato sauce. You have to learn a lot of things. Next come all the vegetables; also, ratatouille, preparing different meats, poultry, fish, seafood, lobster, shrimp, even game rabbits, kidneys, liver, and sweetbread. There is a long list, and it all depends on what the chef likes to offer the clientele. As you can see it takes time to get familiar with everything and then to handle it all.

Cooking is a trade, and you must like it; otherwise, it will eat you alive. It involves long hours and no instant gratification. But if you can take the heat, it is very rewarding.

It took me over ten years to become an executive chef. When you see a person working in a fast-food place who calls him- or herself a chef, think again. I have nothing against fast-food workers, but there is a big different between them and a trained chef.

I worked in many places around the globe, and in every place, I gained more knowledge and experience. The fascinating thing, if you have the desire to do so, is that a good chef travels the globe, and people are looking for a good, qualified chef.

You can see how the international kitchens have evolved over the years, but the basic structure is definitely the classical French kitchen. From that, new types were born, such as the nouvelle kitchen, then came the *minceur* kitchen, which plays a big role in today's diet, and even organic food is used.

And a lot of restaurants are specializing in certain concepts to maintain their niche in the field—French classical, seafood places, steakhouses, Chinese, Italian, Korean, Japanese, and the list goes on and on. Unfortunately, a few of them want to be all of these types, and usually it is impossible to so.

I would like to show you what my résumé looks like. After my basic training and a short winter season in Sils Maria, in 1961 I did my obligation in the Swiss Army. It took three months, then I worked in Bad Ragaz as an assistant to the sauce cook for the summer season. Then in 1962 I again had the title of assistant chef to the sauce cook at the Hotel Belvédère in Davos, Switzerland, under Chef Huber. A lot of the cooking was done to enhance the flavors by reducing the brown sauce with wine and herbs. Mr. Huber had a lot of connections, and he later became my mentor in 1992.

I took a job in Geneva, Switzerland, as a relief assistant cook at the Hôtel du Rhône. The chef's name was Mr. Guyard. I worked first in the cold kitchen, then there was a rotation cycle among the entire assistant cooks to cook for all hotel employees. The chef was very fussy about what went out of the kitchen. It was normally for just one week, but if the chef thought it was not up to his standards, you had another week to improve.

When my turn came, I made sure it was just for one week. I rounded up everything under the sun to make sure it was just for one week.

One item I had to cook was pig's feet. First the feet have to be cooked well in stock, then remove the meat, top it with herbed garlic spiced bread crumbs, and then serve with a mustard-laced brown sauce.

Next, I worked in the rotisserie. Everything was cooked on a spit and was done strictly to order. I also worked in the pastry shop and main kitchen.

It was like musical chairs, and it was very hard. If you did not have any knowledge in the pastry department, you were not even allowed to enter the pastry shop, period.

My intent was to improve my French and then to go to Montreal, Canada, to the Queen Elizabeth Hotel. I had my visa and a job, but as my parents found out, it was a no-no. They did not trust me. I studied hard to master the French language so that I would be able to survive, but my parents thought that I would not earn enough money, based on the information they got from the Canadian embassy.

In 1963 I then took a job at the Movenpick Restaurant at Sihle Porte in Zurich, Switzerland, as second fiddle to the cold kitchen chef. The concept was unique for me—it was the introduction to the hamburger. The place where it was promoted was called Silver Kugel. It was geared toward the lighter fare of cooking. Mainly just one item served on a plate, such as beef stroganoff on a bed of noodles and nothing else. It was very successful. They served big salad combinations, and during asparagus season you could eat as many asparagus as you could for one price, and they were served with different hot and cold sauces.

There was a contest among the young chefs to see who could peel a large case of asparagus in the shortest amount of time, and the winner got to choose any bottle of booze. I got my fair share. They opened several other units in Germany in late 1963.

I then got an offer from the Hotel Chantarella in St. Moritz, which is affiliated with the Waldhaus in Sils Maria, as a relief station *chef tournant*. I filled in all the stations to accommodate others' day off. One time the chef de cuisine, Mr. Troxler, had me working in the vegetable station, and the vegetable for the dinner service was glazed baby carrots that had to be cut in a shape like a very small football. It took me just several hours to do, and when I was about done, the chef came over to check on me. He took a handful out of the container, looked at it, and said it was a lousy job. He called the person who cooked for the hotel help and said to him, "Those are your vegetables for tomorrow."

The whole kitchen crew was stunned and could not believe it. I was told to redo all of the carrots and that they had to be done for the dinner service.

I was ticked off! I then went to get a new bag of carrots, and while everybody went on their break, I kept on working on my dinner vegetables. As soon as I saw the chef leaving the hotel, the whole kitchen crew showed up and helped me complete all the carrots for the evening. It was the first time that I had the position as *chef de partie* (station chef), and I was told later that this was my introduction to my new title.

The sauce chef at the hotel was Mr. Zogg. During the season, the chef had a hard time writing balanced menus. He was inconsistent in constructing a menu and would wind up with an imbalance in color combinations—in other words, the soup was white, the vegetables were white, the potatoes were white, and even the dessert was white.

Prior to the season, I was told by Mr. Zogg, to look out for this issue. This was in St. Moritz during the winter season. I told the chef about it, and he got ticked off. He threw his menus at me and told me to write the menus. I did so, and he even accepted my suggestions.

In 1964 I became chef sauce cook and also sous-chef at the Waldhaus in Sils Maria. When I arrived in Sils Maria, my contract called for cold kitchen chef, and to my surprise there were three Arabs in the kitchen. The chef did not trust them to take over the sauce station.

I worked at that station as relief chef in St. Moritz before and during the time the sauce cook in a previous season, Mr. Zogg, broke his ribs while lifting a heavy pot and fell. So the chef upgraded me to the sauce station till Mr. Zogg could return.

This was the first time that I was exposed to the Arab lifestyle. The oldest one was the boss in the family, and they had their praying sessions. And when something went wrong between them, they had brawls that were viscous.

The season went by smoothly despite a few run-ins I had with the chef. He tried to sabotage me on several occasions by turning off the stove during the service, but I just got back at him. We had a so-called cold war. He called me names of disrespect, and I said to him that if I used words like this to my father, he would spank me. The chef got even more irritated, so I cut out his conversation by being silent. During the lunch or dinner service, when he was expecting me to call out what customers ordered, I just took down the dishes needed to serve the food. Then he got pissed off and started to throw complete dishes ready to be picked up by the waiters. I practiced this system all through the whole season, and it worked out fine. By the end of the season, Chef Troxler was fired.

The town of Sils Maria is near St. Moritz and has a mountain lake. I purchased a fishing license, then early in the morning, at 5:30 a.m., I would go fishing. I sold all my catch to the hotel. I had a portable fish tank and all my catch was alive. It was my hobby during the season.

I kept in touch with Chef Huber after the summer season and was interested in going to Puerto Rico. Mr. Huber used to be the chef at the Caribe Hilton there, and he often talked about it during lunch break. It must have left a good impression on me.

I met with Mr. Huber after the season in Zurich while having a beer at a *gasthaus* near the central railroad station. He thought since I had never been in a foreign country before, it would be wise for me first to go to London to improve my English and to see if I would be able to cope with such a big change.

Mr. Huber made a phone call to the executive chef at the London Hilton. His name was Joseph Bazani. I got a contract as a relief station chef for one year. This was in 1964.

My promise to my father of never returning was becoming a reality.

London was rather a big change for a small-town boy. The size of the city went from 10,000 to 10 million, the language was English, the traffic was on the left side, and the currency was in British pounds. The hotel, which was with Hilton International, was very large and had 650 rooms.

I arrived in London by Swissair around 2:00 p.m. After I got off the plane, I went through the customs office. And then I was faced with all the double-decker buses trying to get to the London Hilton Hotel.

I finally asked a cab driver to take me to the hotel. He helped me load my suitcase—they are kept outside the cab—then he started to drive. It seemed to take forever, but then all of a sudden, we wound up in front of the London Hilton Hotel. The driver helped me get my luggage into the hotel lobby, then he told me what I had to pay for the fare. It was five pounds. I had no idea if that was right or not.

I then asked the front desk how to go to the main kitchen to meet the chef and let them know of my arrival. While going through the main kitchen, I recognized a person I knew before, Hans Zach from Davos. Next the secretary of the head chef sent me to the personnel office to fill out papers so that I could start the next day.

The person in the personnel office gave me a business card on which was an address for the place where I was to room. Also written on the card was the number of a bus I supposed to take, and directions for where to go to catch the bus. It was the Hyde Park corner.

I got on the bus and off I went, and I had no idea where I was going. I kept looking at the street signs. It seemed endless. I finally decided to get off the bus. Before I did so, the conductor of the bus came by, and I gave him sixpence. I was unaware of the way the fare was collected. I did hear numbers being thrown around, so I went by the lowest denomination, which was a sixpence. I got off the bus and then kept on walking, and it looked like I was going in circles.

Finally, I decided to ask an older gentleman who came around the corner where I was going. It was already pretty dark, and I showed him my card with the address written on it. He said that it was just around the corner, and he even walked me to the place. I thanked him, and off he went.

I rang the doorbell, and a gentleman answered the door and said that he was waiting for me. He took me upstairs to the second floor. He showed me my room and said that if I had any questions, he would be downstairs.

I then tried to take a shower—yes, the water was running for a few seconds, then off she went. I went downstairs and told the landlord about it. He said that I would have to feed the meter and gave me some change. I finally got to bed but did not sleep too well.

The next morning, I got up and was ready to shave, but to my surprise the socket in the outlet was different than the plug on my razor. I looked through my luggage and found two small keys that I stuck into the outlet and was able to shave. Then I got dressed and was on the way to the bus station.

I still had a hard time figuring out that the traffic was on the left side, but somehow, I got on the bus. Then I heard some people complaining, and I recognized my ignorance. Europe has the traffic on the right side.

I again gave the conductor sixpence. I was lucky that I was on the right bus. There were several buses with the same numbers going in different directions.

I finally saw the Hilton Hotel and was able to relax. I found the employee entrance, got my uniform, and reported for duty. I was quickly introduced by the morning sous-chef and ended up in the cold kitchen.

I was able to figure out how the money system works and was told by one of my British coworkers that I had been taken to the cleaners by the cab driver. I was told that if I had his cab number, the driver could lose his license. It was too late, but the lesson was well learned.

I was living at the place given to me by the personnel office for a couple of days, then I found a flat (room) very close by the hotel, on Oxford Street. The hotel was in walking distance. Yes, it did cost more, but it was worth it.

I had many positions during a single day, sometimes three or four. I remember my first day, I was assigned to the cold kitchen and was told to make grapefruit sections out of a case of grapefruit. I was very familiar with it, and when I was finished I reported to the chef of the cold kitchen, Franz Kuhne. He was pleasantly surprised to see that one person could actually do the job right.

The next day I took over the chef position in the steakhouse. The regular person, Mr. Schlumpf, was due for his vacation. The first item to prepare was steak and kidney pie. I had never before made such an item but was told just to make a beef stew and then add the veal kidney and mushrooms to it. I got all my ingredients from the butcher shop and did as I was told. My pie was A-OK. I filled in at the steakhouse for the next ten days.

Then the sauce chef in the main kitchen, Mr. Stocker, had to be operated on for his veins. So I took over his station for ten days. This was more European-style cooking and was not too hard. The layout in the kitchen was more American style. During that time, we had several chefs from the Istanbul Hilton Hotel, and there was an exchange of cultural cuisine. A lot of different curry dishes were featured for a whole month, and I was able to learn how to cook proper curry dishes. We also had several other countries represented, including Argentina, plus all the British cuisine.

Then I worked at the vegetable station, out of the main kitchen. The morning sous-chef, Mr. Myer, was German. He told me to make one hundred portions of *spaetzli* (German homemade noodles) on a wooden board. It was not exactly strange to me, because I had made it a few times in Switzerland, but it takes some skill to make it. The German supervisor wanted to see if a Swiss guy knew how to handle it.

I also worked in the butcher shop, pastry shop, and banquet kitchen on different days. Later on, I was introduced to the night shift as night chef, working 10:00 p.m. to 6:00 a.m. Working these hours will definitely upset your equilibrium and was hard on me since I had English classes five days week from 2:30 to 4:30 p.m. I was one of the first students at the newly opened school of English, which had all kinds of nationalities, including Indian, French, Spanish, German, and Swiss. A lot of bottle parties were going on during the week, and all you had to do was bring a bottle of some kind of booze and you were invited and got introduced quickly to the British lifestyle.

Ham display for the food show in Washington D.C.

Seafood display for the food show in DC.

Ham display for the food show in Boston Rose truffle drawing.

Seahorse sculpture for buffet display.

CHAPTER 5

TESTING YOUR WILL

The school was located at 25-27 Oxford Street. My professor's name was Charles Quinn. He was Scottish. Overall, I had a very busy time in London.

One time I prepared a roast leg of lamb for the students. I was doing it at my teacher's house, together with a French student. It was a hit. We had lessons in Hyde Park just to get into conversations about what was going on. We also went to the wax museum and visited all the major attractions in London.

There was one morning when the breakfast chef did not show up after my night shift, and I was asked to fill in for him by Mr. Myer. I had to cook a British breakfast of lamb kidney, Scottish banger, and smoked haddock poached in milk. I got overtime pay, which helps when you are on a small paycheck.

Before I left Switzerland, I had applied for my green card in Bern, the capital of Switzerland, at the American embassy. By the end of my contract in London, I had received my green card.

During my last month at the London Hilton, I got the OK from the executive chef, Mr. Bazani, to finish my time in the cold kitchen, where I practiced carving ice and butter sculptures. Once again, Mr. Huber made a phone call, this time from Switzerland to Puerto Rico, and I was hired by the Swiss Chalet Hotel Company. I worked there for three months, till there was an opening at the Caribe Hilton. The chef at the Swiss Chalet was not happy about my sudden departure from the Swiss Chalet Hotel Company.

I transferred over to the Caribe Hilton and became the cold buffet chef at the nightclub showroom. I also purchased my first brand-new car. It was a Triumph Spitfire. A friend of mine, Bruno Brandli, gave me a loan to purchase the car.

The chef at the Hilton was John Scharer. I met Mr. Schlumpf again at the Caribe Hilton. He also came from the London Hilton and was now the sous-chef at the Ocean Terrace Restaurant.

The food in Puerto Rico is Latin cooking with a lot of seafood, and since the Hilton is international, a variety of food was on the menu. The currency is US dollars, and the English language is common. I was able to use my talent on more artistic work such as ice carvings, butter sculpturing, and fancy food displays. I worked there from 1965 to 1966. Then, together with the sous-chef from the Caribe Hilton, Freddy Schare, I opened the Estate Carlson Country Club in St. Croix with the Swiss Chalet Hotel Company.

In 1967 I totaled my car in St. Croix. It was a freak accident. St. Croix has the same traffic situation as London, also on the left side. The car turned over because the road was under construction and I got caught up in the uneven road. I had State Farm Insurance, and it covered everything. By the time the police report was filed, the insurance had paid the total cost of the purchase price. Lucky me!

From St. Croix I moved to Boston. The Boston Bruins won the Stanley Cup that year. I became *chef garde manger* (cold kitchen chef) for one year at the Sheraton Boston Hotel under Chef Fuchs. He then took the chef's job at the Washington Hilton. I followed him to Washington, DC, and I became his night sous-chef over two restaurants. Then came the Statler Hilton, where I was sous-chef. I had the pleasure of feeding the newly elected President Johnson.

Then briefly I was cold kitchen chef at the Sheraton Park Hotel in Washington, DC.

Before I got my first real chef's job, I worked from 1969 to 1971 in Rochester, New York, at the five-hundred-room Sheraton Hotel. The facility was rapidly deteriorating. Many things were out of order, even the service elevator to the top floor. I often had to carry food up fifteen flight of stairs.

At the Rochester Sheraton, I surely was tested on my stamina. I ended up with an ulcer. They took advantage of my good nature. But I surely got all the experience I would ever need for any future chef's position.

During this time, I took a three-week vacation in Switzerland. When I arrived in Zurich, my father picked me up at the airport and asked me, "What's wrong with you? You look skinny."

He made arrangement for me to see a specialist doctor, and it turned out to be an ulcer. I spent two weeks going back and forth twice a day from Mannedorf to Zurich to run several tests. I was put on a strict diet. No booze, and I ate small portions, easy on the salt, five times a day.

The doctor I visited in Zurich did his study in Rochester, New York, and was familiar with the town. At the end of my treatment, he gave me my X-rays and told me to tell my boss that I could no longer work all those long hours.

While I was in Switzerland, I was the best man at my brother Fritz's wedding in Hombrechtikon. It was a rainy day. He had a horse-drawn carriage, and it was cold, but it is today an old-fashioned, classical wedding. He chose a nice restaurant where we had individual hors d'oeuvres plates with meats, cheese, and cornichons. It was all nicely arranged.

The Rochester Sheraton Hotel was sold later on, and I was transferred to Niagara Falls, Canada, as head chef for the summer season. I was hired to prepare a cold buffet, because the dining room was

Finishing details on my show piece before it was sent to Frankfurt Germany.

very long and with the air-conditioner running, it was difficult to serve hot food. This was at the Sheraton Foxhead in 1971.

Then the summer season came to an end. The general manager, Mr. Sullivan, was very pleased with the job I did in Canada. I was then transferred to the Moana Surfrider Sheraton in Honolulu, Hawaii, for one year.

The word *day off* was not in the dictionary. Once again, I took a real beating that year—long hours with no days off. It looked like I was cursed, and again I took three months off just lying on the beach to recharge my battery. It took a toll on me. I was burned out and needed to come back to reality; in other words, become a human again.

A friend of mine who had an employment agency and was also a liquor salesman was aware of an opening at the Ilikai Hotel. So from February 1972 till December 1973, I was the head chef at the Ilikai Hotel. It was a job with dignity. I improved the food concept, and the overall food revenue was very respectful again. The food revenue per month was about $75,000. I made a new menu by asking some businesses located near the hotel what they were looking for, and I combined their input with mine. After two months of the new concept, the revenue more than doubled to $180,000. I was in like Flynn!

A month after I left the Surfrider Sheraton in disgust, Sheraton had offered me any new hotel opening in 1973 within the company. I was interviewed at the Sheraton Waikiki by the vice president of food and beverage for the corporation. His name was Mike Waffel. I chose Hong Kong, and while I was waiting for my starting day, I got a phone call from the home office. They said that they had hired a chef from Hong Kong. This was another disappointment.

At that time, I had already purchased two plane tickets to fly to Hong Kong. Lily, who was then my fiancée, and I took the opportunity to take a vacation to Hong Kong. We flew out of Honolulu on a Pan Am 747 plane, and it had a *Clipper Magazine* on board. I saw that there were four new hotels in Hong Kong to be opened in 1973. I had a couple of my résumés with me and said to Lily that I would become the chef of one those hotels. She said to me, "You are nuts!"

While we were staying at a hotel with the Peninsula group where Lily's friend was the general manager, he left a note in our mailbox that he wanted to talk to us.

While flying to Hong Kong, it was for Lily and me a vacation trip. But the situation was so overwhelming for me. I could not believe that again I was left out. I was determined. I had an intuition and it was real that this time I would succeed. I always believed in myself.

I also was visiting the chef from the Hong Kong Hilton, Rolf Hardmeier. Sheraton had planes for me to go to the Hilton for a couple of weeks to get acquainted with the Oriental cooking and purchasing. I had heard of Mr. Hardmeier in Switzerland from his nephew, who was working at that time in Sils Maria.

The Sheraton job fell through, and I was able to talk with Mr. Hardmeier while having a beer in his office. He told me at time that I would become the chef of the Plaza Hotel, which was then under construction in Hong Kong. This was a couple of days prior to me talking with the management of the Plaza Hotel, which was under construction.

It seemed to be unreal, but after talking with the manager at the hotel where we stayed for two weeks, before we flew back to Hawaii, I signed a contract to open the Plaza Hotel as executive chef. My wish had come true. And, what a coincidence—Lily's friend became the general manager of the Plaza Hotel.

During the time I worked at the Ilikai, I entered the Culinary Olympics in Frankfurt, Germany, sculpturing the emperor of China with tallow, which is a combination of fat, paraffin, and beeswax. I was awarded a gold medallion for the sculpture.

I got married in Hawaii to Lily Pai in 1973. While Lily and I were dating, we had spent good times together enjoying good company, good food, good conversations, and dancing at the Kahala Hilton. We usually dated twice a week, Wednesdays and Sundays, for over a year. She also worked in the hotel field, and I was told by her father that I was extremely timely, like a train—you could count on me.

Now I would like to share with you a story I found that my wife wrote in 2006.

21 ROSES

In my lifetime, I only noticed two drastic changes Father made to adapt to the American way of life. The first one was that mother suddenly decided that she was not going to cook Chinese food every day (which was composed of two stir-fry vegetables, a meat dish, and soup). She wanted the weekends off. Father was shocked but accepted her request. So on the weekends, they like to go eat at McDonald's or Burger King.

The second change was Karl's fault. While we were dating, on

Valentine's Day I got one dozen roses from Karl. Mother asked Father why people give flowers and chocolate on February 14. After father explained the meaning of Valentine's Day, Mother said how come she did not get any flowers. From that day, Father follows the tradition and remembers to buy flowers for Mother. Mother loves being an American—she thinks American women have a lot of freedom in thinking and making their own decisions.

Now let me tell you the story of the 21 roses. The first time, when I received the dozen roses on Valentine's Day, the note Karl wrote said, "The day you receive 21 roses, that will be the sign that I am ready to settle down."

Promotion for the Ilikai hotel on Oahu.

CHAPTER 6

CHANGING TRADITION & MOVING TO HONG KONG

*G*uess *what—it did not happen until about eight months later. When I came home from work, Father and Mother were excited and told me that Karl had invited them to dinner that night and asked me why he sent such a big bunch of roses. I gave them a mysterious smile and said, "Be patient, you will find out." During the six courses of Chinese dinner, Karl did not say anything. I thought his purpose was to ask my parents' permission for my hand. When the dessert of candied apples came, I had lost my appetite. I just kicked his leg under the table to give him the hint—diner is over, where is the proposal? He just continued his meaningless (to me) conversation with my parents. I think my father was a wise man. He sensed something and invited Karl for after-dinner drinks in our house. In my mind I thought he had changed his original idea. When we all got our brandy, Father made a toast to thank him for the delicious dinner, and then it was Karl's turn to toast. He smiled at me and winked his eye, and he finally asked my parents for their permission to marry me. What a relief I felt!*

This year Valentine's Day fell on a Tuesday—our day off. It was the first time in our career that we did not have to work on this important business day. We know how hectic the restaurant business is on Valentine's

Day, so we gave our peers a break and had a quiet, romantic dinner
out on Monday night, checking out our competition at the same time.

We are satisfied that we did a good job and proud that our restaurant
can represent Grass Valley and Nevada County without red in our faces,
and it all began with 21 roses.

Before we moved to Hong Kong, Lily and I spent three weeks on
our honeymoon in Kauai, ten days in Taiwan, and five days in Tokyo.
Then I opened the Plaza Hotel from 1974 to 1975. We arrived in
Hong Kong on Chinese New Year. It was crazy; everything was
closed. Yes, we had an apartment, but it was poorly furnished, and
we ate in American-owned hotels. Everything else was closed till
the Chinese celebration was over. Only then was it possible to get
organized in our own apartment.

Hong Kong was very successful. It was like getting a second
degree in teaching the Chinese European cooking, and they taught
me the Chinese way to cook. The people were very loyal, and I
found myself at home.

While I was working during the opening, Lily was staying home.
She explored the Chinese street markets and purchased all kinds
of food. I remember one time she brought home live shrimp in a
bag of water, and as I returned from work, I heard her screaming
in the kitchen over the sink while trying to peel the shrimp. They
were still alive and jumping. I decided to take over and finished
making the meal.

Most of the time we went out to eat. Lily's father used to work in
Hong Kong as a district manager for the Mobil gas company, and
through him we had good connections. Lily worked as a secretary
in Hong Kong at that time and knew several people.

Ice carving demo at the Hyatt Regency in Dearborn Michigan.

She found a job with the Sheraton Hotel where I was supposed to work as the chef, but she could not see herself in a disorganized place. It lasted one week. Then she found a job working for the Wu family as a manager of one of the restaurants. They had a chain of Chinese restaurants. Lily knew Miss Annie Wu from Hawaii.

The Plaza Hotel was a Chinese-Japanese venture. During the opening process, I had to explain every item we needed to run the food operations. It was a task of its own, coming from the United States. The equipment standards were completely different. We had a project manager from Australia named Mr. Mottram, and he thought he could run roughshod over me.

My sous-chef, Frederick Ott, and I looked at the blueprints and found out the exact size of all the refrigeration units we had. We decided to mark every unit with chalk on the floor, and we came to the conclusion that the room was way too small. We notified the management, and the project manager was released from his duties. Then a German consultant from another local hotel, Lee Garden, was brought in, and the proper adjustments were made. At the end we got what was necessary to run a proper food operation.

I was the first chef in Hong Kong to purchase most of the food items from the United States. We implemented US standards, which were consistent, and it was well accepted. Today it is common practice.

Opening a hotel in Hong Kong was very special for me, and I will cherish it for the rest of my life.

All the chefs in the major hotels there were Europeans, and before my two-year contract with the Plaza Hotel came to an end, once a month we got together and had an extended lunch in some of the very best restaurants. We took turns eating in each other's restaurants. Mr. Hardmeier was like the godfather and was the corporate chef for the Pacific division for Hilton Hotels. He was well known in the local food industry and spoke perfect Cantonese. We received a lot of favors through him.

One of the other chefs worked at the Hyatt Hotel in Kowloon as the executive chef. His name was Bob Hauser, and he knew of a chef position opening in Sydney, Australia. I applied and got the job, but before I was supposed to go there, the hotel burned down. Bob said not to worry, the vice president of industrial relations of Hyatt USA, Mr. Lombardi, was coming to Hong Kong. Bob made an appointment for me to meet with him at the Hyatt Hotel in Kowloon.

I gave Mr. Lombardi a couple of my résumés. He flew back to the United States, and ten days later I got a phone call at 6:00 a.m. local time. I was asked if I had the money to fly to Honolulu for an interview. The meeting would be poolside and would last for about an hour at the Hawaiian Regent Hotel on Oahu. The meeting was with the vice president of food and beverage for the American division, Mr. Berkowitz. That same day, Lily was able to get me a ticket, and the next day I was on the way.

After the interview, I was given the reimbursement for the plane ticket, and in the envelope was a note saying that I was chosen to open the Hyatt Regency Hotel in Dearborn, Michigan. I flew back to Hong Kong, packed up my belongings, and flew back to Hawaii for a ten-day vacation. Then we moved to Dearborn. The move from Hong Kong to Dearborn was reimbursed by Hyatt.

From October 1975 to August 1977, I opened the Hyatt Regency Hotel in Dearborn. The hotel is owned by Henry Ford Inc. Opening a new hotel in the United States was completely different than it was in Hong Kong. In Hong Kong I was in charge, but not in Dearborn.

Dearborn had its challenges. You basically had to go by your estimation because Dearborn was a small town and people did not think that there would be much demand for that type of food venue. It had eight hundred rooms and was the first major hotel of this size in Dearborn.

The employees that were hired were young and did not have much experience, and during the opening not too many could take the stress. Procedures changed several times, even during the same day. All the interviews for the basic staff were conducted at the Community Center. It took a couple of days to conduct all the interviews, which were arranged according to the different departments—food and beverage, housekeeping, and so on. Then the qualified candidates were chosen and some training began. The corporate office was heavily involved in deciding the food concept. The food and beverage manager, his assistant, and I flew to Chicago for consulting on the final decisions.

We met Mr. Denis Berkovitch, vice president of the food and beverage division of Hyatt USA, and the general manager of the Chicago Hyatt. The menu items were discussed, and presentations were made. Training was for about ten days, and stations in the kitchens had to be set up so that it was practical to work. On the day before the opening, we had a dry run and the Ansul sprinkler system went off. All the food was ruined.

Then came the situation of proper equipment. The home office had purchased equipment based on their estimation from a similar-sized hotel, and we had to go with whatever we had. It was difficult, but first you had to convince them the equipment was inadequate. After observing during the dry run, they had to admit that improvements needed to be made. I really at times had to bite my tongue. It was a daily grind, and only people with patience could handle it. I had a few very loyal young chefs, which made it possible to stay organized and get things accomplished.

The hotel turned out to be the highest moneymaker at that time. It made $10 million the first year, and I was chosen the department head of the month.

After the opening, while I worked at Hyatt, Lily worked at the Magic Pan as manager at the Fairlane Center. I felt that after the opening, I needed a change of scenery. I got an offer for the Caesars Palace Hotel in Las Vegas as executive chef. But when Hyatt found out, I had to decline and was transferred to New Orleans instead, also with the Hyatt Corporation.

While in New Orleans, I worked during the Super Bowl, Mardi Gras, and also the Food and Beverage Convention for the Hyatt Corporation, all within a couple of months.

I stayed at the Hyatt Hotel for a few days till I could find a place of my own. On my third day, I went up to my room around 10:00 p.m. and my phone was blinking. I was told that somebody had been shot in the kitchen and that I should come down to the kitchen and make sure everything was all right.

It was tough. I should have left right then and there. The kitchen was always understaffed. We had a lot of sick calls and could not get replacements.

There was a certain attitude among the different department heads against me, and I was on my own. It was political. I became somehow abused. My food cost was very low. I worked very closely with the purchasing manager, Robert Scholten, to purchase wisely. I was told that I did not give the costumers the proper portions. When I left they Hyatt in 1977, five of my loyal workers gave their notice the same day in disgust, and I was accused of having a following, which would be bad. The Hyatt would lose good, loyal employees. But it was also proof the employees supported me and were disgusted by the management's decision.

After I left the Hyatt in New Orleans, in 1978 I became the executive chef at the Royal Lahaina Hotel on Maui, Hawaii. It was challenging. There were eight restaurants over forty acres. I had a golf cart to check on all the restaurants. Lily was working as assistant manager at the Kapalua Bay Resort Hotel during this time.

We had a good time in Maui. I went deep-sea fishing every Sunday. Once I caught a couple of mahi-mahi, and another time I caught a Hawaiian lobster right off the beach. Often at night we would cast our fishing line from the beach in the ocean and enjoyed life while having a few beers. Sometimes it lasted till 6:00 a.m. the next day.

As a white person with a foreign accent in Hawaii, it can be difficult. You are called "haole," which is Hawaiian slang for a white person.

During this time, I attended the national food show in Chicago, and after returning from the show, I sensed some sort of resentment. I was told to pay more attention to the place.

The general manager in Maui, Jack Dallas, and I got along fine. Quite often we had a cigar while checking the place before closing for the night. We had a good relationship.

As a going-away present, I made a large lion tallow sculpture for the dinner buffet. They could not believe it. The general manager left shortly after me.

From October 1979 to 1984, I worked as the executive chef at the nineteen-hundred-room Sheraton Waikiki Hotel. I had 120 employees. I hired two sous-chefs from Maui to work for me at the Sheraton for four and a half years. At one time I had five European

The go away Lion sculpture at the
Royal Lahaina in Maui.

sous-chefs working for me, and I was asked to make them chefs in smaller Sheraton hotels. During this time, Lily was the manager at La Mer Restaurant at the Halekulani Resort Hotel.

At Sheraton Waikiki a lot of things needed to be corrected. Food cost was 39 percent, and labor cost was also far too high. All new menus were implemented, and all of them needed to be calculated so that the cost was under control, and new presentations came to be more modern and eye catching.

There was little discipline in the food operation. I was hired to make corrections and communicate with the general manager, Mr. Schweibert. I knew him from when I worked at the Sheraton Park in Washington, DC. I sent him a weekly progress report so that he could see what was accomplished. We also had daily meetings between the two of us without the food and beverage manager to make sure we were on the right track.

There was a strong union to deal with. My car was vandalized on several occasions, and many times I was escorted by the security guard to pick up my car. I made quick changes and was not exactly their best friend.

After two years we had a new general manager, named Mr. Brogan, because Mr. Schweibert had skin cancer. By that time the cost was under control. Then I got into a union dispute, and it ended up in arbitration.

I had a butcher who went to Florida and needed to be replaced, so I promoted one fry cook, Mr. Tolentino, who claimed to know how to work with meats and said that he cut meat at the local Safeway store in Honolulu. Later on, I found out that he was fired by Safeway because he was dishonest. The union gave him their blessings.

I worked with him for a couple of weeks, and then he was on his own. It just so happened that he was also the shop steward, and he tried to give me a hard time. He said that I was sending bad meat to the food outlets, and he claimed that I did not know how to cut meat, despite the fact that I had trained the guy for a couple of weeks.

A lot of meat was unaccounted for. There were no controls whatsoever. Frequently, at the end of the day, several pieces of meat such as fillets and New York steaks were missing.

I implemented a cart with padlocks on it and an inventory sheet based on the menu item for the outlet in question. The restaurant chef ordered from the butcher, then the butcher had to verify the order and sign off when the order was complete, and it was then picked up by the restaurant chef prior to his shift. The chef had to check that the order was correct.

By the end of each shift, the orders were matched up against the guest checks. Then again, the restaurant chef had to sign for it so that I could see what was going on even at 11:00 p.m.

Food display arrangement for the Sheraton Waikiki hotel promotion.

My first tallow sculpture at the London Hilton

CHAPTER 7

THE HAOLE IN HAWAII

I secured the cart with a padlock, and the key was then kept in the chef's office. Each morning, the sous-chef opened it, and the butcher was able to fill the order for the day. Again, the butcher had to sign, and then the padlock was applied. The restaurant chef then took the cart to his outlet and had to present it to the restaurant manager before the service. Finally, we had strict control.

It was corrected almost overnight. I did daily briefings with the food and beverage manager, Mr. Brown, and records were kept. The butcher turned me in to the union after he was disciplined and fired. A grievance was filed by the union, and it became an arbitration case.

I thought I was in a criminal court. I had resigned from the place prior to the arbitrator arriving from Oakland, California, and I was called back to the hotel to testify. The hotel lawyer was called in, and it became a really nasty case. But it was eventually settled, and I won.

You can see I had my ups and downs, and that comes with the territory.

The Sheraton Waikiki was finally brought under control, and it showed on the profit and loss statement that the food cost had come down to 30 percent. The payroll was 9 percent. One percent of the food cost was ten thousand dollars in 1985. During the weekly department head meetings, Mr. Brogan mentioned that I was able to keep cost at 30 percent for over two years, and he was proud.

Before I left the Sheraton Waikiki, the vice president of food and beverage for the Pacific Division, Max Wilhelm, offered me a job as corporate chef for his division. But I had always wanted a place of my own. So I took some time off and began looking for a restaurant of my own.

The chef from the Kahala Hilton in Honolulu, Martin Wyss, had a friend who was an accountant for a man who was looking for someone to take over his place. It was the Chicken Shake Restaurant in Santa Isabel, California. The owner's name was Franz Dolder. I visited him and also worked for him for six months. Then my wife called me from Hawaii and said that the owner of Scheidels Restaurant in Grass Valley, California, wanted to retire.

I got in contact with the owner, Serge Bartolome. We used to work together sometime in the past, and he wanted to talk to me. He was in a wheelchair because he had broken his neck in a plane accident. I drove to Grass Valley and worked for him while trying to buy his place. The realtor's name was Kurt Buckholz. After a long negotiation, the deal fell through.

Then I found the then-called Empire House Restaurant in Grass Valley, which I bought. And I opened my own restaurant on Thanksgiving Day in 1985.

It was a lot of work to do all the cleaning, painting, and repairs. It took us almost four months. We had to put up with all the hassle of the government requests that never seemed to end. Next came the health department, and they had some more requests, and that went too far. I told them one more request and I will tell you what I spent so far on the place, and you can pay me back and I will be glad to get the hell out of town. Finally, they backed off.

The previous owner, Mr. Schaller, had Mexican food, steak, and seafood. I changed the whole concept, and it took quite an effort to educate the locals, but as they started to realize what we were trying to do, they accepted it. A couple of years later, it became the Swiss House and had Swiss German food with some European flavor.

I never wanted a hash house, and as a real professional chef, everything was done the proper way, no convenience food. We were well known for excellent food. Before I opened my own restaurant in Grass Valley, I gained all my experience working for different hotel chains, including Hilton, Sheraton, Western, Hyatt, and a couple of private companies.

Showpiece for the Chaine des rotisseure Goument dinner.

Chaine des Rotisseure dinner display.

My very first hotel promotion at the Ilikai in 1967.

CHAPTER 8

DON'T BE AFRAID TO WASH DISHES

We operated Swiss House for 30 years. Unfortunately, I had to close the place after my wife Lily passed away in November 2014. She cannot be replaced; her death took the wind out of my sails, but I know she is watching over me.

We were a good team, and we could count on each other. She was well experienced and knew exactly what it takes to be successful. She deserves some credit for my success having a restaurant for over thirty years. She made sure that the dining room was flawless and the front of the house had the attention it needed. We were a good team and knew exactly what we had to look for in order to stay in business for so long.

Today very few chefs will take the time and effort to travel and move around to gain experience. Instead, they buy cookbooks and even use the internet. You can also buy CDs that will show you step by step how to do it, but there is always a catch—hands-on experience cannot be replicated by just looking through books. You will need special items, and the terms the books use can be confusing.

In most of the United States, you can find places where you can sign up for classes, such as the Culinary Institute. The campus is located in Napa Valley. It is mainly for chefs ready to open their own business.

The younger generation prefers to go out to eat or mother does the cooking, maybe the kids help with the dishes, I hope.

In all of the different styles of kitchen, there are some basic rules in order to arrive at the expected results. Most homemakers are not up to working all day long just to make a stock or sauce. Yes, there are many products on the market you can buy of reasonable quality, but if you want something special, it will take effort.

Even in some of today's restaurants, they use convenience foods because there are not enough qualified chefs on the market, and this way at least it will taste as close as possible to the real thing.

In today's supermarkets such as Costco, Trader Joe's, and other food outlets, you can get almost anything you can think of. But all the books in the world with different recipes at times can be very confusing. You have to have a good basic knowledge in order to come up with a good result.

Most of the Swiss chefs from 1955 onward were looking for a career and worked in different countries, which gave them the opportunity to become diversified and have international experience. They were placed all over the globe.

I never had to look for a job. I was always referred by chef to chef or associates. I basically traveled twice around the globe with my profession. People think a chef is born in two to three years; it took me over ten years, and the learning goes on. I also entered several culinary competitions to measure my skills. It is much more than just flipping hamburgers and making sandwiches.

I think to become a good chef, you have to have some talent for it. I trained several apprentices and was a member of the Chaîne des Rôtisseurs. I won a gold medallion at the Culinary Olympics in Frankfurt, Germany, in 1972 by sculpturing the emperor of China in life size with tallow. I copied it from an ivory carving I borrowed from a jewelry store at the Ilikai Hotel and had to pay seven hundred dollars in case I broke it. Then I sent it on my own to Frankfurt and spent another eight hundred dollars.

In every place I worked, I learned new things and added to my repertoire and résumé. There was a nice collection of items that were beneficial and gave me the variety to prepare daily specials in my own restaurant. Each country is full of culinary treasures—it's endless.

Unfortunately, today everybody is trying to improve the old classical kitchen, but do not be fooled. An apple is an apple, period. It takes discipline to stay true. Just work on one concept. At the Swiss House, we had the old classical kitchen; the new fusion style and reduction approach was used on some special occasions.

If you know what a real pepper steak should look like and then you visit a restaurant that carries such an item on the menu and you get something completely different, what a shock! Now we have many fast-food places and lots of convenience food is being used. It all tastes the same. It takes the fun out of eating out.

There are very few classical places such as French restaurants or Swiss or Japanese kitchens. They have a hard time competing with the chain outfits. Competition is fierce. The younger generation of today is seldom ready to work that hard.

Fast food is not too healthy. Most people do not take the proper time to eat right, instead eating a meal in twenty-five or thirty minutes and even on the run. For a really good meal, it will take about two hours because it is cooked to order and quality ingredients are used. You should really enjoy your meal with a good glass of wine.

Even in the so-called fancy restaurants with a lot of seats, dining is handled as a mass feeding. They need the turnover to pay all the bills. Also, these restaurants are often very noisy.

I was the only assistant chef from the German part of Switzerland at the Hôtel du Rhône in Geneva, and the French chefs did not have too much confidence in me. They used the nickname *Stoffifs* for young chefs from the German part of Switzerland. It was some sort of almost discrimination.

There was a French assistant cook named Allan who cooked for the help for three weeks. His performance was not up to the standard of the chef, usually one week was OK, but more than that was punishment.

We had a French vegetable chef named Raymond, and one day the daily special called for dauphine potatoes, which is cream puff dough mixed together with dry mashed potatoes and then deep-fried. The chef asked the vegetable chef before he went to lunch if the potatoes would hold up in the fryer. Raymond answered, "*Oui.*" The chef then said to him to fire up one portion and see if it was all right.

To Raymond's dismay, the whole deep fryer started to foam up, and he began to panic. Then the chef asked me if I knew how to make such potatoes. Yes, I said. That week it was my turn to cook for the hotel employees, and I was dishing out the food from the kitchen while the whole kitchen crew had their lunch. By the time lunch was over and I completed the potatoes, the chef was happy and offered me a shot of his best brandy he kept under his desk in his chef's office.

We had a young Jewish assistant chef, Roland Ozbold. He was ready to go to Canada, and on his last day of work the chef de cuisine told him to prepare an order of grilled lentils during the guests' lunch service. The chef gave him a requisition for the lentils, then Roland got the lentils out of the storeroom, and then the chef told him how to grill them.

Roland tried very hard to put the lentils on the electric broiler, but they would not hold on to the very thin rods. Then the chef told him to get some egg white and dip the lentils into it. That did not work either. The chef started to laugh and said, "You idiot, this will never work. It was a prank."

This was funny, and all the cooks around the stove started to crack up. It sure was good entertainment.

I was also in Geneva with the intent to go to Montreal, Canada, but it never materialized despite the fact that I had all the papers. My father thought that I would not earn enough money there.

If you want to be successful in life, you first have to know what you want to do with your life, then get a good basic education. When you have chosen your trade, find yourself the proper place where your interest is being taught or practiced. Work there till you know the ins and outs or even move around in first-class places.

Look for a possible promotion, or build up your confidence so that you can be promoted. Make sure you always check out the very best places, and never go for just OK. You might not make a lot of money, but as time goes by you will make up for it in the long run with the experience you will gain. This will give you the opportunity to venture out on your own.

You need to know every detail toward your ultimate goal in order to avoid pitfalls. Then always choose the right size for your start-up— it should be no bigger than you can handle by yourself. Do not take on more than you can handle by yourself. The basic rules of success are quality, consistency, honesty, and knowledge.

Strive for the very best in your field. Yes, there are always big dreams, but be wary of mousetraps, such as economic fluctuations, competition, ability to perform consistently, loss of control over market share, demand for products, loyalty, and being undermined by your competitors.

Keep it simple so that you do not lose control. Check your operation periodically. To avoid inefficient performance, control your overhead and don't spend more than you can afford.

A sound business plan has to be in place. Do not mimic your neighbors. Be your own brand. Believe in yourself. There are a lot of imitators, but only the fittest will eventually survive.

I always improved my operation by looking for more efficient ways of doing business. Do not cut corners; when you jeopardize quality to improve your bottom line, it could cost you dearly.

Yes, a business is there to make money, but do not think you will get rich overnight. Check the records and see how many ventures have come and gone. Be honest and sincere. Public relations are important, as are customer service and feedback. Criticism keeps you honest and is a necessary evil. Stay on top of things, making sure you stick to your plan. Do what you do the very best, and check with your competition.

Honest and trustworthy workers are a must. If they do not perform, let them go. Always seek the best you can get, and give them a probation period; then you will see if you have chosen wisely.

Never promise your workers anything you cannot do. Most people are followers and not leaders. Do not give in to shortcuts. Delegate only as much as they are capable of handling. Let them become comfortable before you add on an extra load. People are creatures of habit and are completely satisfied with their normal routine.

Keep a clean environment, and do not allow any drugs, ever. For hiring purposes, check references. Everyone tells you that they are the best, till you take them to the task.

Job descriptions are important. Cover all the bases. Take nothing for granted, because your reputation is at stake. I believe a strict, decisive, and firm approach will do you good.

Do not have holes where workers can slip through or even attempt to do so. Employees will always know where they stand, and it prevents a lot of grief and headaches. If you tolerate small things, before you know it, they will get bigger and bigger. It is like first the little finger, then the whole arm. Make sure you run the show, no doubt about it. In other words, you are the boss.

All the challenges you will face will make you stronger and even more determined to become successful. There is no golden goose;

everything has to be earned. Only this will make you appreciate your hard work and in turn take care of your achievement. Easy come easy go—sound familiar? Mediocre lackadaisical indecisiveness will cost you in the long run. Your own pride is the barometer toward your own success. Staying on top of things and having satisfied customers will lead to the sustainability of your business.

I took the road of traveling to different counties and by doing so building a career and reputation. This gave me the chance to improve my status in my field while I learned pastries first, then I topped it by also learning to become a chef. This gave me extra qualifications for the job market and my future employment.

Proper learning and taking the time to become knowledgeable and secure in all phases of the trade are important. During the 1950s to 1970s, there was very little convenience food at best. One had to know how to do almost everything. Everybody can cook hamburgers, but those so-called chefs cannot carve ice, make sculptures, or do any related fancy work. Yes, you can learn these things, but in this field, you will see the difference between just OK and excellent. It takes as many years to become a certified chef as it takes a doctor to get a license to practice medicine.

The Swiss are well known for producing excellent all-around chefs who are well traveled. It's important for individuals to set themselves up to be of value to the industry worldwide. You have to have the desire to become excellent, not just go through the motions.

For me, my trades are more like a hobby and not just a job. I never lost interest and pushed myself constantly forward to improve myself. As I grew older, I did get tired, but I have never lost interest in this business.

Never lose your basic principles. You need tenacity and stamina to resist temptation. Always keep your eyes on the big picture and plan for the long run. It is very easy to fall in a pit, but that would be the end of your dream. You build a business for years, but you can also lose it in a few days. Take the same care with your smallest job as you would with a masterpiece.

There will be always ups and downs. The only thing that matters is how you deal with things.

A chef has to be good at multitasking. Business requires a keen business sense. Haste is waste and can become your enemy.

Choose a concept, then stick with it and fine-tune it as you move along. There are four seasons you can play with.

There are so many styles of cooking, and you will be amazed at the choices you have. There are also a lot of trends, and they will put your head into a tizzy and confuse you quickly. I found out over the years of doing business that you must become a person of many hats, and each one is part of the puzzle for success.

Do not be afraid to wash dishes, clean floors, service equipment, or scrub pots and pans—whatever helps you keep costs under control.

Tallow eagle sculpture food show Washington Hilton D.C.

CHAPTER 9

MY URGE TO TRAVEL

The responsibility and risks of a business owner scare away many people, who worry they might fail. This is the challenge; only a few people will take it on, but the reward is sweet. You have to have the desire and a good background with previous experience, which will give you the confidence that will help you toward success.

The Swiss kitchen is pretty international, and you can build on it. Switzerland is surrounded by Germany, France, and Italy. Switzerland is well known for all-around good food. You can go through all the continents and you will be surprised by what you will find.

Food is based many times on climate; food will keep you warm and also keep you cool. You eat heartier in the winter than in the summer. In warmer climates people are more relaxed and need less clothing, which affects their whole lifestyle and habits.

The economy also dictates a lot, and incomes will determine what people spend. Holidays will boost your business, as well specialty items and unique dishes that draw customers. Ambience is not always the main reason for success. The products you sell surely will be.

The environment has to be clean and fresh. People will judge a restaurant on its clean restrooms and kitchen. A foul smell will turn them off.

Word of mouth is the best source for building a solid clientele. Television, newspaper, and radio advertising can get expensive, and if you do not have a good product to sell, it will be tough to attract business.

Convenience food was created because of a shortage of properly qualified professionals. It is almost impossible to turn out as many chefs as the number of new places that are opening. Check out your supermarkets—today you can put a meal together in minutes without even preparing anything. Just open cans, boxes, pouches, and reheat it, period.

This will give you a greater challenge because people always look at the food in the supermarket and think we are doing the same thing. Nothing could be further from the truth. We make our own ravioli, soups, and sauces from square one, and it takes knowledge and qualified labor to do so.

Fast-food outlets have commissaries that standardize all the food for them and deliver most of their food, such as French fries, hamburgers, hot dogs, salad dressings, shredded cheese, and so forth. Yes, a lot of average restaurants also have to look into those sources because of the lack of qualified employees.

Restaurants of my class and quality slowly but surely are becoming very rare to come by. Today you go to many restaurants and the food all tastes the same. Once or twice a week, you will see the trucks from Sysco or US Foods making deliveries, and that's your answer. It's good most of the time, but if you are looking for something better than that, you will have to look for a place where the chef is the owner and practices classical cooking without just convenience food. Yes, it will cost more, but you will be satisfied.

Good food costs money. I do not buy convenience food except tomato paste, flour, eggs, butter, milk, and cream. I even cut all my meats, chicken, and fish. I made all the salad dressings, stocks, soups, and sauces, including desserts. No steam table service—everything was done to order. I did all this with pride and consistency daily.

When I started as a chef, European chefs were known as technicians and not politicians. You got the position because of your professional knowledge, not just because you were a good talker.

My dream was always to travel as a chef, and the opportunities were presented. I had the qualification, and I took advantage of it. My guardian angel sure was with me and kept me out of trouble.

As I grew older and my childhood wounds started to heal, I was able to achieve something nobody in my family thought I could do. I am the only one who became a chef in the family and traveled as far as I did. And I was able, together with my Oriental wife Lily, to open a restaurant in Grass Valley, California, called the Swiss House. Where there is a will, there is always a way.

As a kid I was a rabble-rouser. I vandalized things, drove my mother crazy, and got into trouble with next-door neighbors. I paid a price for it and also took the punishment. It made me even more determined to become successful in whatever I would do.

I was the first one in the family who was able to swim, ride a bike, and ice-skate. I was already very industrious back then.

I got married in Hawaii to my Chinese wife Lily in 1973, and we had forty-one good years together. We both traveled quite a bit, and we both benefited from doing so. We had no children; it was not meant to be.

I always could count on Lily. As a chef you move very often. You get transferred a lot, sometimes to places you never thought of going. Lily had a degree in hotel management from Michigan State University, and she knew my situation as a chef. I guess that's like a quote from Frank Sinatra: My way or the highway. That could be the name of my book, or chef owner's how-to, because of my extensive traveling.

I never deviated from my principles. My pride kept me honest, and at that time everybody was doing the new style of cooking. Quite often my customers told me not to change my old classical cooking because they always knew exactly what they would get and it was very consistent. Yes, I could have copied one of my competitor's concepts, but that would be against my principles. I did sometimes have a special where I opened my approach to the new style.

I concentrated on good soups, nice classic demi-glacé (brown sauce), fresh pasta dishes, and homemade desserts. When I served food, the salad plates were cold and the dinner plates were very hot, as it should be. Unfortunately, in so many places that is not true anymore.

Lily paid special attention to details in the dining room as well in the bar, and she remembered customers' names and also what they had to drink without asking them. She had good customer relations and was well received. She even took care of the small children as if they were her own while their parents had dinner.

We planned our retirement and wanted to visit all the places that had meaning in our lives, including Australia. Even though my job there fell through, it is still a dream of mine to visit Australia. Who knows, it may still become reality if my health holds up. God only knows.

Now I would like to explain what I did in every place I worked, even as an apprentice, then explain the reason behind my menu concept. You have to have all the basic items such as beef, lamb, chicken, fish, pasta, shrimp, veal, vegetables, soups, salad, and desserts just to cover all the bases. Then you might add specials to give even more variety to your concept. Sometimes I even had one month of Italian, French, Polynesian, Oktoberfest, or many other pleasing concepts.

You have to find out what will bring you new business. Maybe even banquets for special occasions and birthday celebrations—anything to generate extra income. Make sure it does not get overwhelming, because it could jeopardize your quality and also the service.

If you are dealing with banquet functions, make sure it is well planned and everything is in writing, and have an exact count so that you do not end up with a lot of waste. At the same time, coordinate it properly so that it can be handled without shortchanging your regular customers. It might even look confusing if everybody runs around like chickens without heads.

You have to know what the kitchen is able to handle. It is much more than just carrying food into the dining room. If you want to have a successful service, it has to be conducted from the back of the house—in other words, from the kitchen.

Wait help like to chat and often forget when to cut it out. If you remind them, then they get ticked off. You have to set the tone right from the beginning so that there will be no dispute and everybody will benefit from it.

You also have to have proper rules and regulations for how your employees conduct themselves while working for you. Certain standards have to be met, such as proper appearance, manners, and knowledge of the trade. All the basics have to be applied and the train of service followed to a T. No shortcuts or even the thought of it. Excuses such as I do not feel good today do not cut it. Your customers deserve the very best, and that will take a lot effort. But if you can do so, you will be rewarded and feel good after your shift.

In the dining room you often have to work as a team, especially when you have large tables of ten or more people. The customers all wish to get the same attention. It's like conducting an orchestra in harmony to make it sound good.

Often, I witnessed employees—especially with guests who come often and are good tippers—hang over their tables and never know when to cut it out. And at the same time, they would forget to serve dessert and coffee or not even clear the table or replenish the water or wine. Some employees would show up late for work and have a weak excuse, or they would not even show up at all and not even bother to call.

There are all kinds of hurdles and hoops you will have to jump through in order to run your business, not to mention the cost of doing business and all the rules and regulations, plus all the taxes you must pay. And that's one reason why so many restaurants fail, and on top of that they hire too many employees and do not know how to control the costs. Instead, they sit outside or in the bar and smoke cigarettes. There is no productivity, and everything starts to fall apart.

When frustration takes over, people lose interest quickly. You have to be able to keep them motivated at all times. A business has to be run respectfully. In many places it is run by the employees, and the bosses are in the bar having a good old time and not really knowing what's going on. Supervision and knowledge of the trade from the inside out will make your business sustainable.

My first time getting my feet wet before I came to Grass Valley was in Santa Isabel, California, at the Chicken Shake Restaurant. It had seventy seats, and on Fridays and Sundays, we served seven hundred customers from noon till 8:00 p.m. The menu included fried chicken, chicken cordon bleu, prime rib, and baked chicken. These came with soup, salad, and fresh biscuits, and some had fresh mashed potatoes, French fries, and vegetables.

The kitchen crew were all high school kids who did not have much knowledge, and it was often a real test to get things done. The restaurant was open five days a week, and I was able to see what else was in the neighborhood. The owner was Franz Dolder, and he thought that I would take the restaurant over since he wanted to retire. But I was looking for a place of my own, with higher standards.

I left the Chicken Shake Restaurant at the end of March 1985, when I heard from Lily about the accident that Serge Bartolome, the owner of Scheidels Restaurant, had suffered. He broke his neck in a plane crash and was paralyzed and in a wheelchair. We had worked together in Canada at the Foxhead Sheraton. Lily said maybe I could see if I could buy his place. I started working for him on April 3, 1985. He asked me to start on April 1, but I never took a job on April Fool's Day.

I made him an offer, but the deal fell through. So then I ended up at the then-called Empire House, which I bought. I started working on the Empire House on August 3 to get it ready for the opening on Thanksgiving Day. This was my first experience as an owner of my own restaurant, in Grass Valley.

It ended on November 18, 2014, when Lily passed away. We operated the place proudly for thirty years and made many improvements and sacrifices to bring the place to what it is today.

I decided to sell the place. It is a turnkey operation with a full liquor license. It is well equipped, kept very clean, has a lot of parking, and also has potential for any future owner. You just have to be willing to work it.

My present concept is Swiss German food with a few international dishes such as Hungarian goulash, osso buco, rack of lamb, and Mongolian lamb.

Whoever takes it over will have a lot of possibilities. We had very good clientele who were very loyal and had a good reputation in town.

At the beginning we served lunch and dinner five days a week. Then after about twenty years, my doctor told me to take it easy. So we served dinners only. Then I had a hip replacement, and from then on we went down to four days a week, dinners only.

I always liked the business and always will, but when Lily passed it became hard for me. It feels like somebody cut my leg off, and the energy was missing. I am sure I will find a good way to overcome this feeling and do something that brings enjoyment and satisfaction for the rest of my life, in order to fulfill a few of my unfilled dreams.

I worked since I was sixteen, and I know this will be somehow rewarded. I am living a clean life and basically mind my own business. Yes, I have a few hobbies and special interests, which will keep me occupied for a long time if my health holds.

When I look back on my life, I can say so far it has been very rewarding indeed. I lived my dream and then some, and it all started with a childhood dream in 1946 in a small town called Mannedorf, Switzerland. I also cooked several dinners for the Chaîne des Rôtisseurs, a high society of chefs founded in France. It was originally just for chefs, but today it is taken over by doctors and lawyers and other food connoisseurs. It is very prestigious, and you have to be inducted to become a member. I was inducted in Hawaii at the Ilikai Hotel in 1971. I opened several hotels and traveled the globe. I was always true to myself. I never pretended to be others. I took the good and the bad. If you are not honest with yourself, you are living a fantasy, and eventually it will catch up with you and I guess it is not funny.

The same applies to business. You can fool some of the people some of the time but not all the time. I am living a simple life. I stay away from temptation, do what I think is allowable, and do not want to become the talk of the town. I always stand up for what's right. What you see is what you get, and you can take it to the bank; in other words, no BS.

Over the years, I learned a lot and put it into practice. It gave my place a certain personality, and I was always checked out by my competitors. Some of them tried to copy some of the items I had on the menu. Quite often I was told by my competitors that they could not afford an expensive chef like me and had to make do with what they had.

Our place is not exactly in the middle of town. I always try to stay away from all the politics, but every now and then I got caught up in the crosshairs of the so-called lawmakers. Yes, they will always find something you have to comply with. Most of the time it was just little things they were concerned about.

I guess that's the nature of the game. In order to maximize your success, stay on top of things as much as possible. Do not wait till something becomes overwhelming.

Being from Switzerland, having a clean place was never an issue. We are raised to be neat and organized and to clean as we go along in every possible way. People appreciated us for that.

Lily was raised in China, and her dad had a position with the Mobil gas company as a supervisor. Her family had servants and a chauffeur. After completing her schooling at Michigan State University, she was quickly introduced into the hands-on world. She did an excellent job at the restaurant and even enjoyed it immensely. She also helped out in the kitchen as much as she could.

Yes, we had long hours but also had many good times together. We took some trips to Germany, Austria, and Switzerland, where I introduced her to my family. They did not know to whom I got married, despite sending them an invitation from Hawaii. It was too far for them to travel. I always made my own decisions after I left the old country. I made a good choice, and we got the OK when we arrived in Switzerland.

Lily had a very close family and enjoyed trips to Hawaii now and then. Grass Valley became her adopted hometown, and she felt very comfortable here.

Her father gave her his Volvo 760. It was a very sturdy car, and she felt secure driving it. To the last day, she never would have given it up.

CHAPTER 10

LEARNING AND THEN PRACTICE

Yes, I have given you a lot about me, but let's go back and make a good chicken stock. Most of the homemakers never think of it, because it takes too much time.

First, get yourself a fresh 3- to 4-pound chicken. Then get all the needed items ready, also called *mise en place*, or setup. Take a large 3- to 4-gallon pot, fill it with hot water, set it on the stove, and bring it to a boil. When it boils, place the chicken in it and slowly bring it again to a boil, then remove the chicken. Cool the chicken in cold water. Empty the water from the pot you used to blanch the chicken. Wash the pot clean, then fill it with water again. Bring the water to the boiling point, then place the chicken in it. When the water starts to boil again, reduce the heat so that it just simmers.

If there is some foam showing up, skim it off. Then add your vegetables, such as carrots, celery, leeks, onions, one or two cloves of garlic, cracked white peppercorn, salt, parsley stems, and a twig of fresh rosemary.

Slowly simmer the chicken till it is done. When the legs are starting to have a hint of cracking, that means the chicken is cooked.

Remove the chicken and vegetables with a large chef's fork, place them in a deep dish, and strain some of the stock over them. The stock will keep the chicken and vegetables warm while boil a few noodles al dente in lightly salted water. Then divide the chicken; each portion should be a half of a 2-pound chicken. Combine the stock, noodles, vegetables, and the divided chicken. Now you have stewed chicken with vegetables and noodles, or *pot-au-feu*.

Strain the rest of the stock and cool it. You can also freeze it, and you will have a good stock when it is called for in your next recipe.

If you buy canned chicken stock, choose Swanson and make sure it is low sodium and without MSG.

Now let's make a clear beef stock. And at the same time, you will have a meal you can enjoy. The procedure is very similar to that for chicken stock, but this time we are going to use beef. I would suggest using a tri-tip, but first you will have to trim off some of the fat and the silver skin. Then follow the same steps as you did for the chicken stock.

Here you might use some more vegetables, such as white cabbage, celery root, turnips, or Chinese cabbage. It also may need extra cracked black peppercorn, and if the stock is somewhat weak, fortify it with some MSG-free beef base. Make sure you do not over season it with salt.

The stock again can be chilled and then frozen and can be used for anything you wish where clear beef stock is asked for. Onion soup comes to my mind. Or just use it as a bouillon—it's good soup.

I know it will take some extra effort, but if you like to cook, it is worth the effort.

If you do not eat all the beef the same day, prepare a vinaigrette sauce, slice the beef thin, then pour the sauce over it.

You may be concerned about not knowing exactly when the beef is done while boiling it. The beef will float on top of the liquid, and to make sure it's done, use a bamboo stick or a kebab skewer and stick it into the meat. When the juice comes out clear, that means it is well done.

In order not to overcook your vegetables, check them while they are simmering. When the vegetables are done, take them out and keep them warm in a separate dish till your meat is done, then combine as you wish. You can use horseradish sauce, mustard, or any other kind of sauce, even salsa. Be creative, as the saying goes. Remember, cooking has a lot of possibilities. It all depends on what you like.

Make sure you do not slice your meat too thick, because it may be tough and chewy and you will be disappointed.

A lot of people like to cook seafood dishes that require fish stock, and since you do not have all day to make the stock, I recommend purchasing low-sodium clam juice or fish bouillon. At the same time, it will not be too fishy.

When you poach fish, make sure you buy a sort of fish that is meant to be poached. Ask the butcher at the supermarket about it; he or she will be glad to tell you.

To poach fish, you will need some dry white wine. It can be done by adding shrimp, mushrooms, scallops, clams, mussels, or any combination that will go with seafood. You can add shallots, sweet (unsalted) butter, salt, and ground white pepper.

To poach your seafood combination, use a stainless steel pan and make sure you have enough wine to cover the food. Then bring it to a boil on top of the stove, cover with a lid, and complete the cooking in the oven at 400 degrees. Make sure you do not overcook it; when you touch it with your finger, it should be still firm but not mushy.

When it is done, take the seafood out of the pan, place it on a plate, and keep it warm. You may use the same lid to cover it. If you want to make a sauce, put your liquid back on the stove and reduce the heat. Add heavy cream and a few drops of lemon juice, and check the seasoning. Then reduce it till it is lightly creamy. Place the seafood on serving plates and pour your sauce over it. Serves it with your favorite vegetables. Seafood also goes well with potatoes.

If it is done right, it is a delight. Cooking seafood is a specialty thing and needs to be done properly. This will take some skill, and even in some restaurants it is sometimes questionable. There is a saying: to be or not to be. Take your pick.

Only experienced chefs will have the knowledge to be consistent, and sometimes there is a lack of them. The time it takes to prepare a decent meal is definitely worth it, but you have to have the passion to do so. It is not fast food. Remember!

Over all these years, we had quite a few customers who requested special items, such as rabbit stew, rack of lamb, sweetbread, chateaubriand, braised lamb shanks, formula-fed veal chops, whole prime ribs with Yorkshire pudding, calf liver, salmon poached in romaine lettuce, and Chinese steamed vegetables in a bamboo steamer. Some people even asked for rösti with *geschnetzeltes*, a specialty from Zurich, whole lobsters, and many more items.

They all ordered in advance and never asked what it would cost. They had confidence in me and also knew my background.

The same applied to our dessert section, which had hot chocolate soufflés and flamed bananas. I had a baker's rack in the dining room and furnished items according the season—egg bread, Christmas stollen, all kinds of cookies, and even chocolate candies.

We had seasoning salt and hot pepper jelly. And we sold salad dressings and had to-go orders.

The Swiss House has a banquet room that can accommodate seventy guests. During the year, we featured special events, such as Oktoberfest, Polynesian month, Italian month, April in Paris, and even August 1, which is the Swiss national day. You can see there was never a dull moment, but you have to have all the knowledge to do so, or as they say in my profession, to be or not to be.

I guess in this business you can do different things all through your life, and it looks as if you'll never run out of new ideas. The only thing is that you have to love what you are doing, and if it becomes a job then it is time to get out of it. For me it was a dream come true. I look at it as a hobby; this way you never get tired of it.

There are very few restaurants that stay in business for thirty years, and with the same owner. I never was looking for a hash house. We stressed quality and consistency all the time. We had a good following, and we stuck to our guns.

You always knew what you are getting—no guesswork, period! I am in good standing with the police department and health department, and we always paid our bills.

Grass Valley was good to us, and I plan to retire here. There are still a few things I wish to accomplish, now that I have sold the restaurant, but first I still need to settle in. I sold the restaurant in 2017.

I like to stay busy, and I do not see myself sitting in a rocking chair and waiting till the days are gone. I hope to travel sometime in the future, but I have some limitations because of my hip replacement, and recently I tore my right shoulder ligaments, which will take a long time to heal. But have no fear, Karl will be here.

It is amazing how much stuff you accumulate over the years. I surely will amuse myself for quite some time. I intend to find a way to organize myself so that I feel comfortable and enjoy life to the fullest as long as I have it.

For me life is a journey, and I will make the best out of it, despite the ups and downs we all face. I know the sun will always come up again. It's just a matter of belief and trust and faith. It is not just me; we all have to stick together to make it work.

With good health life is wonderful, and as you get older it has meaning, and you will be able to reminisce over all the things you have seen and done. It's just like a movie, but it is real and not just make believe.

I cannot imagine why so many people in this day and age are not exited by life. You have to look for that excitement, and eventually you will find it.

There is more to life than just eating and sleeping. Enjoy the simple things you find out there. Believe me, it is amazing. It is better than a lot of school learning.

And it is yours to keep.

Your life will be fulfilling, and every day you can build on it. I remember when we started thirty years ago what the prices were and what is going on today. I kept many menus to illustrate exactly what I mean by that—not only the change of the restaurant's name from Empire House to Swiss House but also how we evolved along the way.

Changes are not easy, and it requires passion and money. First, we had to give the place a new look. But since the place is a historical site, we had to apply for permits, which was a task by itself. On the inside it is less complicated—the rules were completely different.

We took some time off, since trying to run a restaurant while construction is going on does not work out too well, as you can probably imagine. When it was done, our guests really appreciated it and gave us a boost in business.

The whole process was just like raising a child, and to keep it that way you have to cherish the progress and investment. It took us some time to convince our employees to be gentle on our investment. We did not want to make it look like it was done many years ago.

To take over an old business surely has a hefty price tag. My father told me one time that if you want to get rid of your money quickly, then just buy an old house. He spoke from experience. He did exactly that when he was younger.

I consider myself a handyman and was able to do a few things on my own. I saved some money that way. If you totally rely on everybody else, it will be overwhelming. As they say in the old country, every penny counts, and if you do not respect the penny then the dollar has no meaning.

As kids, when we saw a penny on the street, we picked it up. When the head showed up, that meant good luck.

A penny saved is a penny earned.

We did not have any allowance when I was growing up, but if we ever had a few cents we made sure it was used wisely. It was clear to me then and ever since that whenever I bought something for myself it had to be something that would last for a long time, not just for the fun of it. Cheap things are usually short-lived and very expensive in the long run.

Osso Buco   Serves 5

Osso buco is an Italian dish, and we had it on the dinner menu from day one. It became a favorite dish for many of our loyal guests. As time went on, it became pricey and very hard to get; nevertheless, I made it as a special now then, and it was very popular. I would like to share the recipe with you in case you would like to try it at home yourselves.

First you have to find a place where you can get milk-fed veal hind shanks, maybe in a supermarket that is willing to get it. Go to the meat department and ask the butcher if they have it, and if not, the butcher may know where to get it. The butcher shop can also cut it into portions for you.

This is for five people, and it will take five 12-ounce or smaller milk-fed veal hind shanks.

I make my own seasoning salt, but you can get some at the store—just make sure it is without MSG. You will need the following ingredients:

Flour to dust
5 ounces cottonseed oil
6 ounces finely chopped onion
1 ounce minced garlic
6 ounces root celery cut into fine dices (called brunoise)
6 ounces carrots, also brunoise
3 ounces tomato paste
4 ounces flour
5 ounces dry white wine
½ gallon clear brown veal stock (you may substitute a low-sodium light beef stock)
Thyme
Rosemary
Basil
Marjoram
Ground white pepper
Seasoning salt

You need a large saucepot with a thick bottom. Heat the oil on high, then add the seasoning salt and flour. Dust the veal shanks and brown on both sides but do not burn. Remove from the pot and keep on the side on a plate.

Reduce the heat and let the saucepot cool off so that when you add the garlic and other vegetables it will just smother. With a wooden spoon, stir till all the baked-on crust has dissolved. Add the seasoning salt, spices, tomato paste, and flour. Blend well. Pour in the stock and use a wire whisk till everything is completely lump free. Heat the sauce slowly while occasionally stirring so that it does not burn.

When it boils, reduce the heat and place the shanks in it. Simmer till they are tender—about 40 minutes. You can take one out and squeeze it with your finger. It should feel soft but not overcooked.

If the sauce is too thin, reduce it till you have the right consistency. It should cover the meat nicely and not be watery.

⚜   ⚜   ⚜

Gremolata

It is time to make the gremolata, which is actually a special seasoning to enhance the flavor of the veal but is only put on top of the marrowbone.

½ bunch parsley
½ ounce fresh garlic
¼ ounce caraway seeds
½ lemon rind
½ orange rind
all the above items need to be finely chopped

Mix the ingredients together. Serve with noodles, spaetzli, or risotto rice. Broccoli is a nice Italian vegetable with it.

Once again, it will take some labor of love to cook osso buco, or maybe there is a place where they have it on their menu.

Blue Cheese Dressing

2 pounds blue cheese crumbs
2 pints buttermilk
1 gallon mayonnaise
5 ounces white vinegar
Salt
Ground white pepper
Tabasco sauce
Worcestershire sauce

Blend all ingredients together, making sure that the cheese is properly broken up. Otherwise, you might have one big lump of cheese on the bottom of your mixing bowl. If the dressing is a bit too thick, add some cold water to make it thinner.

Store it in the fridge. It will last for a long time but must be kept in the cooler.

I make it with 30 pounds of mayonnaise. Use 1½ ounces of dressing per small salad.

Brandy Cocktail Sauce

½ gallon mayonnaise
1½ cups ketchup
1½ ounces horseradish
2 ounces mango chutney, finely chopped
¼ ounce ground white pepper
¼ ounce English mustard
1 teaspoon white salt
3 ounces brandy
3 ounces whipped cream
Tabasco sauce
Worcestershire sauce

This is the European style of cocktail sauce, also called Calypso sauce. Use 2 ounces per serving.

Spaetzli   Serving size 3 ounces

In Switzerland we call it chnöpli.

1 pound white flour
1 teaspoon white salt
12 whole eggs
Dash of ground nutmeg

Put all items together in your mixing machine, then blend it with the hook attachment at low speed. It should look like a thick pancake batter.

Use a food mill with a medium blade and let the batter drop into the boiling water, but make sure you do not dip your mill into the hot water. Do it in small quantities, using a rubber spatula to scrap off extra batter.

With a spoon, stir it lightly to separate the nuggets. Bring it to a boil, then with a skimmer remove it and drop it into a container of ice water.

When you have used up all the batter and everything has cooled off, strain it into a colander. If you are ready to serve your spaetzli, sauté your product in butter and season lightly with salt.

You can also freeze it in a ziplock bag. This way you will have some for your next occasion.

Meat Sauce

Bolognese sauce is the Italian name for it.

2 pounds lean ground beef
5 ounces finely chopped onions
1 ounce finely chopped garlic
3 ounces celery
3 ounces carrots
3 ounces medium leeks, finely chopped
2 ounces tomato paste
10 ounces fresh, peeled, diced tomatoes
3 ounces dry red wine
½ gallon demi-glacé (brown sauce)
Seasoning salt
Marjoram
Thyme
Bay leaf
Paprika
Ground white pepper

You can substitute brown beef stock for the demi-glacé, but you may have to thicken it with cornstarch diluted with some red wine.

In a heavy saucepot over high heat, brown the ground beef in a small amount of salad oil. It has to sizzle but not smoke. Make sure the meat takes on a brown color and looks like it has been cooked properly, because this will give you extra flavor.

Then add the garlic and all other vegetables and seasonings. You might need a little bit more oil, but be frugal so that the oil does not float all over the intended sauce.

Sauté for a few minutes, then add the tomato paste and pour in the wine. Stir well, and make sure you reduce the heat so that it does not burn. Add the brown sauce and bring again to a simmer. Cover the pot with a lid and let it simmer for about 1 hour.

Frequently check the sauce—it may need some more seasoning and liquid. You can fortify it with some beef base. The end product should look like a rich but not dry sauce.

If the sauce is too thin, take some cornstarch, dilute it with red wine, and slowly pour it into the sauce. Stir constantly while adding the cornstarch so that the end result is smooth.

This sauce goes good with spaghetti. Top it with Parmesan cheese and a pad of sweet solid butter.

If you do not have time to chop all the vegetables, you could use a food processor but make sure it is coarse, not mushy. You could also use a Crock-Pot to cook it. This way it will be safer to handle, but you still have to brown the meat first. The Bolognese sauce can also be frozen.

Caramel Custard   **Serves 12**

    12 soup cups
    1 quart milk

14 ounces of sugar total
7 medium eggs
8 ounces sugar
½ ounce vanilla extract
Pinch of salt

Caramelize 8 ounces of the sugar by adding a small amount of water to it then heating it in a small saucepot over low heat till the sugar is golden brown. Add another small amount of water and let it dissolve so that you have a thick syrup.

Take 12 regular soup cups. Divide the caramel liquid evenly into the cups. The bottoms should be well covered.

In a mixing bowl combine the remaining 6 ounces of sugar, vanilla extract, the eggs, and a pinch of salt. Blend well with a whisk till nice and creamy, then bring the milk to a boil and slowly pour the boiling milk into the sugar, vanilla, and egg mixture while constantly stirring. Then strain it though a fine sieve.

Fill the caramelized soup cups evenly with the milk, vanilla, sugar, and egg mixture and poach the filled cups in a water bath in a 400-degree oven for about 50 minutes. Check for doneness with a bamboo stick or a kebab skewer. Put a folded newspaper on the bottom of the pan where you will place the soup cups. This will prevent bubbles in your custard.

If the stick comes out clear, that means it is done. The water bath will also prevent the custard from having small bubbles in it. Make sure you do not over poach. If you over poach, it will get dry. It should look like a firm custard sauce. Let it cool completely, then with a small knife cut along the rim of the cups, put a service plate on top, and turn it upside down. It should fall out onto the plate.

Garnish with whipped cream and fresh berries.

⚜ ⚜ ⚜

Polenta

> 2 pints milk
> 1 cup water
> 3 ounces cornmeal
> ⅛ teaspoon salt
> 2 ounces Parmesan cheese
> 1 ounce butter

Bring water, milk, and salt to a boil in a heavy saucepan, then slowly pour in the cornmeal (polenta). Reduce the heat and stir constantly with a wooden spoon till you have a consistency like thick oatmeal. Beware, it could splash and hit your arm, and you may get burned.

Then pour the polenta into a slightly oiled shallow pan, cool in the fridge till completely cold, and cut it into portions.

Panfry it or even broil it. Sprinkle with Parmesan cheese.

Saltimbocca Romana with Chicken   Serves 1

> 3 each 2-ounce chicken breasts, boneless and skinless
> 3 each ½-ounce thin-sliced prosciutto ham
> 3 each large fresh sage leaves
> 8 ounces au jus
> 2 ounces dry white wine
> 1 ounce salad oil
> Salt and ground white pepper to season

First trim the chicken breasts, then take a piece of clear plastic wrap and pound the breasts thin and even. Season them, but be aware the ham is salty. Place one sage leaf in the center of each chicken breast, then top it with the prosciutto ham and gently press down on it.

Preheat a cast iron pan. It will keep the heat better and gives a rusty look. When the pan is good and hot, pour in the oil. Then fry the chicken breasts ham side down first for a couple of minutes, then turn over.

When the chicken breasts are done, remove and place them on a warm plate. Pour out the extra oil, bring the pan back to the heat, add the wine, and let it deglaze. That means the meat residue will blend with the wine. Add the au jus and reduce till you have a light syrupy texture.

Garnish the serving plate with the polenta, broccoli florets, and the chicken breasts. Pour the reduction over it. Garnish with a twig of fresh rosemary. Bon appétit.

You could also use veal instead of chicken.

Jaegerschnitzel

Jaeger means "hunter," and the hunting is done in the forest, where you find wild mushrooms.

> 6 each 1-ounce well-trimmed pork tenderloin, pounded like piccatas
> 2 ounces white sliced mushrooms
> 2 ounces baby portabellas, sliced
> 1 ounce oyster mushrooms
> 1 medium fresh tomato, peeled and diced
> 1 ounce dry white wine
> ½ teaspoon chopped parsley
> 2 ounces demi-glacé (brown sauce)
> 1 ounce clarified butter
> Flour to dust
> Seasoning salt

I prefer a cast iron pan for this dish. This is also an à la carte dish and needs a bit of heat; otherwise, the meat will be tough.

Season the meat with seasoning salt, dust with flour, and quickly panfry it on both sides. It should look golden brown.

Remove from the pan and place it on a warm plate. Add all the mushrooms and sauté for a minute or so, then deglaze with the wine. Pour in the brown sauce and tomatoes and let it reduce so that it covers the mushrooms and tomatoes nicely. This dish goes well with spaetzli and fresh mixed vegetables. The last touch is some chopped parsley.

Pâte Brisée

> 2 pounds sifted all-purpose flour
> 16 ounces sweet solid cold butter
> ¾ ounce salt
> 1¾ to 2 cups cold water

In a mixing machine, add the flour, salt, and cold cubed butter just out of the fridge. On slow speed, let it mix till you have a product that is crumbly looking but not sticking together—it should be loose and flaky. Add the cold water, then just barely mix it together. Do not work it too hard. The dough should be easy to roll out without shrinking.

This dough can be used for pie and quiche.

Chocolate Mousse

> 12 ounces semisweet dark chocolate (Swiss Lindt is available at Raley's or Trader Joe's)
> 2 ounces confectioners' sugar
> 3 ounces sweet solid butter
> 2 eggs
> 1 pint whipping cream
> 1 ounce Kahlúa liqueur

First, melt the chocolate and butter in a double boiler. This means you take a medium-size pot, add some water, and place it on top of the stove. Then place a stainless-steel bowl with the chocolate and butter on top of the pot. Use a wooden spoon to stir, and make sure that it is not hot, just melted.

In another bowl, first separate the 2 eggs and keep the whites separate. Add half of the sugar to the egg yolks, add the Kahlúa, and whisk it to a creamy mixture. Continue till everything is well blended.

In your mixing machine, first whip your cream, but do not make it too stiff; otherwise, it will be hard to blend it together. Take the whipping cream out of bowl and wash the bowl really well so that there is absolutely no fat remaining and the bowl is cold. Pour the egg whites and the remaining part of the sugar together in the bowl, then whip the mixture so that when you turn the bowl upside down it does not fall out.

Check the chocolate and butter mixture. It should be runny and a bit warmer than body temperature. Add it to the egg mixture, and with a rubber spatula fold in half of the whipped cream and egg whites. When it is smooth, add the second half of the whipped cream and egg whites to the mixture and fold in.

You can spoon the mousse into glass dishes and decorate with whipped cream and strawberries.

The mouse can be done the day before if you plan to entertain.

❧   ❧   ❧

Curried Noodles   Serves 1

3 ounces chicken breast fillets
2 ounces red bell pepper, cut into strips
1 ounce root celery, cut into julienne
1½ ounces bock choy strips
1 ounce sliced fresh mushrooms
2 ounces butter
2 ounces white wine
3 ounces heavy cream
2 ounces sliced banana
½ ounce yellow raisins
¾ ounce curry powder
¼ ounce cut green onion
½ ounce toasted sliced almonds
Salt
Pepper
Flour for dusting
Cottonseed oil

Season the chicken fillets with salt and pepper. Flour dust and quickly panfry in cottonseed oil. Set aside.

In a separate pan, sauté all the vegetables in butter. Deglaze with the white wine. Pour in the cream and add the fruits, curry powder, and chicken fillets. Rotate till everything is well coated. Pour all of this on a bed of linguine. Garnish with the almonds and green onions.

Cucumber, Swiss Cheese, and Onion Salad

1 pound skinny fresh Japanese cucumbers
3 ounces real Swiss cheese
3 ounces white onions
Ground white pepper
Light soy sauce

Olive oil
Rice wine vinegar

Peel and seed the cucumber, then cut it into julienne. The same will be done with the cheese and the onions.

Marinate all the ingredients in the pepper, soy sauce, olive oil, and rice wine vinegar. When you are ready to plate the salad, garnish it with slices of boiled eggs and chopped parsley.

Kartoffelpuffer

My first dish prepared on the stove as an apprentice in the kitchen was kartoffelpuffer for the help. It is German potato pancakes.

6 medium raw potatoes, about 2 pounds (preferably baker's potatoes)
2 whole eggs
2 ounces finely chopped onion
2 ounces flour
1 teaspoon salt
Cooking oil for frying

First you have to peel the potatoes, then place them into cold water right away so they will not discolor.

Beat the eggs in a large stainless steel bowl. Add the chopped onion, flour, and salt and mix into a smooth batter.

Remove the potatoes from the water and dry each one with a paper towel. Shred the potatoes medium fine. Place the potatoes in a colander and squeeze out all the water.

Combine the potatoes with the batter, then panfry it small batches about 5 inches in diameter, using a cast iron pan. Use a good amount of oil. The oil has to be hot so that the puffer will get nice and crispy on both sides.

With a spoon, form them into 5-inch rounds. They really should look like pancakes. Serve with applesauce. Kids will love them too.

There are also potato pancakes made with a flour batter, and then you add the cooked potatoes to it. In order to make them tastier, add green chopped onions, finely chopped white onions, chopped parsley, eggs, salt, white pepper, and maybe some nutmeg. Then also fry it, but this time over medium heat. This dish cannot be kept too long because the pancakes will get soggy. In other words, cook and eat.

One of the next items I was taught to make was omelets with chicken liver. This is not for breakfast. It is served as an appetizer.

To make a proper omelet takes some skill. It is not just like folding it over. It has to be soft inside, and you roll it out of the rim of the frying pan onto your serving dish. It should look like an even, oblong, smooth product.

For a first course (appetizer), you use only two eggs, and the chicken liver is sautéed after being blanched in brown butter and a brown red wine sauce. The chicken liver is usually served in a sauceboat on the side.

Again, I practiced first by cooking farmer's omelets for the help. It gave me the proper experience to be able to cook for the hotel guests. It just so happened that when I was an apprentice in the pastry shop, we had a tearoom, and there we had omelets on the lunch menu. I was chosen to make the omelets, and already it was not exactly strange to me.

A lot of learning requires a lot of practice, and the way to practice and not waste money was by cooking for the help. It was not always glamorous, but it surely did the trick. The most important thing was to gain confidence in what you needed to master consistently and, in some ways, to become second nature.

I started on the bottom, and again it's like building a house—it needs a proper foundation. Once you are comfortable with something, you can go on and expand your knowledge to make it possible to pass your upcoming exam.

It's much more than just chopping parsley. If you learn anything that maybe one day will earn you a living, you better take it seriously. Just getting by does not cut it in any trade or profession. If you wish for longevity in anything, you will have to become very efficient and be sure you are on the right track.

Geschnetzeltes Nach Zücher Art   Serves 3

I said that I am from Zurich, Switzerland. We have a special there called geschnetzeltes nach Zürcher art, which is a veal dish. This recipe makes 6 ounces total, or 3 servings.

> 3 ounces white mushrooms
> ½ ounce finely chopped shallot
> 2 ounces veal kidneys
> 2 ounces veal tenderloin
> 1 teaspoon seasoning salt
> 2 ounces demi-glacé (brown sauce)
> 3 ounces heavy cream
> 2 ounces dry white wine
> 1½ ounces brandy

First trim and slice the veal, cleaned veal kidneys, and white mushrooms. Then sauté the veal, kidneys, and mushrooms over high heat so that it does not simmer. It has to seal quickly; otherwise, it may be tough.

Remove the pan from the stove and clean out all the loose residue.

Then add some butter and sauté the chopped shallots. Deglaze with the brandy and white wine, then pour in some demi-glacé and heavy cream.

Bring it to a boil, place all remaining items in it, and heat it once again before you are ready to serve it. Make sure that it does not boil because it could get tough. In Switzerland we serve it with rösti.

Rösti Potatoes

This is Swiss hash browns. Using a nonstick pan, sauté finely chopped onions and thin slices of bacon in butter, then add the cold, cooked shredded potatoes and season with salt. While you brown it, make sure you rotate it several times—in other words, flip it over several times before you let it get nice and golden brown on both sides. The end product should be round and crispy on both sides. Make yourself a nice mixed green salad and you have a wonderful dinner.

In Switzerland we have specialty restaurants that strictly serve specialties from all twenty-six cantons, which are like states but on a smaller scale. Remember, Switzerland is small, but the Swiss are decisive and proud of what they do.

Veal Sweetbreads

This is a very special dish, and very seldom can you find a place where it is done properly. Often it is deep-fried.

My recipe is very different because I blanch the sweetbreads first and let them cool off in the stock. I use pickling spices and some salt to blanch, then I cut them into medallions and panfry them in clarified butter till they are nice and brown.

I sauté chopped shallots and white sliced mushrooms, add cracked black peppercorn, flame it with cognac and white wine, then add demi-glacé, heavy cream, seasoning salt, and a few drops of lemon juice. The sauce is then poured over the sweetbreads. I served it with spaetzli or rice.

The secret for a good outcome is the properly made demi-glacé. No purchased product can compare to it; it is the personality of the chef. Every chef has a different one.

Frozen Lemon Soufflé

> 3 lemon rinds and juice, soaked overnight
> 6 whole eggs
> 1 egg yolk
> 9 ounces sugar
> 16 ounces heavy whipping cream

Add the 6 eggs and the yolk to the sugar and mix together well in a stainless steel mixing bowl. Then grind the lemon rind and juice together in a blender and place it in the top of a double boiler. Create a *sabayon* and continue to whip it until it is completely cold. Put your finger in it; the temperature should be about 100 degrees. Make sure you do not overheat it. It's like making a hot biscuit cake. Then fold in the stiff heavy whipping cream.

Pour it into the desired serving dishes or glasses and freeze overnight. Before you serve it, dust with sweet cocoa powder, and serve with raspberry *coulis*.

Béchamel Sauce

This is a white milk-based ground sauce, which is a basic sauce that can be used to make many different types of sauces.

> 1 quart milk
> 2 ounces butter
> 3 ounces flour
> Pinch of nutmeg
> Dash of salt

First melt the butter, then add the flour. This is called a *roux*. Let it cook for a couple of minutes, then put it to the side and let it cool down. Heat the milk but do not completely bring it to a boil. Slowly pour the milk into the roux with the help of a wire whisk. This makes a smooth and creamy sauce. Add the seasoning and let it simmer for about 30 minutes. To make sure you have no lumps in the sauce, strain it through a cheesecloth.

Add grated Parmesan cheese to it and now you have Mornay sauce.

Crêpes Suzette

Glazed delicate French crêpes

> 1½ cups flour
> 1½ cups cornstarch
> 12 fresh eggs
> 2 cups heavy cream
> ½ pound brown butter
> ½ cup of sugar
> Râpée of 1 orange (very finely grated orange)
> 1 lemon, finely grated

Mix the sugar, flour, cornstarch, lemon, and orange râpée together. Then add the eggs one by one. Whip vigorously with a wire whip. The batter should be thin and lump-free.

Pour in the heavy cream and then slowly blend in the brown butter. To make the crêpes, use a nonstick pan and make them very thin. You do not have to add any nonstick spray because the butter you put in the batter will do that for you, but make sure the pan is not too hot, just warm; otherwise, it will stick or even burn. This is a large amount, and you may reduce the quantities according to your needs.

Syrup

For the syrup to flame the crêpes, you need the following ingredients:

1½ ounces sweet (unsalted) solid butter
1 ounce white sugar
1 ounce orange juice
½ ounce lemon juice
½ ounce Grand Marnier
¼ ounce kirschwasser
½ ounce brandy
2 ounces heavy cream

Caramelize the sugar and butter, then flame it with the brandy. Add the Grand Marnier and kirschwasser, pour in the orange and lemon juice, and let it reduce over low heat till it becomes a light syrup. Then add the cream, and then coat the crêpes with the syrup. Fold the crêpes into quarters, then place them on dessert plates and enjoy them with a glass of champagne.

There are very few places where this type of dessert is still served. It is a real classic. Most of the time it is done tableside.

⚜   ⚜   ⚜

Semmelknoedel   Serves 4

Bread dumpling for 4 people

> 8 each day-old French rolls
> 2 cups hot milk (to soak)
> 2 strips finely diced raw bacon
> 1 medium finely chopped onion
> ½ teaspoon chopped parsley
> 2 eggs
> Nutmeg
> Salt
> 1½ quarts chicken stock

First cut the rolls into ½-inch cubes and soak them in the hot milk till the bread is complexly mushy. Then add all other ingredients and blend everything well together. Form it into 1½-inch balls. Poach your dumpling in chicken stock. When they float on top of the chicken stock, that means they are done.

Knoedels go good with pot roast. You can buy the chicken stock in a supermarket.

Fillet Goulash Stroganoff   Serves 1

> ½ ounce Hungarian paprika
> 4 ounces beef tenderloin
> 1 small chopped shallot
> ¼ clove garlic, finely chopped
> 1 ounce julienne of dill pickles (not sweet)
> ¼ ounce vodka
> 1 ounce demi-glacé (brown sauce)
> ½ ounce heavy cream
> ½ ounce oil
> ½ ounce sweet solid butter
> 1 teaspoon small diced red bell peppers

1 teaspoon chopped parsley
1 ounce sour cream
1 ounce sliced white mushrooms
Salt to taste

Cut well-trimmed beef tenderloin into ½-inch cubes and season it with salt and paprika. Heat the oil in a cast iron skillet good and hot, then quickly stir-fry the meat nice and brown. It should be medium on the inside and brown on the outside.

Remove the meat from the skillet and pour out the oil. Then melt the butter in the skillet and add the shallots, mushrooms, and garlic. Simmer and for a minute deglaze with the vodka. Then add the demi-glacé, heavy cream, and pickles, bring to a simmer, and at the end add the meat and give a short boil.

Pour the goulash into a serving dish and top it with the sour cream and the chopped parsley. Serve the dish with egg noodles or spaetzli and a glass of good red wine.

English Sherry Brandy Trifle   Serves 6–8

Use a piece of sponge cake 5 inches long, 4 inches wide, and 3 inches high. The cake should be one or two days old. Buy it in the store or make your own if you wish.

3 teaspoons raspberry jam
5 ounces white sliced toasted almonds
¼ pint sweet sherry wine
4 teaspoons brandy
1 pint whipping cream
2 teaspoons powdered sugar
1 pint custard sauce (see below)
1 pound fresh raspberries

Cut the dry sponge cake into ½-inch-thick slices and coat with the raspberry jam. Use only as much as it takes to lay out the bowl. Place the cake slices jam side up in a glass bowl about 8 or 9 inches across.

Cut the remaining cake into 1-inch cubes and scatter over the slices, then sprinkle half of the almonds on top. Then generously pour the sherry wine and brandy evenly over the cake cubes and let stand for about 30 minutes at room temperature.

Whip the cream in a bowl with a whisk until it is half thick, then add the powdered sugar and continue to beat until the cream is stiff enough to form unwavering peaks on the whisk when it is lifted out of the bowl.

To assemble the trifle, set 10 of the best raspberries aside and scatter the rest over the cake.

Spread the custard sauce across the top with a spatula, then gently smooth half of the whipped cream over the surface of the custard. Pipe the rest of the whipping cream decoratively around the edge using a pastry bag.

Garnish with the 10 berries you reserved and the almonds. Refrigerate for an hour prior to service.

Custard Sauce

> 1 pint milk
> 1½ ounce sugar
> 4 medium eggs
> ½ teaspoon pure vanilla

Heat the milk in a saucepot, but do not boil it. Combine the sugar, eggs, and vanilla and whip well till it looks real creamy. Then pour the milk into the mixture while whipping constantly. Then return to the pot you used to heat the milk and slowly start heating over low heat. When it starts to get creamy, remove the pot from the burner and let it cool, stirring every once in a while. You do not want a crust on it.

Hot Chocolate Soufflé

1 pint milk
4½ ounces sugar
3½ ounces butter
4 ounces flour
8 egg yolks
8 egg whites
9 ounces dark semisweet Swiss chocolate

In a saucepan bring the milk to a boil. In a second pan mix the flour and butter, then pour in the hot milk. Mix the milk and flour combination with a wire whisk till nice and smooth. Do not remove it from the stove yet! Reduce the heat when everything is nice and smooth, then take it from the heat and let it cool off. You do not want scrambled eggs. Then add the egg yolks one by one till everything is completely blended. Pour in the melted chocolate and mix again till it looks like chocolate pudding.

Prepare the dishes called *cocottes* by brushing the insides with melted butter and add sugar; it should look as if you have crystals. Pour out the extra sugar—you only need enough to coat it.

Now it is time the get the egg whites ready. Beat them together with the rest of the sugar to a firm peak. Then slowly fold the egg whites into the chocolate mixture.

Fill the cocottes ¾ full. Bake the soufflés in the oven at 325 degrees for about 29 minutes, then turn up the heat to 350 degrees and continue baking till they are done; about 35 to 40 minutes.

To check for doneness, stick a bamboo stick in it. If the stick comes out dry, then it is done.

For the chocolate sauce, melt about ½ pound of the same type of chocolate with heavy cream.

Shrimp Lil

This dish was created in honor of my wife Lily and became a very popular special.

> 6 each U-15 tiger prawns
> 3 ounces sliced white mushrooms
> ½ ounce finely chopped shallots
> 1 ounce clarified butter
> ½ ounce medium-finely chopped fresh basil
> ¼ ounce chopped parsley
> ¼ ounce brandy
> 1 ounce dry white wine
> 2 ounces heavy cream
> A few drops of lemon juice
> Salt

First you have to peel the prawns and devein them, but leave the tails on. In a stainless steel skillet, pour the clarified butter and sauté the prawns till they look nice and red, but do not overcook them. It is OK if they look like they are half done.

Remove the prawns from the skillet. Add the shallots, mushrooms, and basil and sauté for a couple of minutes. Flame it with the brandy, then add the white wine and cream and reduce till you have a light creamy sauce. Add salt and a few drops of lemon juice.

At the end, bring the prawns back into the sauce and quick boil them. Transfer the so-called Shrimps Lil onto a serving dish and sprinkle them with the chopped parsley. You are good to go. Enjoy.

Portuguese Bean Soup

Ham hocks
Kidney beans
White onion
White cabbage
Watercress
Diced potatoes
Elbow macaroni
Portuguese sausage
Tomato sauce
Salt
Pepper
Beef or chicken stock

The soup is prepared like a minestrone soup, but you have to precook the ham hock and the beans. I make a large quantity of this soup, and to break it down is difficult so use your judgment as to how much of each ingredient to use. All the vegetables should be of equal proportions.

Cut the ham hocks into small chunks after cooking. When you serve it, each portion should have some meat in it. Use the liquid from the precooked ham hocks.

It is a soup for cold days and served with a hearty type of bread. This soup can be considered as a full meal.

Chinese Omelet

Crabmeat
Bay shrimp
White mushrooms
Broccoli florets
Green onions

Eggs
Peanut oil
Salt
Pepper

First, sauté the mushrooms in peanut oil, then add all the other items. Heat everything till all the ingredients are hot, then pour in the beaten eggs and flip over a couple of times till your dish looks like it is done.

Do not overcook it, because it will get dry. The final product should look like egg foo young—in other, words flat. Serve soy sauce with it. If you wish, you could serve white steamed rice. Use 3 eggs per person.

Tournedos Flambé Swiss House

4 each center-cut well-trimmed beef tenderloins, 6 ounces and about 1½ inch thick
Finely chopped shallots
Brandy
Demi-glacé (brown sauce)
Dijon mustard
Pinot noir (red wine)
Madeira wine
Fresh, sliced white mushrooms (a good amount)
Heavy cream
Finely chopped parsley
Ground thyme
Salt
Pepper

Season the beef tenderloins with salt, pepper, and the thyme. In a cast iron skillet, sear the tenderloins over high heat on both sides till they look as if they are rusty. They will be medium rare.

Remove the meat from the skillet and reduce the heat. Add the shallots and mushrooms and sauté till they become slightly brown. Flame with the brandy, then pour in the red wine, Madeira wine, and the demi-glacé. Flavor with the mustard. Add the cream and bring to a soft boil till you have a light creamy sauce. Then return the meat to the skillet and bring to a quick boil. Place the meat onto a serving plate and top it with the sauce and the chopped parsley.

Serve the fillets with your favorite side dishes.

Steak Diane   Serves 1

 6-ounce beef tenderloin, flattened to about ½ inch
 Finely chopped shallots
 Freshly ground black pepper
 Salt
 Fresh, sliced white mushrooms
 Dijon mustard
 Demi-glacé (brown sauce)
 Heavy cream
 Chopped parsley
 Worcestershire sauce
 Brandy

In a gueridon-style skillet (flat pan), season and sauté the fillet briskly on both sides, then keep the meat warm while you sauté the shallots and mushrooms. Flame with the brandy, then add the demi-glacé and mustard. Bring to a simmer again, then pour in the cream. Add Worcestershire sauce. Check for seasoning.

Return the fillet to the sauce and quickly boil it. Serve by putting the meat on a plate, then pouring the sauce over it. Serve with *pommes* sauté and broiled tomatoes.

This is tableside cooking. Tableside cooking is now mainly done in the kitchen because it takes skill and is time consuming; it is also a safety problem because of the flame it creates in the dining room. In the olden days the maître d'hôtel used to handle that type of challenge.

Onion Soup with Three Types of Onion

White onion, sliced
Red onion, sliced
Green onion, sliced
Chicken stock
Clear beef stock
Apple jack
White wine
Oil
Fresh garlic
Bay leaf
Thyme leaf
Oregano leaves
Caraway seeds
Cracked white peppercorn
Salt

These are all the items you will need to prepare the soup. You will have to determine how much soup you will need to make, based on the onions being the main ingredients to consider. My recipe is for use in a restaurant and is based on about 1½ medium onions (about 6 ounces), half white and half red. The green onions and the applejack are placed into the container before you pour in the actual soup and then baked in the oven or a cheese melter (salamander), if you have one. The garlic and the spices are put into a spice bag and removed by the end of cooking.

To prepare the soup, first you sauté the white and red onions in some oil over low heat till they start to look like they are being caramelized but not burned. Then pour in the chicken and beef stock. Then fill a spice bag with the garlic and all other seasonings. Add the wine and spice bag to the soup and bring to a boil over low temperature. Simmer for about half an hour. Top the soup with a slice of toast, Gruyère, and real Swiss cheese, and bake at 400 degrees till golden brown but not burned.

Green Goddess Dressing

This is a mayonnaise-based dressing.

Fresh garlic purée
Green onions
Washed parsley tops
Wilted watercress
Anchovy fillets
Mayonnaise
Worcestershire sauce
Ground white pepper
Cider vinegar
Tabasco sauce
Lemon juice
Salt
Sour cream

In a food processor, blend the garlic, green onion, parsley, watercress, and anchovies to a medium fine mixture. You need to still see small speckles, not too fine. Then mix together with all the rest of the items. If the dressing is too thick, add a little cold water to it.

Hungarian Goulash   Serves 1

> 8 ounces lean cubed beef stew meat, about 1 inch in size
> 6 ounces white onion, sliced fine
> ½ ounce fresh garlic purée
> 3 ounces sweet Hungarian paprika
> Thyme leaves
> Ground cumin
> ¼ ounce Caraway seeds, finely chopped
> ¼ of a lemon rind, finely chopped
> ¼ of an orange rind, finely chopped
> Salt
> Ground white pepper
> Clear beef broth

In a heavy-duty saucepot, first add the stew meat, onion, garlic, paprika, thyme, cumin, salt, ground white pepper, and a small amount of clear beef broth. By hand, mix all the items together really well so that it is bright red from the paprika.

Next, put the so-called raw goulash on the stove over low heat and bring it to a boil. Make sure you pay close attention to it and don't let it burn—that means you have to stir it every now and then. When it reaches the boiling point, reduce the heat, cover it with a lid, and simmer it till the meat is tender but not overcooked.

The orange and lemon rind, garlic, and caraway seeds need to be finely chopped and added last to the goulash. This will give the dish its personality. Goulash is usually served with sour cream, rice, or pasta.

Vegetable Soup
You can add a ham hock to the soup for extra flavor.

> Onions
> Carrots

Leeks
White cabbage
Raw potatoes
Fresh peeled and seeded tomatoes
Celery root
Zucchinis
Clear beef stock
Finely chopped garlic
Olive oil
Salt
Pepper

Cut all the vegetables in medium-sized dices or slivers. Keep the potatoes raw in cold water till everything is prepared. You will add the potatoes when the soup is halfway done.

First, sauté the vegetables and garlic in some olive oil over low heat until they look transparent. Pour in the beef stock and season with salt and pepper. Bring to a boil, reduce the heat, and add the precooked ham hock. Halfway through cooking, add the diced potatoes. Do not overcook the potatoes—it is part of the presentation. Before you serve the soup, sprinkle with chopped parsley. Serve Parmesan cheese with it.

Garlic Butter

This is a compound butter.

¼ ounce fresh peeled and chopped garlic
3 pounds sweet solid butter
½ bunch thyme leaves
Finely chopped parsley
1 teaspoon salt
¼ teaspoon ground white pepper

Lemon juice of 1 lemon
2 ounces white wine
½ ounce Worcestershire sauce
1 teaspoon English mustard

Mix all the ingredients in a mixing bowl and whip slightly, but not fluffy. When you are done putting everything together, taste it and add seasonings as needed. Then roll in parchment paper and freeze it.

When you have a use for it, take it out of the freezer and cut as much as you need, then return the rest to the freezer. It will last a while.

Cooking is an art where your taste buds come into play. If you wish to play pharmacist and always make the same amount, weighing every item on a scale, it will give you a very consistent product.

All my recipes were tested in big quantities, and I go mainly by weight. If you have the patience, it will pay off. And if you are running a restaurant, you need to know what the cost will be for every item. This will make it possible to know what price to set your dish.

Roasted Honey Glazed Duck   Serves 2

5-pounds Maple Leaf brand whole duck
Seasoning salt
2 ounces sweet (unsalted) butter
1½ ounces sliced almonds
2 ounces honey
Chopped parsley
Some oil to roast

First, roast your oven-ready duck at 400 degrees till completely done, about 1 hour or so. When done, remove it from the oven and let it cool till you are able to handle it.

Cut the duck in half lengthwise. Break out the bones and keep it warm in the oven. Next, melt the butter in a skillet. Add the almonds and let them get brown. Almonds get brown quickly, so be careful not to burn them. Then pour in the honey. Glaze the duck with the honey, almond, and butter combination.

Coq au Vin　　　　　　　　　　　　　　　　　　　　Serves 4

2 each 3½-pound whole fresh chickens
8 ounces red wine
2 ounces carrots
3 ounces celery
3 ounces onion
¼ ounce garlic
1 ounce cracked black peppercorn
1 quart brown chicken stock
1 ounce tomato paste
3 ounces butter
2 ounces flour
4 ounces bacon lardoons (bacon sticks)
4 ounces pearl onions
4 ounces fresh mushrooms
Seasoning salt

First, bone the chickens. You will have 2 breasts, 2 drumsticks, and 2 thighs per chicken. Total 12 pieces.

Marinate the chicken in the red wine with the carrots, celery, onion, garlic, and peppercorn. It is OK to do this step the day before so that the chicken gets properly marinated.

Then drain out the marinade and keep it on the side. It needs to be boiled because the chicken will bleed into the marinade and your sauce will look like it is being curdled. When you boil blood, it will curdle and look like small flakes in the sauce. That is the reason to boil the marinade separately and then strain it through a cheesecloth before you return it to the sauce.

In a saucepot melt the butter, then panfry the towel-dried chicken on all sides nice and brown. Remove the chicken. Add the *mirepoix* (the vegetables from the marinade) and let it roast for a couple of minutes. Then add the tomato paste and flour.

Pour in the chicken stock and the boiled strained marinade. Then stir with a wire whisk till all the lumps are gone. When the sauce begins to boil, reduce the heat. Place the chicken in it and let it simmer till the chicken is done.

A sign of being done is when the drumsticks starts to crack on the end. Before you serve, add some red wine to the sauce.

In the meantime, blanch the lardoons and pearl onions, cut the mushrooms into quarters, and then quick sauté the garnish in butter and top the chicken with it. Sprinkle some chopped parsley on top as a final touch.

Serve with noodles and your choice of vegetables.

Gazpacho Soup

This is a Spanish cold soup.

1 medium cucumber, peeled and seeded
5 ounces tomato juice
½ small garlic clove
½ medium white onion
3 slices trimmed white bread
½ ounce olive oil
2 small fresh tomatoes, peeled and seeded (5 ounces)

2 ounces green seeded bell peppers
½ teaspoon salt
Dash of ground white pepper
10 drops of Tabasco sauce
Homemade croutons as a garniture

First, cut all the items into small chunks. In a blender, pour in the tomato juice, olive oil, cucumber, garlic, onion, bell pepper, sliced white bread, and seasoning. Put the lid on the blender and start on low speed to create a smooth soup. Chill well before you serve it, and add your kept garnishes (diced cucumber, diced tomatoes, and the croutons).

Thousand Island Dressing

½ gallon mayonnaise
3 ounces mixed sweet relishes
½ cup chili sauce
½ cup ketchup
½ ounce Worcestershire sauce
15 drops of Tabasco sauce
4 medium eggs, boiled and chopped
1 teaspoon salt
¼ ounce ground white pepper
½ cup apple cider vinegar

Mix all the items together. If the dressing is too thick, add some cold water.

Ceviche

This dish is of Latin origin and is usually served as an appetizer.

3 ounces fresh medium scallops
Juice of ½ a lime
½ ounce finely chopped onion
½ ounce diced green bell peppers
¼ ounce diced red bell peppers
½ ounce diced yellow wax pepper
½ ounce sliced Spanish olives
Dash of fine white sea salt
¼ teaspoon ground white pepper
6 drops of Tabasco sauce

Cut the scallops in half so that they still look like a whole piece, not diced—like a wheel. Then dice all the peppers and chop the onion. Combine everything together, add seasonings, and blend well. Refrigerate it. It is to be served cold, even on ice.

Pork Chow Mein   Serves 1

3 ounces pork butt
1 ounce cornstarch
1 ounce onion
½ ounce celery
½ ounce carrots
1 ounce bean sprouts
½ ounce water chestnuts
2 ounces chow mein noodles
1 ounce light soy sauce
2 ounces peanut oil
2 ounces chicken stock
½ clove of garlic, chopped

First, trim the pork butt, then cut it into thin slices. It should look like small leaves. Cover it with some soy sauce and a bit of cornstarch, then let it marinate for 15 minutes.

Meanwhile, cut the onion, carrots, celery, and fresh water chestnuts. If you cannot get fresh nuts, use canned water chestnuts.

In a small wok, stir-fry the meat in peanut oil. It has to be hot so that it sizzles. Remove the meat and reduce the heat. Stir-fry the onion, celery, carrots, chopped garlic, bean sprouts, and water chestnuts. Pour in the chicken stock, dilute soy sauce, and cornstarch and make sure it is completely blended together; it has to be done quickly. Add it to the meat and vegetables and bring it to a quick boil. Serve it over the crispy noodles.

To make crispy noodles, fry them in a separate skillet with a little bit of oil. They should look like round hash browns. The noodles you can prepare ahead of time and keep warm in the oven till you are ready with the meat and vegetable combination.

Beef Tips with Oyster Sauce   Serves 1

3 ounces beef tenderloin tips
½ ounce cornstarch
1½ ounces soy sauce
¼ ounce fresh garlic
2 ounces peanut oil
1 ounce bamboo shoots
1 ounce pea pods
1 ounce sliced white mushroom
2 ounces oyster sauce
¼ teaspoon sugar
1 cup clear beef stock

First, slice the beef tenderloin into even slivers and marinate it in the soy sauce and cornstarch. Put it to the side.

Then slice the bamboo shoots, pea pods, and mushrooms. Then stir-fry the meat first in the peanut oil over high heat.

Remove the meat from the pan, reduce the heat, and continue to fry the garlic, pea pods, and bamboo shoots. Here you also mix the cornstarch but this time with the beef stock. Pour the sugar in and then combine all the ingredients and finish it by pouring the oyster sauce over it. This dish deserves steamed rice or Chinese noodles.

Steak au Poivre

This was a house special.

> 1 each 12-ounce US Prime New York steak
> 1 ounces cracked black peppercorn
> ½ ounce cottonseed oil
> 1 ounce cognac
> 1 ounce dry white wine
> 1½ ounces demi-glacé
> 1½ ounces heavy cream

Make sure the steak is well-trimmed and studded with a lot of cracked black peppercorn. Then panfry it in a cast iron skillet over high heat. It should look like rust when it is done, but do not use excessive oil—the peppercorn has to stay on the steak.

When the meat is done—rare, medium rare, medium, or even well done, whatever your choice is—remove it from the pan and let it rest on a plate, keeping it warm. Pour out the remaining oil. Deglaze with cognac, white wine, and demi-glacé, and add the heavy cream.

Reduce till you have a velvety sauce. Pour the sauce over the steak and sprinkle with chopped parsley. Serve with Lyonnaise potatoes, home fries smothered in onions.

Chicken Cordon Blue   Serves 1

1 each 6-ounce fresh skinless chicken breast
1½ ounces real Swiss cheese
1¼ ounces sliced Black Forest ham
1 small whole egg
Salt
Ground white pepper
Bread crumbs
Flour to dust
Seasoning salt

First, take out the fillet-looking part of the breast and butterfly the breast, then slightly pound both sides with a piece of plastic so that it does not tear.

Then wrap the ham around the cheese, place it on one side of the chicken, and cover with the second half of the breast. Press it down so that it will hold together.

Season, dust with flour, then dip it into the beaten egg and bread it with bread crumbs. Push heavily into the crumbs so that it will hold together. Then brown it in clarified butter on both sides and complete the cooking process in a 350-degree oven for about 15 minutes, until the cheese has melted but is not leaking out.

Serve with a lemon star and your choice of side dishes.

It is well known that the classical kitchen began in Europe, especially in France, then the Italian kitchen followed suit. The Chinese were always somewhat in the background; remember Marco Polo introduced spaghetti to Italy when he returned from China, and so the whole world enjoyed a variety of different cuisines. There were a lot of chefs who came up with their own special ideas from Russia, Japan, India, Australia, England, and now even around the whole globe. We have a total smorgasbord.

In many countries you can enjoy whatever your heart desires. Many foreigners have entered different countries and influenced the variety of new food concepts. This has also brought many different nationalities in the form of legal immigrants who opened their own specialty restaurants. Unfortunately, it also created many fast-food places, and as a result people have forgotten to enjoy really good food. If you eat fast food every day and wonder if you can stay slim, look in the mirror. You will be surprised at what you see.

I guess all the so-called progress we have made over the years has sometimes left us with few choices. I still today enjoy a really good meal, but this takes some time. You don't just gobble up your food in a few minutes while having a good glass of wine and even a delicious dessert. In this case I would say, speaking words of wisdom, let it be. Take your pick.

I gained a lot of experience working in Hawaii and Hong Kong. I will show you a few well-tested recipes in this area. Polynesian and Chinese cooking require a lot of preparation, but the dishes really cook fast.

People say Chinese food is low calorie, but think again. In many places a lot of oil is used to make it look shiny. If you try to cook it at home, be aware of the cleaning job you will have to do. It splashes a lot. The splashing oil is calling for your elbow grease later, but I still enjoy this food immensely. I know exactly what I will get, because I will get the best using only the best ingredients. Now let's make some hot pepper jelly.

Hot Pepper Jelly

2½ cups red bell peppers, washed and cleaned
1¼ cups green peppers, washed and cleaned
¼ cup jalapeño peppers, cleaned
1 cup apple cider vinegar
1¾ ounces Sure-Jell pectin
5 cups white sugar
A few drops of red food coloring

Clean all peppers and completely remove the stems and seeds, but for the jalapeño peppers use gloves and do not wipe your face or eyes because it will burn. Chop all the peppers medium fine so that they do not turn into mush.

Pour sugar and half the vinegar together, then add the peppers and cook over low heat, stirring constantly, for about 10 minutes. Do not burn. Then add the rest of the sugar and the pectin, bring to a boil, and add few drops of red food coloring to it. Cook over low heat for about 3 minutes till everything is blended together.

Pour a few drops of the jelly on a small plate and let it cool so that you can see if it jells properly. If not, add some more pectin.

Next prepare the jars and lids according the instructions listed on the box of jars you have purchased. The jars can be found at the hardware store or even at the supermarket during canning season. Keep the jars hot while you fill them with jelly to within about a half inch of the rim. Put the lids on and heat the jars in boiling water for about 10 minutes. When done, take the jars out of the water and place them on a tray covered with a towel. Cools the jars in a draft-free place overnight.

Inside the pectin box, there is some more information that will help you be successful in preparing your own hot pepper jelly.

The jelly is used with lamb, chicken, pork, and even fish. Some people I know put it on toast for breakfast. Try it, you'll like it.

You can find all kinds of gadgets in a hardware store to help make canning easier, especially items to protect you from burning your hands. If you do canning, you know what I am talking about.

Fried Shrimp with Walnuts

    10 ounces medium shrimp (16 to 20 shrimp)
    8 ounces walnuts
    2 ounces green peas
    6 small slices fresh ginger
    6 medium carrots
    3 stalks spring onions
    1 teaspoon Chinese wine
    8 cups oil
    ¼ teaspoon sesame oil
    Water
    1¾ teaspoons cornstarch
    1½ teaspoons salt
    Dash of pepper flakes

Shell and clean the shrimp. Rub the shrimp with 1 teaspoon of salt, then rinse and allow to dry. Marinate with ¼ teaspoon salt, ¼ teaspoon cornstarch, a few drops of sesame seed oil, and the pepper flakes.

Cook the walnuts in hot water for 10 minutes. Add 1 cup of water and bring to a boil again. Drain.

Heat 4 cups of oil in a wok. Deep-fry the walnuts for 4 minutes, then put aside. Rinse the wok.

Add the shrimp to 4 cups of boiling water, fast boil until cooked, and put aside. Rinse the wok again.

Boil the green peas for 2 minutes in a cup of water and put them aside. Rinse the wok again.

Heat 4 cups of oil. Quickly stir-fry the shrimp, then put them aside.

Drain the excess oil and stir-fry the carrots, ginger, spring onions, and peas quickly, adding the wine and the shrimp. Mix 1½ teaspoons of cornstarch diluted with water and ¼ teaspoon of salt. Pour a few drops of sesame seed oil into the wok and stir-fry thoroughly. Add the walnuts and stir-fry quickly. Serve.

Flying horse sculpture London Hilton

CHAPTER 11

WORKING IN HONG KONG

While working in Hong Kong, it felt like a student exchange program. I got another degree for my résumé. First of all, it was another continent, a different language, and a complete change in culture. And I was able to teach my Chinese kitchen crew the European type of cooking, and they in turn thought me the proper way to cook Cantonese Chinese food.

I had a bit of a head start because I worked in Hawaii for some time prior to moving to Hong Kong. My wife Lily was born in Beijing, China. I had the privilege of opening the Plaza Hotel in Hong Kong and had a special visa to do so for two years. This experience was the dream of a lifetime, and I must say that Hong Kong was probably one of the best places to work besides Switzerland.

The local Chinese people are hardworking and also very loyal. It took almost two years to do the opening. Together with my Swiss sous-chef, Fred Ott, we set up the whole food and beverage operation. I brought my sous-chef and pastry chef Al Frieden from Hawaii, and we all worked well together. The opening was very successful, and I still have fond memories.

I often cook Chinese food, and I know what it should look like because I was instructed by the Chinese chefs in Hong Kong. When you order food in any restaurant, you have no idea what you will get from that kitchen. But the wait help is aware of the shortcuts being done. You will hear from them saying that they don't know the difference. Being from the trade, it makes one wonder.

Chicken in Lemon Sauce

1 fresh 2½ lb. chicken
1 lemon sliced into 12 slices
2 egg yolks, well beaten
1½ cups white vinegar
2 cups oil
3 tablespoons oil
8 ounces cornstarch
6 teaspoons custard powder
12 teaspoons sugar
4 teaspoons salt
Bicarbonate of soda

Slit the chicken and removes the bones, then spread it out on a plate. Marinate with 3 teaspoons of the salt, bicarbonate of soda, and 6 teaspoons water.

Coat the chicken with the egg yolk, then the cornstarch. Heat 2 cups of oil and fry the chicken in the wok until golden yellow. Cut into pieces and put on a plate.

Rinse the wok, heat 3 tablespoons of oil, and add 1½ cups of water, the vinegar, the sugar, 1 teaspoon of salt, and the lemon slices. Mix the custard powder with 12 teaspoons water, add to the wok, and stir constantly until cooked. Pour over the chicken and serve.

Fried Mixed Vegetables

8 ounces bamboo shoots
2½ ounces straw mushrooms
2½ ounces button mushrooms
2½ ounces black mushrooms
2½ ounces carrots, sliced
2½ ounces dried tree fungi
2 ounces snow peas
2½ ounces baby sweet corn
8 pieces Chinese choy sum
1 tablespoon ginger extract
¾ tablespoon oyster sauce
1 teaspoon soy sauce
1 tablespoon rice wine
6 tablespoons oil
1 teaspoon cornstarch, with water to dilute
¼ teaspoon sugar
1¼ teaspoons salt

Soak the back mushrooms and fungi in water for 20 to 30 minutes, then slice thinly. Remove the roots and heads of the bamboo shoots and cut into chunks. Halve the straw mushrooms and button mushrooms and slice the black mushrooms.

In the wok, boil the carrots in 5 cups of hot water. Add the bamboo shoots, mushrooms, fungi, and corn. Season with the ginger extract and ¼ teaspoon salt. Boil for 3 more minutes, then put the vegetables aside.

Rinse the wok. Stir-fry the choy sum in 3 tablespoons of oil; add ½ teaspoon of salt and 2 tablespoons of water. When it is cooked, arrange on a serving dish.

Rinse the wok. Stir-fry the mixed vegetables in 3 tablespoons of oil; add the peas and ½ teaspoon of salt. Mix the cornstarch with 2 teaspoons of water. Add the sugar, oyster sauce, wine, and soy sauce. Stir thoroughly. Mix the cornstarch with 2 teaspoons of water and add to the vegetables. Stir-fry until the juices thicken. Transfer to the serving dish. Enjoy.

Walnut Vinaigrette Dressing

1 gallon red wine vinegar
2 gallons cottonseed oil
1 gallon olive oil
½ gallon water
2 ounces thyme leaves
1 ounce oregano leaves
½ ounce marjoram leaves
5 ounces finely chopped carrots
8 ounces finely chopped walnuts
Sugar to cut the acidity
Ground white pepper
Worcestershire sauce

Blend all the ingredients together. The dressing should be tasted with lettuce. Dip a few pieces of lettuce into the sauce and if it is too sour, make the proper adjustments, but be careful not to over salt.

Tartar Sauce

⅓ gallon mayonnaise
3 cooked eggs, chopped
5 ounces cornichons (small dill pickles), chopped
3 ounces capers, chopped
1 ounce finely chopped parsley
1 ounce finely cut chives

2 ounces finely chopped onion
Salt
Ground white pepper
Dijon mustard
White vinegar
Worcestershire sauce

Mix all the ingredients together with the mayonnaise. Serve with fried seafood.

Pork Stew with Lentil and Dill

Lean pork from the neck, cut into 1-inch cubes
Finely chopped onions
Finely chopped garlic
Tomato paste
Flour
Dash of paprika
Salt
Ground white pepper
White wine
Brown, clear beef stock
Finely chopped fresh dill
Lentils, precooked
Oil to brown the meat

Season the meat cubes with salt, pepper, paprika, and flour. In a heavy saucepot, heat the oil till it starts to smoke, then brown the meat till it is good and brown on all sides. Remove the meat from the pot and put it aside.

Let the pot cool, then sauté the onions, garlic, tomato paste, and flour. Let it take on a bit of a brown look. Then deglaze with the white wine. Pour in the beef stock and quickly whisk it into a smooth-looking sauce. Bring it to a boil. Reduce the heat and add the browned meat to it. Let it simmer till the meat is cooked but not mush. Check a piece by taking it out of the pot and cutting it in half. It should be cooked but not raw. Then add the precooked lentils and complete the cooking process. Check for seasoning and then stir in the finely chopped fresh dill and serve.

You can brown the meat nice and brown in a saucepot, or you could use a Crock-Pot because it is easier to control.

This is a so-called comfort food, and you could easily prepare a larger amount. It can be reheated and will bail you out when you do not have time to cook for hours after a long day. I had this dish on the menu as a special. I learned to prepare it from a Swiss chef in St. Moritz at the Chantarella Hotel, Florian Zogg.

✤   ✤   ✤

Poached Alaskan Salmon in Romaine Lettuce

7-ounce center-cut skinless, boneless portion of salmon
¼ ounce fresh ginger, cut into fine julienne
1½ ounces carrot julienne
1 ounce sweet solid butter
Dash of salt
3 ounces dry white wine
1 piece romaine lettuce, big enough to cover the whole portion of fish
2 ounces heavy cream
5 drops of lemon juice

In a stainless steel fish pan, spread the butter nice and even. Add the salt, sprinkle the julienne of ginger on top, and place the fish with the out side up (the side where the skin was cut off). Pour the wine over it and cover with the green lettuce leaf.

Next, bring the prepared fish to a boil on top of the stove. Cover with a lid and cook in a 350-degree oven. Cooking time depends on the size of the fish. Do not overcook it; it should still be a bit moist in the middle. When the fish is done, remove it from the pan, place it on a plate, and keep warm.

You still should have a good amount of liquid in your fish pan. Add the carrot julienne and the heavy cream. Reduce the liquid so that you have a nice and creamy sauce. A couple of drops of lemon juice will lift the taste of your sauce.

Garnish the plate with *pommes natures* (steamed potatoes). Place the fish next to the potatoes, pour the sauce over it, and sprinkle it with chopped parsley.

The ginger for cooking fish will reduce the strong fish taste. It's a Chinese trick that I learned in Hong Kong.

Did you know that white vinegar is a miracle ingredient? In the kitchen, you can cook with it, clean with it, marinate with it, and even use it when you do laundry and many more uses—just think of it. And it is also organic. If you have a sunburn, it can take out the sting. Spray in on weeds in the garden—it is safer than Roundup.

Now let's make satés—skewered grilled meat.

Satés

You can use beef, chicken, and pork to make satés.

For the marinade, use granulated sugar, lemon grass, sliced finely chopped ginger, garlic, toasted and ground coriander seeds, salt, ground cumin, and ground cinnamon. Mix all ingredients together.

Cut the chicken, pork, and beef into strips. Some people cut it into small cubes. Thread the meat onto bamboo sticks. Marinate each type of meat separately for about 2 hours.

When you cook the satés on a barbeque broiler, spray the broiler with Pam so that they will not stick. Cooking time depends on the type of meat you cook. Serve with sate sauce.

Saté Sauce

> Arbor peppers, chopped
> Salt
> Minced garlic
> Chopped ginger
> Red miso
> Peanut butter
> Sugar
> Soy sauce
> Some lemon juice

Blend all the ingredients together.

Pork Chops Crusted with Sage and Fennel Crust

> Use center-cut boneless chops.
> Finely chopped fresh sage
> Ground fennel seeds
> Lemon rind, chopped fine
> Salt
> Chopped parsley
> Olive oil
> Ground black pepper

Blend all the ingredients together and rub it onto the meat evenly. Place in a porcelain dish, cover with clear plastic wrap, and let it marinate overnight.

To cook, heat the olive oil in a cast iron pan good and hot. Let the chops sear on both sides till done. Serve with fingerling potatoes and a nice mixed green salad. And if you like, even with applesauce.

Poached Chilean Sea Bass Swiss House

7 ounces boneless, skinless sea bass
1½ ounces sweet solid butter
Finely chopped parsley
Finely chopped tarragon
Fresh chopped thyme
Finely chopped basil
3 ounces dry white wine
2 ounces heavy cream
Lemon juice
Salt
Ground white pepper

Cover the bottom of a stainless steel sauté pan with the soft butter. Add the salt, pepper, parsley, tarragon, thyme, and basil. Place the fish on top. Pour the wine in, bring it to a boil, place a lid over it, and poach the fish in a 350-degree oven till done. Do not overcook; it needs to be slightly moist inside.

When the fish is done, remove from the pan and keep it warm. Add the heavy cream and 3 or 4 drops of lemon juice to the pan and let it reduce till you have a velvety sauce. Place the fish on a serving plate and garnish with pommes natures and asparagus spears.

Shrimp Fajitas with Sabor

Serve with hot flour tortillas.

Large jumbo shrimp peeled and deveined, U-15
Ground cumin
Freshly ground garlic
Ground black pepper
Fresh oregano
Brown sugar
Chili powder
Salt
Olive oil
Onions, sliced
Fresh poblano peppers
Cilantro
Lime wedges
Sour cream

In a small bowl, combine the cumin, garlic, pepper, salt, chili powder, brown sugar, oregano, and shrimp. Coat well.

Heat a sauté pan medium hot and add olive oil. Add the onions and smother till transparent. Add the chili peppers and continue to sauté. Add the remaining spices, then place in a bowl and garnish with the cilantro.

Return the skillet to the stove. Add the shrimp and cook through over medium heat. Add the sautéed vegetables, toss to combine, and reheat.

Place on a serving platter and serve with flour tortillas, cilantro, lime wedges, and sour cream.

Poitrine de Volaille Princesse   Serves 1

(Chicken Breast Princess)

4-ounce boneless, skinless chicken breast
1½ ounces creamed fresh mushrooms
1 egg, beaten
Salt and ground white pepper to taste
2 ounces all-purpose flour to dust
3 green asparagus tips
2 strips red cooked pimentos for garnish
2 ounces brown rice
1 piece baby bock choy cooked al dente

Cut the chicken breast in half (butterflied), then pound it evenly under a piece of clear plastic wrap. Fill the two halves of chicken breast with the creamed mushrooms. It should look like a pouch. Season with salt and pepper, dust with flour, then dip into the beaten egg and panfry it in clarified butter over medium heat till both sides are golden brown.

I advise you if you are not sure the chicken is done properly, finish it in the oven at 400 degrees. Have the vegetable and rice hot, then plate it and at last you add the chicken topped with the pimentos and the asparagus tips.

Creamed Mushrooms

Sauté the washed and sliced mushrooms in butter with finely chopped shallots. Season with salt and pepper. Deglaze with some white wine. When you sauté mushrooms and add white wine, it becomes soupy, so you need to pour about as much heavy cream in as the liquid from the mushrooms and wine. Then let it reduce by half. Use some cornstarch diluted with white wine to be sure it is firm when cold, not runny. I recommend that you do the creamed mushrooms the day before you prepare this dish.

Chicken Normandy with Walnut Sauce   Serves 3

6 each 3-ounce boneless, skinless chicken breasts
2 ounces butter
2 ounces peanut oil
2 ounces calvados or regular brandy
4 ounces hard cider
4 ounces brown chicken stock
4 ounces whipping cream
3 ounces chopped walnuts
2 large Granny Smith apples sliced into ¼-inch wedges (leave the skin on)
Chopped parsley
Flour to dust
Seasoning salt

Sprinkle seasoning salt on the chicken breasts and then dust with flour. Sauté the chicken breasts in a combination of half oil and half butter till golden brown on both sides.

Put the breasts on a plate and keep warm. Remove the oil and butter mixture and deglaze with the calvados.

Add the hard cider and brown chicken stock, then reduce the sauce by half. Pour in the cream and the walnuts, then bring back to a boil.

Place the chicken into the sauce; simmer till the entire breasts are covered evenly. Keep warm.

In a second pan, brown the apples in butter on both sides, then arrange them nicely side by side on a heated platter. Overlap the sautéed chicken with the apples without covering the green color of the apple. Spoon some of the sauce over the chicken and serve the remainder separately. Sprinkle the chopped parsley over the chicken before serving.

Beef Shish Kebab

This dish can be made with beef, chicken, pork or even shrimp wrapped in prosciutto ham. Let's start with beef.

I use New York strip loin because I cut my own meat, and when it gets toward the end of the loin there is a part that has a vein in it and cannot be served as a perfect steak. So I cut it up into 1½-inch cubes without having the tough part in it

I marinate the meat with olive oil, ground black pepper, fresh thin-sliced garlic, thyme leaves, curry powder, and broken bay leaves. I marinate it for about 10 hours.

Then I cut red and green bell peppers and white onion into 1½-inch square pieces and blanch them in boiling water for a couple of minutes. Select large, fresh white button mushrooms, cut off the stems, and sauté in butter and white wine. Cool all the items and then use metal skewers to poke first one mushroom cap then one piece of meat, red pepper, green pepper, onion, and even sometimes a short piece of bacon. It usually takes about 5 pieces of meat, and I alternate between meat and vegetables. On the last end, add the second mushroom cap.

When you broil the kebabs, put some salt on them and spray with Pam so that they do not stick on the broiler.

Some people serve kebabs with barbeque sauce and coleslaw.

Chicken and pork are different types of meat to try, and you can use your imagination. You could even use teriyaki sauce and use different vegetables, including hot peppers. You ever heard of corn on the cob? Tickle your fancy. Asparagus is also a good idea.

German Potato Salad

For this dish you should buy yellow potatoes because you do not want to have mush as the end product.

First you wash and then boil the potatoes in lightly salted water. Meanwhile, chop some onion, bacon, and a little bit of finely chopped garlic. In a stainless steel pan, sauté the onions, bacon, and garlic, then add a good amount of clear beef or chicken stock. Bring it to a boil and let it simmer for a few minutes.

In a separate stainless steel bowl, combine mustard, salt, pepper vinegar (white wine vinegar), and oil. Mix together and combine with the beef or chicken stock mixture.

Once the potatoes have cooled off a bit and you can peel them without burning your hands, do so and slice them. As you go along, add them to the still hot dressing while constantly shaking the pot.

As you proceed you will see that it becomes slightly creamy. You may have to check on the seasoning. Make sure you do not use too much oil. At the end, add some freshly chopped parsley to it.

This salad is consumed warm. If you have extra, refrigerate it and you may have another helping for the next day or so.

Ratatouille Provençal

    Red and green bell peppers
    Zucchini
    Eggplant
    Fresh tomatoes, peeled and seeded
    Finely chopped onions
    Garlic
    Tomato paste
    Olive oil
    Salt
    Ground white pepper
    Thyme leaves
    Oregano
    Marjoram

Dijon mustard
Some uncooked rice
Mango chutney
A small amount of water

The vegetable proportions should be equal, except the onions and garlic.

First, cut the peppers. Get rid of the stems and seeds, and cut the peppers into ¾-inch pieces. Then cut the eggplant and zucchini into the same size pieces. Cut the tomatoes into about ½-inch squares. Finely chop some onion and mince the garlic.

In a heavy pot, pour the olive oil and sauté the onions on medium heat together with the garlic. Add the pepper, thyme leaves, oregano, and marjoram. Add the tomato paste and stir constantly over low heat; don't let it burn. Next add the vegetables, including the tomatoes. Season with salt and pepper and a small amount of uncooked rice. The rice will absorb the liquid from the vegetables while the ratatouille cooks.

Keep stirring every now and then while the process of cooking is going on. Make sure that it is not overcooked. The vegetables should stay intact. At the end, chop the mango chutney and add to the stew, along with a spoonful of the Dijon mustard. This will enhance the flavor.

Chefs Karl's Fried Rice

Usually, I cook some pilaf rice first and then let it cool overnight.

The next day, cut root celery, carrots, and ham into small dice shapes. Finely chop a small onion; mice a clove of garlic and get some green peas and also a few raw peanuts.

Add a small amount of peanut oil to a wok and roast the peanuts slightly brown. You have to pay attention because nuts burn fast and then taste bitter.

Remove the nuts from the wok, reduce the heat, and add the onion, garlic, celery, carrots, and ham. Quickly fry all the items, then add the rice. Pour in soy sauce and a little bit of water. Rotate quickly with a metal spoon and make sure the rice is not burning. The green peas and some chopped green onion go in last; they should not look brown.

As a final decor, beat an egg, and in a nonstick frying pan, cook the egg in a thin pancake, then cut into julienne and sprinkle on top of the rice.

Scampi Amoureuse

Check for scampi in the seafood section. Scampi is not shrimp but is in the family between lobster and shrimp.

> 4 pieces raw scampi
> Brandy
> Lemon juice
> Butter
> Shallots, finely chopped
> Champignons (white mushrooms), finely sliced
> Dry white wine
> Heavy cream
> Finely chopped fresh dill
> Pernod
> Salt
> Dash of cayenne pepper

Peel the scampi and then cut in half lengthwise. Devein, wash, and then marinate with brandy, salt, and lemon juice.

Sauté the finely chopped shallots in butter, then add the

marinated scampi and finely sliced white mushrooms. Season with salt and a small dash of cayenne pepper.

Deglaze with dry white wine. Pour in a good amount of heavy cream and simmer for a couple of minutes. Then add some finely chopped fresh dill and a shot of Pernod. Fold everything together and serve it with rice and a green salad.

Stuffed Cabbage Rolls

To make the meat filling, use half ground beef and half ground pork. Mix together with salt, pepper, bread crumbs, whole eggs, chopped parsley, half and half, some Italian seasoning, and cooked rice. The filling should not be too dry—maybe like meatloaf.

To prep the cabbage, remove the outer leaves and then cut out the core and blanch it in hot water. Put the cabbage in cold water, then break off one leaf at a time and lay them out on towels on a table. Fill the leaves with the meat filling. Fold the ends and roll into the same size portions.

Brush a fireproof baking pan with soft butter. Place the rolls side by side and top them with chicken stock and some tomato sauce. Cover with parchment paper and bake in the oven at 400 degrees for about 1 hour, but make sure you keep an eye on it. Some ovens are not properly calibrated. Respect your hard work and I am sure you will enjoy the product of your labor.

Ravioli Dough   Serves about 10

1¾ pounds flour
½ ounce salt
¼ cup oil

4 eggs
½ to ¾ cup water

Sift the flour and salt together and make a well in the center. In a separate bowl, combine the oil, eggs, and water, then mix lightly. Pour into the well and work it together to a smooth dough. The dough should be firm. Do not work it too much.

Let the dough rest for about 1 hour. Use a ravioli board if you have one. Otherwise, you can improvise by rolling out two sheets and filling one side with the filling, then topping it with the second side.

Ravioli Stuffing

1 ounce shallots
3 ounces butter
10 ounces cooked chicken meat
7 ounces cooked veal brains
5 ounces cooked spinach
3 egg yolks
⅛ teaspoon ground nutmeg
1 teaspoons salt
¼ teaspoon pepper

When the chicken meat and brains are cold, add the spinach and grind with a fine blade in a meat grinder. Season and then add the egg yolks and blend well. Assemble the ravioli, then cut with a ravioli wheel.

Now you bring lightly salted water to a boil. Use enough water that the raviolis float in the water; the amount of water should be five times the amount of raviolis. Add some oil to keep the raviolis from sticking together. Place the raviolis into the boiling water and simmer till they are done al dente. They should float on top of the boiling water.

Remove with a skimmer and place in a buttered baking dish.

Arrange the raviolis in layers and sprinkle with Parmesan cheese, then pour brown butter over them and bake in the oven at 350 degrees for 15 minutes.

You now have ravioli Milanese, and if you use tomato sauce it's called Napolitaine.

Hasenpfeffer

This is rabbit stew.

4 to 5 pounds fresh rabbit
1 quart dry red wine
2 cups red wine vinegar
Mirepoix: 2 ounces each carrot, celery, and onion
2 bay leaves
10 juniper berries
20 black peppercorns
3 ounces tomato paste
2 quarts clear beef stock
4 ounces all-purpose flour
3 ounces salad oil
3 ounces sweet butter
4 ounces lardoons
12 pearl onions
10 mushrooms, cut into quarters
Butter-toasted croutons

The fresh rabbit may be purchased from a local farmer. Cut the rabbit hind and front legs in half, then the rest into 1½-ounce portions. Marinate with red wine, wine vinegar, *mirepoix* (roasted vegetables), bay leaves, juniper berries, peppercorns.

Marinate the rabbit for about 8 days. Then separate the meat from the marinade and brown the meat pieces quickly in hot oil. Remove the meat.

Add the mirepoix to the pot and sauté for a couple of minutes. Dust with flour and add tomato paste. Continue to sauté until the flour is brown.

Bring the marinade to a boil and strain though a cheesecloth. Return the marinade to the pot and add the clear beef stock and some more red wine. Season to taste. Bring back the meat and braise till the meat is tender. If excessive evaporation occurs, add more stock.

Remove the meat from the sauce. Strain the sauce through a fine strainer and pour it back over the meat.

Arrange a garnish of lardoons, pearl onions, mushrooms cut into quarters, and butter-toasted croutons. The garnish is sautéed in butter and will complete the hasenpfeffer.

For the stock, you may use clear beef broth. In the old country we used pig's blood and cream to thicken it.

I worked in Hawaii for ten years, and along the way, I also learned to cook some of their native dishes. A lot of the so-called luaus were prepared by special outfits or catering companies. At the Ilikai Hotel, we were able to do it all. One of the first items was sweet and sour pork.

Sweet and Sour Pork

2 pounds pork neck cut into 1½-inch cubes
3 tablespoons soy sauce
1 teaspoon salt
1½ tablespoons chopped ginger

⅓ cup cornstarch
3 cups vegetable oil
½ cup apple cider vinegar
¾ cup water
¾ cup sugar
Pineapple, cut into chunks
Red bell peppers, cut into chunks

Combine the pork pieces with the soy sauce, salt, and ginger and let stand for 30 minutes. Add cornstarch and mix well. Deep-fry the pork chunks till brown.

Remove the oil after deep-frying. Make a sauce of the remaining cornstarch-soy mixture. Add the vinegar, water, and sugar. Simmer till the sauce is thick. Add the fried pork pieces and cook till the pork is tender. Add the pineapples and peppers last, then bring it to a quick boil and serve.

Pork Adobo with Spinach   Serves 6

6 pork chops, ½ inch thick
2 pounds fresh spinach
½ cup water
1½ teaspoons salt
4 teaspoons apple cider vinegar
½ tablespoon paprika
2 cloves garlic, minced
¾ teaspoon black pepper
1 teaspoon fresh chopped ginger
2 tablespoons sherry wine
2 bay leaves

The pork chops may be cut into 1-inch cubes or left whole. Wash and drain the spinach. Set aside.

Make a marinade of the rest of the ingredients. Place the pork into the marinade, refrigerate, and let it stand for 1 hour.

Pour the pork and marinade into a skillet. Cover and let simmer for 1 hour. Then remove to a warm service platter.

Add the spinach to the hot marinade. Cover and simmer for 5 minutes. Now serve the pork adobo with steamed rice.

Yes, Hawaii has all kind of nationalities, and one could write a whole book on all of them. The West Indies has a strong Latin cuisine. Hawaii also has a more or less Latin approach, including a dish called chicken with rice.

There are all kinds of bananas and even plantains, which are more like starch and not sweet. These are turned into chips sort of like potato chips but thicker. The food is quite rich, with a lot of pork dishes.

Red Cabbage

It's time to address red cabbage. This item is not too common, and a lot of customers have asked me what is in my recipe. I can tell you what I put into it, but I do not think you would cook 20 pounds of cabbage at a time. So I will just list what the ingredients are.

Red cabbage, finely sliced white onion, finely minced garlic, red wine vinegar, red wine, ground white pepper, salt, sugar, applesauce, cranberry jelly, ground cinnamon, uncooked rice, and cooking oil. (Since lingonberries are very expensive, I substitute cranberry jelly for them.) The rice will absorb the liquid during the cooking process.

You do not need to use any other thickening agent. I recommend you use a pressure cooker and check your manual for the proper timing. You do not want to overcook because the cabbage should look red, not brown.

Roast Duck in a Melon

First you make a brown stock with the wings and neck of the duck in a stockpot. Add some mirepoix of celery, carrots, onion, garlic, rosemary, thyme, cracked peppercorn, tomato paste, and a small amount of flour. For the liquid, use water and season it very lightly with salt.

Next you roast the duck rose (pink). Then take off the breasts and keep them warm. Continue to roast the legs and bones and the seedless half a skinned, chopped up melon. Then deglaze with port wine and simmer for another 20 minutes.

Add some more port wine and reduce together with the prepared stock till you have a silky sauce. Pass the sauce though a wire strainer.

Prepare a second melon. Leave it whole, just cut the top in a way that it looks like a star. Remove all the seeds and heat it in hot water, but do not cook it. This will serve as the container when the duck is presented.

Empty the melon and let it stand upside down so that there is no water in it. Arrange the duck in the melon and add some of the sauce. Cover with the star-looking end and serve it with potatoes and vegetables.

Saffron Risotto with Prawns, Fresh Shiitake, and White Mushrooms
Serves 5

2½ ounces sweet solid butter
4 ounces finely chopped onion
Pinch of fresh garlic
28 ounces arborio rice
3½ quarts chicken stock
3 ounces Parmesan cheese
15 pieces of 16–20 count prawns, cleaned but with tails on
5 ounces fresh shiitake
White mushrooms, cut into wedges
A few threads of saffron

Sauté the onions and a pinch of fresh garlic in butter. Add the rice and stir until the rice is well covered with butter and looks transparent. Pour in some boiling chicken stock while constantly stirring. Simmer over low heat for about 10 minutes. Add more stock as needed.

Stir as you reduce the liquid. Add the saffron, prawns, shiitake, and white mushrooms. Add more chicken stock if needed. The rice should be al dente. At the end, add some soft butter and the Parmesan cheese.

Braised Lamb Shanks (Chef Karl's way)
Serves 1

Use a 15-ounce hind lamb shank, well-trimmed and *frenched*. I use domestic meat, but I am sure Aussie or New Zealand will do just fine. You may have to shop around a bit because it is not on the market shelf. Ask the butcher at your favorite supermarket.

Chop 1 medium onion, mince 1 medium clove of garlic, and get 1 tablespoon of tomato paste, ½ cup of all-purpose flour, salt, pepper, a rosemary twig, a thyme twig, and a pinch of oregano.

Since it is not practical to fix a brown lamb stock at home, I recommend you use brown clear beef broth.

Fix a small amount of mirepoix with celery, carrots, and onions cut into dice. You will also need 5 ounces of white wine and some oil to brown the shank.

Using a Dutch oven, heat the oil in the braising pot, season the meat with salt and pepper, and brown the shank all around. Remove and set aside.

Reduce the heat and add the onion and garlic. Sauté for a couple minutes. Add the mirepoix to the Dutch oven. Keep on roasting. Pour in the tomato paste and flour and stir till everything is well covered.

Add the wine and with a whisk work it till it is smooth, then pour in the stock. Add the rest of the seasonings, bring to a boil, and at last add the shank.

When it starts to boil, reduce the heat and cover it. Let it simmer for 1 hour or so. Make sure you keep an eye on it to see if it needs some more stock and also to check for doneness. When the meat is cooked, take it out of the pot and strain the sauce though a wire strainer. Serve with mashed potatoes and green beans.

Bouillabaisse Marseillaise

Usually, this French fish soup requires a good fish stock prepared from the bones of the fish if you wish to do so. Yes, you can buy fish bouillon in the market or simply use some clam juice.

First you cut onion, celery, fennel, and leek whites into julienne. Then peel, seed, and dice some tomatoes.

You will also need coarsely chopped parsley, a dash of minced garlic, a good pinch of saffron, olive oil, salt, a bay leaf, ground white pepper, thyme, white wine, and a shot of Pernod.

For the fish, use sea bass, red snapper, shrimp, black mussels, littleneck clams, some slipper lobster, or langoustines.

The soup is served with garlic toast made with French bread. Spread garlic mayonnaise on top of the toast, then bake in the oven till nice and brown.

Sauté the julienne-cut vegetables in olive oil. Add the garlic, saffron, diced tomatoes, salt, pepper, thyme, bay leaf, wine, and fish stock. Bring it to a boil and let it boil for about 10 to 15 minutes.

The seafood should be added according to the time it takes to be done. Please do not overcook. Make your garlic toast, then finish your soup with the Pernod and some chopped parsley. Enjoy!

I was a member of the Chaîne des Rôtisseurs and prepared three different meals in three different hotels: in Hawaii, the Ilikai, Royal Lahaina, and Sheraton Waikiki on Oahu.

During the time I was learning to become a pastry cook, on April 1 there was always some sort of fooling with the young apprentices to check on their awareness. Between the different businesses in town, we had several candidates, and one weak candidate was in my shop.

My boss told the young understudy to take a flour bag filled with two large stones he had prepared without the knowledge of the chosen candidate and deliver it to our competitor. My boss said that it was an expensive piece of equipment needed to polish the inside of the large baking oven. He also said to make sure not to drop it because it was very expensive.

Off the guy went, and as he arrived at the place where he was told to deliver the equipment, the boss at the other end told him to unpack and start cleaning the oven. Then he figured out that it was a joke.

✿ ✿ ✿

Moules Marinière

This is black mussels poached in wine and herbs. This dish was cooked by special request only, because mussels do not last very long and would come in the same day that we had a request. This for an appetizer.

> About 1 pound of mussels per person
> Salt
> Ground white pepper
> White wine
> Finely chopped shallots
> Finely chopped parsley
> Freshly chopped thyme
> Freshly chopped dill
> Butter
> Lemon juice

First, wash and clean the mussels well, then take off the beards.

Place the mussels in a kettle and add salt, pepper, white wine, and shallots. Simmer covered until the mussels open. Drain immediately.

Add the herbs to the stock and reduce to three-fourths of its volume. Stir in the butter, add some heavy cream and the lemon juice, then check for seasoning.

Remove the top shell of each mussel. Place the mussels in a flat container such as a soup plate, cover with the sauce, and sprinkle with chopped parsley.

If you would like to prepare a larger amount, you can use fish bouillon or clam juice.

Three Fillets Musketeers

This is a combination of beef tender, veal tender, and pork tender. Cook each type of fillet to the proper temperature.

Place a small, cooked artichoke bottom filled with creamed spinach on top of the pork tender.

Place a small, cooked artichoke filled with black peppercorn sauce on top of the beef tender.

Place a small, cooked artichoke bottom filled with tomato *concasse* on top of the veal tender.

Each fillet is topped with a fluted mushroom and served with broccoli and potato croquettes.

Tomato Concasse

This is a sort of tomato sauce but looks funkier.

Use ripe, freshly peeled and seeded tomatoes. Sauté finely chopped shallots and a pinch of garlic in olive oil. Add some tomato paste, oregano, basil, thyme, ground white pepper, and a dash of sugar to take out some of the acid. Pour the coarsely chopped tomatoes into it and simmer for 10 minutes.

Season with salt. If it is too thin, add some cornstarch and cold water to thicken it. This sauce can be used with any pasta dish.

During the season when tomatoes were inexpensive, I bought a lot and then peeled and seeded them and froze them in ziplock bags. This way I saved money.

Paella Valenciana

This is a Spanish rice dish with seafood, chicken, pork, and saffron. It requires a special dish called a paella dish. It is a flat pan that you can get at a restaurant supply store or a hardware store.

Olive oil
Minced garlic
Chicken drumsticks
Lean pork, diced
Onions, chopped
Sweet peppers, all different colors, diced
Long-grain rice
White wine
Chicken stock
Saffron
Tomato purée
Salt
Green peas
Parsley
Artichokes, cut into quarters
Mushrooms

Seafood needed:
Large shrimp
Small lobster tail
Clams
Black mussels
Sea bass
Sole

Heat the oil in the paella pan. Sauté the garlic and then remove.

Brown the chicken and pork on all sides. Add onions, garlic, sweet peppers, and mushrooms. Cover and simmer for 10 minutes. Do not let it get brown.

Add the rice. Heat and stir over low heat until the rice becomes transparent. Add the wine and boiling stock, tomato purée, salt, and saffron. Next, add all the seafood and the artichokes. Simmer covered for about 15 minutes.

At the end, sprinkle with parsley and green peas. Serve in the dish, but do not stir.

The dish cannot be served dry. You may have to add some more stock to it during the cooking process. Just pour the stock over it. You can make your own combination, but the saffron is a must.

Swiss Cheese Fondue   Serves 2

> 7 ounces real Swiss cheese
> 7 ounces Gruyère cheese
> 12 ounces dry white wine
> 1 clove garlic, minced
> 1½ ounces Swiss kirschwasser, not sweet
> ½ ounce cornstarch
> Dash of ground white pepper

In a cheese fondue pot, pour the white wine, pepper, and garlic and slowly bring to a boil. Use a wooden spoon and slowly add the shredded cheese, stirring constantly.

When the cheese is completely dissolved and well blended, add the diluted kirschwasser and cornstarch while still stirring. Remove from the burner and put it on a Sterno-heated stand.

Use long fondue forks and cubed French bread. While eating, make sure you rotate the fondue with your fork. Also check your heat under the pot; you do not want to burn the fondue.

You may serve it with some fruit on the side. White wine is a must.

Wine Braised Beef   Serves 4–6

> 2¼ pounds boneless top sirloin
> 1 bottle dry red wine
> Vinegar
> 1 pint beef broth

1 sliced onion
1 sliced carrot
1 stick celery, diced
1 clove garlic, crushed
1 clove
1 bay leaf
1 teaspoon cracked black pepper
1 sprig fresh sage
1 tablespoon oil
1 teaspoon tomato paste
1 tablespoon flour
Salt
Pepper
12 prunes, pitted

Trim the meat and cut into 3 pieces, then tie each one with a piece of butcher string. They should be about 2 to 2½ inches in diameter.

Put the beef in a nonmetallic container with the wine, vinegar, onion, carrot, celery, garlic, clove, bay leaf, pepper, and sage. The meat should be completely covered with liquid. Leave for at least a week in a cool place, turning occasionally to ensure even marinating.

Remove meat; pat dry with paper towel and season with salt and pepper. In a heavy casserole pan, sear the meat in hot oil on all sides.

Boil the marinade and strain. Set aside. Stir the vegetables, tomato paste, and flour into the casserole and cook for a few minutes. Then add the strained marinade and beef broth.

Bring to a simmer and season to taste. Cover and cook gently for 1½ hours or till done. Add the prunes and continue cooking till tender.

Remove the strings from the beef and slice thickly. Strain the sauce and return it to the casserole. Serve with the prunes and the cooking juice.

You might serve mashed potatoes, spaetzli, and glazed baby carrots with it.

Bircher Muesli **Serves 1**

Dr. Bircher-Benner created this dish, which is meant to help with weight loss.

3 tablespoons rolled oats
1 teaspoon raisins
Grated hazelnuts
Grated walnuts
Grated almonds
¾ cup milk
1 ounce orange juice
1 small, unpeeled, grated apple
2 teaspoons honey
Whipped cream
Banana Strawberries
Raspberries
Blueberries
Any seasonal fruits

First, soak the oats in the milk and let stand for half an hour. Then add the nuts, fruits, and honey. Mix well and decorate it with whipped cream and berries.

CHAPTER 12

TWICE AROUND THE GLOBE

From a childhood dream to reality and how it all began.

Yes, we all have dreams. You need a good base and a solid belief. Unfortunately, a lot of young people have pipe dreams, which leaves them dissolute and easily discouraged.

There is a saying: you can do anything if you set your heart to it. But it has to be realistic to start with it. Sometimes, you may regret your dream and have to change your course of action. But then again, it's better to think realistically.

If you finally find what you think is OK, then you should picture yourself doing it, like some sort of role play. You may have a change of heart, but if you feel strongly about it, then go for it. As you grow older, I am sure things will make sense.

As you may know, life is short, and you do not want to run behind the eight ball. You have to have a game plan and then stick with it. Lots of folks have doubts and think it's too hard. Let me tell you, no pain, no gain. But if you succeed, you will be well rewarded.

Now let's go back to cooking.

173

Mini Pizza Florentine
For the dough, you will need:

> 1 ounce fresh yeast
> ¼ cup warm water
> 1 pound bread flour
> ½ teaspoon of salt
> 1 cup olive oil

To prepare the dough, first mix the yeast and water together, then add the rest of the ingredients and knead it into a smooth dough. Let it rise in a bowl covered with plastic wrap until it doubles in size.

Then punch it down and divide into small balls. Roll it out with a rolling pin about 8 inches in diameter or so. Brush it with the oil, let it rise again, and then top it with tomato concasse, sliced mushrooms, black olives, Spanish olives, precooked spinach, thyme, oregano, Parmesan cheese, Swiss, provolone, Swiss Gruyère, and a few hot pepper flakes.

Bake it at 400 degrees till it is nice and brown.

Lecco Poulet   **Serves 2**
Hungarian chicken

> 1 whole chicken
> ½ ounce salt
> 3 ounces flour
> 3 ounces caraway seeds
> 2 ounces oil
> 1 pint sour cream
> 1 pound chopped onions
> ⅓ ounce ground white pepper
> 5 ounces sweet paprika
> 3 cloves garlic, finely chopped

1 quart chicken stock
1 small can red peppers (pimentos)
2 ounces vegetable margarine

Cut the chicken into 6 pieces: 2 half breasts, and the legs split in half, 2 drumsticks and 2 thighs. Season with salt and pepper, then dust with flour and sauté in oil till golden brown. Remove the chicken and keep warm.

Pour the oil from the sauté pan into a cup, then add the margarine and chopped onions. Over low heat, rotate the onions with a wooden spoon till light brown; about 5 minutes.

Add the sweet paprika, chicken stock, salt, and prebrowned chicken. Cover the pot and simmer over low heat about 15 minutes or till done.

Mix the finely chopped garlic and the caraway seeds into the pan, then garnish with the strips of red pepper, parsley, and the sour cream.

Serve with rice and your favorite vegetables.

Sauerbraten

German pot roast

Use meat as you would for a pot roast, about the same size, but you marinate the meat in vinegar, red wine, mirepoix (roasted vegetables, carrots, celery, onions, garlic), pickling spice, black peppercorn, juniper berries, cinnamon stick, bay leaf, and some fresh ginger.

Marinate the meat for 6 days. Make sure you rotate the meat during that time so that it will marinate properly. The meat has to be covered with the marinade. You can cover it with an old upside-down plate.

When the marinating time is up, separate the meat from the

liquid. You have to boil the marinade so that the sauce does not get curly.

First sear the meat on all sides in oil in a cast iron pot over high heat for a few minutes. Then use a Crock-Pot to cook the sauerbraten; it will ensure that the cooking process is controlled.

Remove the meat. Add the vegetables from the marinade and sauté them in the same pot till the baked-on substance has mixed well with the veggies. Add some tomato paste and flour, and keep on roasting till everything is starting to brown.

Deglaze with the cooked and strained marinade and add brown beef stock and vinegar. Stir well and make sure you do not have a lumpy sauce. Season with salt and pepper. I add lingonberries to the sauce to give a sweet and sour flavor to the dish.

We served red cabbage and spaetzli with it; a lot of people use gingersnaps in the sauce, but I use fresh ginger.

Pork Barbeque Spare Ribs

Let's make some pork barbeque spare ribs. Over the years while working all over the country, I experimented with this type of food.

First, I use only baby back ribs, 3 inches and down. These are available at Costco and Walmart. In my case I purchase them from a meat company.

Skin the ribs. There is a sort of a skin on the inside of the ribs, which makes them difficult to marinate.

I do not put any dry rub on the ribs. Instead, I parboil them halfway through in water with salt, sugar, and pickling spices, then I remove the ribs and keep them in part of the boiling liquid so that they do not dry out. Then I prepare the actual barbeque sauce. The amount of sauce depends on how many ribs you have in mind to cook.

Barbeque Sauce

Ground allspice
Ground cinnamon
Ground mace
Ground black pepper
Hot sauce
Curry powder
Chili powder
Sweet paprika
Apple cider vinegar
Ketchup
Molasses
Instant coffee
Unsweetened cocoa powder
Touch of bourbon

Mix all the ingredients together in a pot, then bring it to a boil and set aside.

I cook the ribs in the oven because I do not own a barbeque unit, but the result is quite amazing.

Take the rib section out of the cooking stock and cut in half. This gives me just the right portion per person. Place in a roasting pan and pour the barbeque sauce and some of the boiling stock over the ribs. Then baste them in the oven at about 350 degrees.

Make sure you turn the ribs several times. It may take 1 hour or so, but every time you turn the ribs, you also baste them again so that you do not dry them out.

Serve with corn on the cob and baked beans.

The extra boil can be used for a good bean soup. And since I boil the ribs, I also at the same time render some of the extra fat.

I often cook several portions, and you can cover the rest with the barbeque sauce and serve them the next day. This way they will not dry out and will retain the proper appearance. If you want the sauce to be sweeter, add some brown sugar.

Baked Beans

> 1 pound navy beans (soak overnight to shorten the cooking time)
> ½ cup brown sugar
> 1 onion, finely chopped
> 1 smoked ham hock
> 1 ounce soy sauce
> 1 ounce Lea & Perrins sauce
> 2 ounces Dijon mustard
> ½ cup ketchup
> Salt
> Pepper

First wash the beans in a large pot and soak overnight, then boil them in water but do not add salt because it is difficult to cook beans with salt. Drain the water when the beans are done. Keep the liquid.

In an ovenproof container, mix all the listed items and add the ham hock. Bring back the liquid from the boiling process, and if needed add some more water because the beans have to be covered completely. Then bake covered in the oven. Do not overbake the beans. Baking time is about 5 hours. Some people use a Crock-Pot.

Beef Rouladen

Swiss House

I use a whole top round of beef and trim it so that there is one large solid piece of meat, then cut off the lower end so that it looks more even. To make it possible to cut it evenly and uniformly, freeze the meat till it is firm enough to be sliced on the meat slicer.

In the meantime, prepare a filling consisting of half pork and half veal and fix a sort of forcemeat as a filling. Season with salt, ground white pepper, Italian seasoning, heavy cream, brandy, and a bit of white wine. You can use a food processor but make sure the filling is not watery. It should look like a sausage filling.

When the filling is done, slice the top round on the meat slicer a quarter inch thick. Lay it out on a table. Spread the stuffing over it and place a small piece of sliced bacon and a small piece of gherkin. Then roll it up and secure it with toothpicks to hold it in place during the cooking process.

In a heavy pan, season the rouladen with salt and pepper, then brown in hot oil on all sides. Remove from the pan and reduce the heat.

Simmer finely chopped onions, some minced garlic, thyme, marjoram, white pepper, and tomato paste. Sauté for a few minutes till everything is blended together. Dust with flour, deglaze with red wine, and add the brown beef stock. Then braise till the meat is tender. Keep an eye on it, and do not overcook.

When the meat is done, remove the toothpicks. Keep the meat warm. Degrease the sauce and reduce so that you have a sauce that covers the meat nicely.

Garnish with julienne of carrots and chopped parsley. Serve with spaetzli and red cabbage.

Basler Zwiebelsuppe
Swiss onion soup from the canton of Basel-Stadt

    1 pound onions
    Bay leaves
    Cloves
    3 ounces oil
    7 ounces flour

3 quarts clear beef stock
5 ounces shredded Parmesan cheese
Croutons made from French bread

Cut the onions in half, then spike them with bay leaves and cloves.

Brown the flour in oil to a dark brown roux; make sure you do not burn it. Let it cool off, then add the hot beef stock to it, but be careful because it may start to bubble while still very hot. Use a whip to smooth out the lumps. Season with salt and white pepper. In Switzerland we add some Maggi seasoning, which is a kind of soy sauce that has a particular flavor and is available in some grocery stores.

When the soup starts to boil, add the spiked onions and let it simmer for about 1 hour or so. Before you serve the soup, take out the onions and skim off the oil. Before you serve the soup, add a touch of red wine, salt, and ground white pepper. Parmesan cheese is usually served with it and even some croutons and a dash of red wine.

German Beer Soup

I will tell you all the items you need to make this soup, but it is difficult to break it down just for a small amount for 2 or 3 persons. Finely chopped onions, some minced garlic, flour, paprika, ground cumin, ground white pepper, salt, thyme leaves, marjoram leaves, clear beef stock, and of course, the beer.

First, roast the flour very lightly in the oven till it gets just a little yellow in color. In a stockpot with oil, sauté the finely chopped onions and garlic till they look transparent. Add all the seasonings and the roasted flour. Stir well so that you have a smooth, lump-free product. Pour in the beer and clear beef stock. Add seasoning and boil for 30 minutes.

Peanut Soup

Unsweetened peanut butter
Sweet butter
Flour
Chicken stock
Salt
Ground white pepper
Some chicken base to fortify
A few drops of Tabasco sauce

You can add some half and half (coffee cream) to make it richer. Garnish with chopped roasted peanuts.

Melt the butter and flour and make a roux. Then add the peanut butter and sauté till all is well blended. Pour the hot stock and bring to a boil again. You will have to use a whisk to get the soup smooth. Simmer for 30 minutes, then check for seasoning. At the end add a few roasted, coarsely chopped peanuts and the cream.

Chicken with Peanuts   Serves 6

3 tablespoons peanut oil
4 cups diced raw chicken breast
1 large clove minced garlic
1½ cups roasted shelled peanuts
2 tablespoons cut green onions
¼ teaspoon hot red pepper, finely chopped, fresh or dry
3 tablespoons soy sauce
½ pint chicken broth
2 tablespoons cornstarch diluted with water
1½ tablespoons sherry wine
½ teaspoon salt

Heat the oil in a skillet and stir-fry the chicken for two or three minutes and set aside.

Add the remaining oil to the skillet and then panfry the garlic. Cook till it gets lightly brown, then discard the garlic.

Add the peanuts, green onions, red pepper, salt, chicken broth, and soy sauce. Cook for a minute, stirring frequently. Pour in the chicken broth, and when it starts to boil, add the cornstarch, salt, and sherry wine. Let it thicken, and serve at once. Steamed rice is the way to go. Aloha.

Swiss Meringues

> 10 fresh egg whites
> 1 pound white sugar
> Dash of cream of tartar

Use the mixing bowl of a stand mixer, but be sure there is no fat or any oil inside the bowl; otherwise the recipe will not work.

Beat the egg whites with 3 ounces of sugar and the cream of tartar real firm, then slowly blend in the rest of the sugar with the help of a rubber spatula. Make sure you get to the bottom of the bowl so all the sugar gets well mixed with the egg whites.

Now dress the raw mixture with the help of a pastry bag and a star tube to place egg-size amounts on parchment paper on a sheet pan. Sprinkle sugar over them so that it looks like little crystals.

Bake in the oven at 230 degrees and leave the door slightly open. It will take about 1 hour. When you can lift them without breaking them, they are done. The meringues should stay white when baked. It would be wise to leave them in the turned-off oven overnight so that they are completely baked.

The meringues can be kept in a warm, dry place for several weeks.

Meringues are served with whipped cream and fresh berries. Meringues glacé are two shells filled with a scoop of ice cream and decorated with whipped cream.

Over the years, I traveled twice around the globe and was exposed to all kinds of food around the world. I also came across some natural holistic remedies to cure various illness. A lot of older people end up with all sorts of pills and do not know what's in them.

Yes, I am sure we have a lot pharmaceutical companies making these remedies. If only people would check on alternative ideas, it would probably be healthier.

We have a lot of health food stores, but you have to do some research to make sure you deal with companies that are legitimate. Check with your doctor before doing so. There are a lot of fraudsters out there. Many books have been written on the subject.

Dark chocolate lowers blood pressure and keeps your brain sharp, but do not overindulge.

Have a cup of hot cocoa before you go to sleep; it also helps you relax.

Cinnamon helps control your blood sugar and blood pressure, but again do not get carried away. Beware of the side effects of too much cinnamon.

Green and black tea are cancer-fighting remedies. Add some lemon rind to the tea to boost the fight against cancer. Tea also helps you relax after a long day of work. It does not have to be booze.

Hawaiian Stuffed Prawns

12–14 count prawns
Melted unsalted butter
Sour cream
Lea & Perrins sauce
Lemon juice
Chopped green onion
Finely chopped garlic
Dried white bread crumbs
Medium chopped macadamia nuts
Oil

To make this dish just for one person would be difficult. I recommend making it for a larger amount, maybe 10 people.

Mix melted butter, sour cream, Lea & Perrins sauce, lemon juice, green onions, and garlic. Then add the bread crumbs and the nuts. The mixture should be firm but not dry.

Slit the unpeeled prawns from the inside three-fourths of the way through. Spread them lightly apart and fill with about a tablespoon of the stuffing. Then place on a baking pan. Drizzle with melted butter and bake in the oven at 350 degrees for about 10 minutes or until the shrimp are opaque and take on a nice brown color. Garnish with fried parsley. This serves as a first course, 3 pieces each.

Goulash Soup

I guess every chef has his or her own way to make goulash soup. Again, I will let you know my way of doing so.

Lean ground beef
Finely chopped onions
Minced garlic
Lightly roasted flour

Paprika
Thyme leaves
Marjoram leaves
Ground cumin
Ground white pepper
Salt
Diced potatoes
Oil
Clear beef stock

This is meant to be the soup of the day. If I prepared it for an à la carte item, we used tender beef and cut it into small dices. Again, the roasted flour gives the soup more body.

Sauté the meat in oil till it gets light brown. Add onions and garlic, sweat for a couple of minutes, then add all the spices and flour. Stir well and pour in the stock. Again, you have flour in the soup, and it has to be made lump-free with the assistance of a wire whip, which will give you the proper result.

Slowly bring it back to a boil. Check for seasoning and skim off the extra oil. At the end, add the diced potatoes and let it simmer till the potatoes are cooked. Total cooking time is about 1 hour.

Mulligatawny Soup   Serves 10

This is a curry-flavored chicken soup. It should look like a thin cream soup, and the way I do it is simple.

2 ounces oil
4 ounces finely chopped onion
1 ounce curry powder
5 ounces coconut milk
2 ounces rice flour
3 quarts chicken stock

2 cups heavy cream
3 ounces cooked long-grain rice
6 ounces julienne cooked chicken breast
Salt and ground white pepper to taste

Sauté the onion in oil till transparent, then add the curry powder, coconut milk, and a rich, clear chicken stock. Bring to a boil. Mix the rice flour with cold water so that it is pourable, then add it to the boiling soup while stirring the soup to avoid lumps during this process.

Simmer for half an hour. Check for seasoning. Skim off some of the foaming residue and add the cream, rice, and chicken fillets. Now you are ready to enjoy.

Dungeness Crab Bisque   Serves 10

1 finely chopped medium onion
2 ounces butter
2 ounces rice flower
1 quart clam juice
2 cups heavy cream
2 pounds crabmeat, picked and chopped medium
Salt
Ground white pepper
Tabasco sauce
1 shot of brandy
Finely chopped parsley for garnish

Sauté the onion in butter till transparent. Add the rice flour and stir for a couple of minutes till well blended. Then slowly pour in the clam juice and with the aid of a wire whip make a smooth sauce.

Simmer for a few minutes. Season to taste. Add the cream, brandy, and crabmeat. Blend with a spoon so that the crabmeat is not torn but still chunky.

Serve with French bread or a loaf of sourdough bread.

Crème Fraîche   Yields 6 cups

    4 cups heavy cream
    2 cups sour cream

Combine the two creams and mix well. Pour into a container and seal well with clear plastic wrap. Let the mixture sit at room temperature for 24 hours. After 24 hours, refrigerate before using.

Mee Goreng   Serves 4
Fried Indonesian noodles

    2 pounds 20-count raw prawns
    8 ounces rump steak
    1 large chopped white onion
    2 cloves chopped garlic
    2 red chilies, seeded and chopped very fine
    1 ounce grated ginger
    2 ounces peanut oil
    12 ounces Singapore noodles
    1 large carrot cut into matchsticks
    2 sticks of celery cut into matchsticks
    1 ounce brown sugar
    1 tablespoon soy sauce
    1 tablespoon tomato sauce

Peel and devein the prawns. Finely slice the rump steak.

Combine the onion, garlic, chilies, and ginger in a food processor and make a medium fine paste. Add a little oil to it. Set aside.

Heat about 2 tablespoon of peanut oil in a wok. Add the noodles and stir-fry over medium heat until they are plump and warmed through.

Place the noodles on a serving plate and keep warm. Pour another tablespoon of oil in the wok, then add the paste mixture and fry till golden brown.

Add the prawns, steak, carrots, and celery. Stir-fry for 2 to 3 minutes, then add the brown sugar, soy sauce, and tomato sauce and season well with salt and pepper. Spoon the combination over the noodles and garnish with chopped green onion.

Shortcake Biscuits

1 pound flour
½ teaspoon salt
2 teaspoons baking powder
3 ounces sugar
8 ounces sweet butter
12 ounces cream

Sift all dry ingredients together. Add the cold butter and rub with a fork till it looks like flakes. Then pour the cream over it and press the dough together. Wrap in plastic and allow to rest in the fridge for 1 hour.

Roll dough ⅓ inch thick and cut circles. Use a floured cutter so it will not stick. Bake at 400 degrees for about 15 minutes.

Baked Apples with Custard Sauce   **Serves 10**

> 10 large apples
> 5 ounces sugar
> 3 ounces yellow raisins
> 1 teaspoon cinnamon
> 5 ounces almond paste
> 5 ounces sweet solid butter
> 10 ounces white wine

Peel the apples, then core and fill them with the almond paste and raisins.

Cover the bottom of a fireproof flat Corningware dish with butter. Arrange the apples side by side in the dish. Sprinkle the cinnamon and sugar over them. Then pour in the white wine and a generous portion of butter flakes. Bring it to a boil over low heat on top of the stove. Cover with parchment paper and poach in the oven at 350 degrees till the apples are very lightly caramelized but not mushy. Serve with rich custard sauce and top with toasted sliced almonds.

Chinese Bamboo-Steamed Vegetables

The steamers can be purchased in Asian stores and come in different sizes. This way you really eat fat free.

The ingredients I suggest are baby bock choy, broccoli, cauliflower, fresh Chinese mushrooms, carrots, fennel, pea pods, and items that do not get mushy when steamed.

The best way to steam them is with a small Chinese wok, but you also can use a pot that fits the steamer. If it is still too big, put a small metal container in it, but make sure the steamer is not submerged in water.

Arrange the vegetables in the steamer and place enough water in the wok so that it can produce steam. The amount of water needed is just enough so that it boils and produces steam. You can always add more water if necessary. Cover with the lid that comes with the container and slowly proceed with steaming till the vegetables are done but still crunchy.

When you deal with steam, be careful not to get burned. With the vegetables, serve a dipping sauce consisting of chopped garlic, ginger, hot pepper flakes, Chinese parsley, soy sauce, and a drop of sesame seed oil. Or serve them just plain.

Cheese and Mushroom Pies   Yields 6 pies

1⅓ ounces sweet butter
2 cloves garlic, minced
1 pound sliced button mushrooms
1 small red pepper, finely chopped
5¼ ounces sour cream
3 tablespoons mustard seeds
2½ ounces Gruyère cheese
6 sheets ready roll puff pastry
2¼ ounces cheddar cheese
1 egg, lightly beaten

Preheat the oven to 375 degrees. Cover two baking sheets with parchment paper.

Heat the butter in a large pan. Add the garlic and the mushrooms, stirring occasionally, until the mushrooms are tender and the liquid has evaporated. Remove and cool.

Stir in the red peppers. Combine the sour cream, mustard seeds, and the shredded cheddar cheese in a small bowl. Mix well.

Cut 12 circles 5½ inches in diameter from the puff pastry. Spread the cream mixture over 6 circles, leaving a ½-inch border. Top each with the mushroom mixture.

Sprinkle each with 2 teaspoons of grated Gruyère cheese. Brush around the outer edges with beaten egg. Place reserved pastry rounds on top of the filling; seal the edges with a fork.

Brush the top with beaten egg. Sprinkle the top with the remaining cheese and bake for 20 minutes or till golden brown and puffed. You can buy the puff dough frozen at the grocery store.

Lasagna Bolognese

This was a house special.

The way I made my lasagna was with three different layers consisting of creamed spinach, tomato concasse, and rich white cheese sauce. Then I topped it with meat sauce (Bolognese sauce) and baked it.

Those are the colors of the Italian flag. You can buy the pasta sheets at your local supermarket. For me it was faster just to make ravioli dough. This gives me bigger sheets that do not fall apart when I assemble the lasagna.

For the spinach, make a creamy béchamel sauce. Use freshly cooked chopped baby spinach and some heavy cream. Figure out how much spinach and cheese sauce you will need. Then divide the sauce in half and separate the two halves. Then blanch the spinach and with the help of a towel squeeze as much water out of it as you can. Then coarsely chop the spinach with a knife. Sauté and season the spinach and add it to half of the white sauce. Set aside.

With the second half of the white sauce, add grated Parmesan cheese and finely diced Swiss cheese. It will look a bit doughy but that's OK. Set this aside as well.

Now you get to make the concasse. Use ripe tomatoes. First you have to peel and seed them. Dice the tomatoes into chunks. Sauté some chopped onions and minced garlic in olive oil with some tomato paste. Then add the diced tomatoes and let it simmer while adding Italian seasoning, salt, and pepper to taste and a pinch of sugar to cut the acid. To make sure the sauce is not too thin, thicken with cornstarch diluted in water.

Now is time to put it all together. Cook the pasta sheets in boiling water. When they are done, cool them in ice water.

In the pan where you wish to assemble your creation, cover the bottom with soft butter. Sprinkle Parmesan cheese on top.

Before you lay down the pasta sheets, lay them on a towel so that there is no moisture on them.

First lay down a layer of pasta sheets, then use the spinach all across the pan, then lay another layer of pasta sheets. Top it with the thick cheese sauce, then continue with the next layer of pasta sheets. Spread the concasse and put the last layer of pasta sheets over it. Cover with meat sauce and Parmesan cheese (use the meat sauce recipe).

Bake it in a 350-degree oven for ½ hour.

I know it is hard work, but it is well worth it. Serve with a glass of Chianti red wine and a salad topped with balsamic vinegar.

Cannelloni Al Sugo
Dough

> 1¾ pounds flour
> ½ ounce salt
> ¼ cup olive oil
> 4 eggs
> ½ cup water

Blend everything together in a stand mixer. Make sure you mix it just for a minute or so; otherwise, your dough will be tough and hard to roll out.

Stuffing

    1 ounce chopped shallots
    1 clove garlic
    3 ounces butter
    10 ounces ground beef
    Beef bouillon
    10 ounces cooked spinach
    3 egg yolks
    Parmesan cheese
    Dash of nutmeg
    1 teaspoon salt
    ¼ teaspoon ground white pepper

The filling can consist of various things.

In a Crock-Pot, slow cook the ground beef together with the shallots, garlic, seasonings, and some beef bouillon till tender. Cool the meat, then grind the meat and spinach with a fine blade. Add the egg yolks and some Parmesan cheese.

Roll out the dough. If you have a pasta roller, cut it into 5 x 5 inch squares. Then cook in boiling water and cool in ice water. Dry the pasta sheets with a towel. Using a pastry bag, fill them evenly and arrange in an au gratin pan. Top with the tomato sauce and Parmesan cheese. Sprinkle with melted butter, then bake in the oven at 350 degrees till it bubbles.

Braised Veal Short Ribs Pizzaiola

    Veal short ribs
    Diced onion
    Minced garlic
    Flour
    Tomato paste

Olive oil
Freshly chopped rosemary
Chopped parsley
Peeled, seeded, and diced tomatoes
Salt
Ground white pepper
White wine
Brown veal stock

As you can see, the first five letters in *pizzaiola* spell "pizza." That may have something to do with a lot of tomatoes—yes, that's true.

First, season the ribs with salt and pepper, then dust in flour. In a heavy-duty pot, brown the meat in olive oil all around and put aside. Normally, veal kidney fat is used to braise the ribs, but it is difficult to get your hands on it.

Next, sauté the finely chopped onion till all the baked-on residue in the pot has worked into the onion. Add the garlic and tomato paste, then let it roast for a couple of minutes. Dust with flour and deglaze with the white wine and the coarsely chopped tomatoes.

Fill up the pot with the veal stock. Add the finely chopped rosemary, salt, and pepper and bring to a boil. Reduce heat and place the ribs in it. You can use the veal kidney fat when you add the ribs. Simmer the ribs till tender, then set aside.

If the sauce is too thin after removing the ribs, reduce till it reaches the right consistency. Skim off the extra fat. When you serve the ribs, top with the sauce sprinkled with extra chopped fresh rosemary and chopped parsley. Serve with potato dumplings and vegetables.

※ ※ ※

Fudge Brownies   Yields about 24 pieces

2 sticks sweet butter
8 ounces bittersweet chocolate
5 medium eggs
3 cups sugar
1 tablespoon pure vanilla
1 teaspoon salt
1½ cups flour
3 cups chopped nuts of your choice (almonds, pecan, walnuts)

Use a 10 x 10 baking pan. Line the pan with parchment paper; it is easier to remove the end product and it won't stick.

Set the oven to 350 degrees. In a double boiler, melt the butter and chocolate, then set aside.

In a stand mixer, use the paddle attachment to mix together the eggs, sugar, and vanilla to a light, creamy consistency. Add the melted butter and chocolate mixture, salt, and flour. Blend just until everything is blended together. Gently blend in the nuts. To bring out the flavor, toast the nuts in the oven first.

Pour the batter into the baking pan and bake in the middle of the oven for about 45 minutes. Use a toothpick or a bamboo stick to check for doneness.

The brownies can be eaten cold or warm. Keep them away from the children.

Orange Hazelnut Biscotti

7 ounces hazelnuts
12 ounces flour
6 ounces sugar
¼ teaspoon salt
1 ounce baking powder

5 eggs
1 large naval orange for zest
1 teaspoon vanilla

First, roast the nuts in the oven golden brown; do not burn them. When they are cold enough, rub off the skins. Discard the skins.

Mix the flour, sugar, salt, and baking powder together. Beat 4 eggs, orange zest, and vanilla together and make a firm dough. Fold in the nuts by hand.

Prepare a cookie sheet with a thin layer of butter dusted with flour. Form 3 logs about 3 inches wide. Brush with egg wash and bake in a 350-degree oven till lightly brown.

Remove from the oven and cool off so that you can remove the logs. Slice them into about ¼-inch thick pieces. Lay out on cookie sheets again and toast them in the oven golden brown on both sides. Keep 1 egg for egg wash.

After they are cold, dip them in dark chocolate.

Fruitcake

Also called tea or coffee cake

7 ounces butter
8 ounces sugar
5 medium eggs
15 ounces all-purpose flour
1 ounce baking powder
½ ounce rum
½ cup milk
3 ounces diced candied fruits
3 ounces raisins

This yields two cake molds 8 x 4 inches. It is advisable to line the molds with parchment paper; this way you can easily remove the cakes from the pan.

In a stand mixer, whip the butter and sugar till nice and creamy. Then gradually add the eggs one by one while still running the mixer so that it is properly blended. Pour in the rum and blend again. Work in the flour, baking powder, milk, raisins, and fruits. Stir till all the ingredients are well combined.

Pour the batter into the molds and bake at 350 degrees for about 1 hour.

Baked Noodles Printaniere (Springtime)

Béchamel sauce
Linguine cooked al dente
Blanched vegetables such as broccoli, carrots, green peas, quartered mushrooms, cauliflower, and some red and green bell peppers. Cut the cauliflower and broccoli into florets.

To put this dish together, first make a good béchamel sauce. It has to be thin because the precooked noodles will absorb a lot of liquid, so you need to accommodate for that. Enhance the sauce with a lot of cheese; this can be done with a variety of easy melting cheeses.

Then blanch the vegetables and cook the noodles. Mix it all together and place in a casserole dish. Sprinkle Parmesan cheese, drizzle with melted butter, and bake it at 350 degrees till golden brown; about 25 minutes.

This dish is best when served as a complete dinner. This is a good vegetarian dish for cold weather.

CHAPTER 13

THE BRASS BELL STORY

I believe real chefs need to be recognized for what they are and what it takes to become a real chef. Good, dedicated chefs are like painters of classical art. Their canvas is the stove, pots, and pans. Their brushes are their fork, ladles, spoons, and tongs. The colors they have are almost endless food items with color varieties, and their art galleries are their dinners plates. Their dishes display the art show.

Like a good artist, it takes many years to become successful. Inspiration, dedication, and willingness to sacrifice long, hard hours will give them the recognition they deserve. People will seek their talent all around the globe. Eventually, all of them will find their own niche in what they are recognized for, and they will stay true to their profession and stay committed to the real thing.

They were guided by good teachers. Their classical background will always be their base. You cannot build a house without a good foundation.

As you can see by now, I get philosophical now and then. It is part of being serious about the trade.

Linguine with Shrimp, Asparagus Tips, and Basil   Serves 2

8 ounces linguine
3 tablespoons olive oil
2 cloves garlic, minced
1 red jalapeño cut into small dice
5 ounces dry white wine
2 ounces butter
12 uncooked large shrimp, peeled and deveined, tail on
12 slender pieces asparagus, trimmed and cut diagonally into 1½-inch pieces
1 tablespoon fresh lemon juice
2 cups fresh basil, cut into julienne
4 ounces heavy cream
Salt
White pepper

First, cook the pasta al dente in lightly salted water.

In the meantime, heat the olive oil in a skillet over medium heat. Add the garlic and the jalapeño and simmer for about 1 minute. Add the wine, lemon juice, and butter and simmer for another minute. Then add the shrimp and asparagus.

Toss until the asparagus are tender and the shrimp opaque in the center; about 3 minutes. Drain the pasta, then add to the skillet. Throw in the basil and toss till the basil is slightly wilted. Add the cream to coat the pasta. Season with salt and pepper.

Divide the pasta onto two pasta plates and add lemon wedges on the side.

King Crab Cioppino   Serves 12

1 pound onions, sliced
1 pound green bell peppers, sliced
2 bunches green onions, sliced

1 cup olive oil
4 cloves garlic
1 cup chopped parsley
1½ quarts tomato purée
1 quart tomato sauce
1 quart dry white wine
1¼ quarts water
2 bay leaves
1 teaspoon fresh thyme
1 teaspoon white pepper
1 teaspoon basil
24 fresh clams
1 pound medium-size shrimp, peeled and deveined, tail on
3 pounds king crab meat
2 pounds whitefish, boneless and skinless, cut into 1½-inch cubes

Slice the onions, green peppers, and scallions, including top parts. Sauté in olive oil along with the chopped garlic. Cook for 5 minutes, then add the parsley, tomato purée, tomato sauce, wine, water, and seasonings. Simmer for 1 hour.

Scrub the clams and make sure you get rid of the sand. Cut the crab legs into 3-inch pieces. Add the crab and clams to the sauce and cook for 10 minutes.

Add the shrimp and whitefish and simmer for another 15 minutes. Discard any clam that does not open. Serve in a soup bowl with sourdough bread.

Jambalaya Louisiana Style   Serves 4

4 bay leaves
½ teaspoon thyme
1 teaspoon salt
1 teaspoon white pepper

1 teaspoon English mustard
¾ teaspoon cayenne pepper
½ teaspoon cumin
½ teaspoon ground black pepper
3 ounces vegetable margarine
6 ounces smoked ham, diced
7 ounces Andouille sausage, sliced
2 cups diced onions
2 cups diced celery
3 ounces diced green peppers, seeded
2 teaspoons minced garlic
2 cups Uncle Ben's rice
1 quart chicken stock

Mix all the seasonings together and put aside.

In a cast iron skillet, melt the margarine. Then sauté the ham and sausage for 5 minutes, stirring constantly. Add the onions, celery, bell peppers, seasoning, and garlic and cook till everything is slightly brown. Scrub the bottom of the pan with the spatula and do not let the mixture burn. Add the rice and the stock and stir well. Reduce the heat and keep on stirring; simmer till the rice is still crunchy, about 15 minutes or so. When everything is done, take out the bay leaves. Portion it onto 4 plates.

Veal Steak with Fresh Morel Sauce (Swiss Style)   Serves 6

6 each 6-ounce milk-fed veal steaks cut from the short loin, boneless
Salt
Pepper
Flour to dust
Peanut oil
3 ounces fresh morels

2 ounces fresh sweet butter
2 ounces chopped shallots
Pinch of fresh garlic
2 ounces brandy
1 ounce Madeira wine
1½ ounces port wine
3 cups heavy cream
1 ounce glacé de viande (meat extract)

Flour dust the meat, then sauté in the peanut oil. The meat should be medium, not well done.

Wash the morels well so that there is absolutely no sand in them. You can also use dried morels, but they have to be soaked till soft and also must be well washed. Cut the morels into quarters.

For the sauce, sauté the shallots and the garlic in butter, then add the morels. Flame with brandy. Pour in the port and Madeira wine and reduce till almost dry. Then add the cream, seasonings, and glacé de viande. Simmer till the sauce has a nice creamy texture. Do not let it boil again; it would break the sauce. Whip in the 2 ounces of soft butter and serve over the sautéed steaks.

Butter Confect (Piped Butter Cookies)

16 ounces sweet butter
16 ounces sugar
8 eggs, medium
4 egg yolks
2 pounds all-purpose flour

Make sure the butter is at room temperature. Mix the butter and sugar till real fluffy with the help of a stand mixer. Then blend in the eggs and yolks one by one. If you fold in the eggs and yolks too quickly and do not let them blend properly, it could separate.

Fold in the flour with a wooden spoon; do not over blend. Next, take a cookie sheet and pipe rosettes with a star tube ½ inch apart. Add half a red candied cherry on top of each rosette.

Bake at 300 degrees for about 20 to 30 minutes, based on the calibration of the oven. Some household ovens vary.

When the cookies are baked, let them cool for a moment. Then with the help of a pastry spatula, loosen the cookies from the sheet and place onto a cooling rack.

If you make cat paws, hold two pieces together and dip into melted dark chocolate, then set on parchment paper. When the chocolate has set, place them into ziplock bags and keep the cookies in a dry, cool place till you feel like eating them.

Arroz con Pollo (Chicken with Rice)

Use thighs and drumsticks, 2 each per person. For this dish I use thighs and drumsticks, not breasts, because breasts are too dry.

Uncle Ben's rice
Finely chopped onions
Fresh diced tomatoes, seeded and peeled
Sliced mushrooms
Dash of cumin
1 small bay leaf
Salt
White pepper
Rich chicken stock
Butter

In a cast iron pot (Dutch oven), sauté the chicken pieces in butter all around till nice and brown, then remove from the pot. Reduce the heat and smother the onions. Add the rice and stir until it looks transparent. Add the mushrooms, cumin, and bay leaf. Simmer for a couple of minutes, then add the tomatoes and seasonings and pour in the chicken stock.

Bring to a boil, reduce the heat, then cover with a lid and cook for 30 minutes. The ratio of rice to liquid should be 1 part rice and 1½ parts chicken stock. You do not want the end result to be too dry.

Grilled Lobster Tail with Cumin, Lime Butter, and Avocado Pico de Gallo

Serves 4

A dish from south of the border

Lobster

> 4 each 8-ounce lobster tails
> 1 stick (4 ounces) butter
> 3 cloves minced garlic
> 1 tablespoon lime juice
> 2 teaspoons ground cumin
> ¼ teaspoon cayenne pepper
> 4 whole limes
> Salt

Pico de Gallo

> 1 cup diced tomatoes
> ½ cup diced onion
> 2 tablespoons minced jalapeño
> 3 tablespoons freshly chopped cilantro
> 1 tablespoon lime juice
> 2 ripe peeled, pitted, and diced avocados

To make the pico de gallo, simply blend the ingredients together.

Next, prep the lobster tails by cutting halfway through from the top. Melt the butter with garlic in a saucepan. Stir in the lime juice, cumin, and cayenne pepper and keep warm.

Brush the cut lobster tails with the melted butter and season with salt. Grill the lobster cut side down first for 3 to 4 minutes, then turn and continue to broil until the lobster meat is just opaque all around.

Transfer to a plate and drizzle with the remaining butter. Garnish with the lime wedges and serve with the pico de gallo. This dish is meant to be for outdoor parties. Have a Corona beer with it.

Tandoori Style Chicken with Mango Jasmine Rice   Serves 4

Use Cornish game hens, about 22 ounces each.
¼ cup cilantro
¼ cup parsley
2 cloves minced garlic
2 teaspoons cumin
2 teaspoons paprika
½ tablespoon salt
¼ teaspoon cayenne pepper
¼ cup olive oil
½ cup plain white yogurt
3 tablespoons lemon juice
2 large mangoes, peeled and cut into wedges
2 cups jasmine rice
3 cups water
¼ cup toasted pine nuts

Use a food processor to make a purée of the cilantro, parsley, garlic, cumin, paprika, salt, cayenne pepper, and olive oil. Transfer one-fourth the mixture to a small bowl and reserve.

Add the yogurt and lemon juice to the remaining portion and

mix well. In a glass baking dish, pour the yogurt mixture over the hens, turning to coat. Cover with plastic wrap and refrigerate for 1 hour or so.

Next get your barbeque broiler ready at medium heat. Butterfly the chicken, cut off the backbone, and then put the split hens on the broiler skin side down. Cover the grill and turn the birds every now and then till they are done.

In the meantime, start your rice cooking. Combine the rice, 3 cups of water, and the set-aside mixture, then blend well. Reduce the heat and simmer covered for about 15 minutes.

Fold in a few pieces of cubed mangoes to the rice, then grill the mango wedges. Remove the breastbone and serve the hens over the rice. Garnish with the broiled mango wedges, jasmine rice, and pine nuts.

Chicken in Red Wine   Serves 6

   2 each 3-pound fresh chickens
   3½ cups red wine
   1 ounce whole black peppercorns
   3 cloves garlic
   2 celery ribs, diced
   1 medium carrot, diced
   1 yellow onion, diced
   1 ounce oil
   10 sprigs parsley
   2 sprigs thyme
   2 bay leaves
   ½ cup flour for dusting
   1 cup flour
   2 cups chicken stock
   Salt and white pepper to taste

½ pound lean bacon, cut into lardoon strips
20 peeled pearl onions
¾ pound button mushrooms, cut into quarters
3 ounces butter
1 ounce chopped parsley

In a stainless steel pot, add wine, peppercorns, garlic, celery, carrots, and yellow onions. Bring to a boil, then remove from heat and let it cool completely.

Cut the chicken breasts and legs in half. You should have 12 pieces. Pour the marinade and 1 ounce of oil over the chicken, then cover and let it marinate overnight in the fridge.

The next day strain the liquid from the chicken and keep the liquid separate.

String the parsley and thyme sprigs together (bouquet garni) and put aside. Pat the chicken dry, then flour dust and brown in oil all around. Set aside.

Add all the vegetables from the marinade and cook till they are soft. Sprinkle in the cup of flour and rotate for 1 minute. Add the reserved liquid and chicken stock and whisk till everything is smooth. Then add seasonings, bring to a boil again, and arrange the chicken pieces in the sauce.

Cover the pot with a lid, then place in a 350-degree oven and braise it for approximately 1 hour.

Now is time to fix the garnish. Blanch the pearl onions and lardoons. Quarter the mushrooms and panfry in clarified butter till nice and golden brown. When the chicken is done, lift the chicken out of the sauce and place on a serving dish, then strain the sauce and pour over the chicken.

Top with the garnishes. Sprinkle with chopped parsley and serve it with noodles and green beans.

⚜ ⚜ ⚜

Cream of Brie Cheese and Leek Soup   Serves 6

½ cup unsalted butter
8 ounces leeks, white parts only, well washed and finely sliced
5 cups low-sodium chicken stock
½ cup all-purpose flour
4 cups half and half or coffee creamer
2 pounds brie cheese, well chilled and cut into cubes, rind on
Salt
Ground white pepper
2 ounces finely cut chives

Melt ¼ cup of butter in a heavy saucepot over medium heat. Add leeks and chicken stock and simmer, stirring frequently, till transparent; about 3 to 4 minutes. Reduce heat, cover and simmer till the leeks are tender. Purée in a blender.

Melt the remaining ¼ cup of butter in a stainless steel saucepan over medium heat. Add flour and stir for a couple of minutes. This is a roux.

Slowly pour in the half and half. Use a whisk to make it lump free. Next add one-fourth of the cheese and blend until smooth and melted. Repeat with the remaining cheese.

Strain the soup though a fine sieve, pressing with the back of a spoon. Return to saucepan. Mix in leek purée and check for seasoning. Serve the soup with the chives sprinkled over it.

Let's go fishing.

Blackened Red Snapper

Today I caught a red snapper, and I will blacken the fish. The fish has to be boneless and skinless.

The fish will be cooked in a cast iron skillet. The skillet needs to be very hot and could create a bit of smoke. Use a thick oven mitt so that you do not burn your hands. You do not need to use a fire extinguisher or call the fire department.

Seasoning

1 tablespoon sweet paprika
½ teaspoon dried oregano
½ teaspoon dried thyme leaves
¾ teaspoon ground white pepper
2½ teaspoons kosher salt
1 teaspoon onion powder
1 teaspoon cayenne pepper
1 teaspoon garlic powder
¾ teaspoon ground black pepper
2 sticks unsalted butter, melted

Mix all the seasonings together in a bowl and set aside.

Put one-third of the melted butter in a wide, shallow dish so that you can dip the fish in it. Dip each portion of fish into the melted butter and lay out on sheet pan covered with parchment paper.

Season the individual fish portions with the seasonings on both sides. Be generous and pat it down so that when you move it, the seasonings will stay on the fish. Put the pan with the butter aside.

Set the oven at 250 degrees. Heat a cast iron skillet till you can smell the pan. Carefully place 2 or 3 fillets of fish into the pan. Beware: the pan is very hot and will smoke. Pour a small amount of butter into the pan and sear both sides of the fish. As you cook the fish, drizzle with butter.

The cooking time depends on the size of the fish. Make certain the fish is done but not dried out. Both sides of the fish should look evenly charred.

If you make several portions, you can keep the fish warm in the oven till you have your side dishes fixed.

Serve with a lemon star and drawn butter.

My wife was Chinese, and I do have a soft spot for Asian cooking.

Mongolian Lamb   Serves 4

2 pounds lamb fillets, derived from a rack of lamb
2 cloves garlic, crushed
1 teaspoon grated fresh ginger
1 teaspoon hoisin sauce
1 teaspoon sesame oil
1 teaspoon sesame seeds
2 teaspoons peanut oil
4 onions, cut into wedges
3 teaspoons cornstarch
3 teaspoons soy sauce
1 ounce sherry wine

First, trim the meat of any fat and skin, then slice across the grain into thin slices.

Mix the hoisin sauce, garlic, ginger, and sesame oil. Coat the meat well and let it marinate for about 1 hour in the fridge.

Toast the sesame seeds in a dry pan on medium heat 2 to 3 minutes. Remove quickly; do not let them burn. Pour onto a cold plate.

Heat the peanut oil in a wok on a small fame and stir-fry the onions for 10 minutes till they are soft and just start to get a bit brown. Remove from the wok and keep warm.

Reheat the wok and cook the meat over high heat, but do not cook it totally through—just medium. Mix the cornstarch, soy sauce, and sherry wine; it has to be completely solidified. Then add to the wok over high heat till the fillets are completely covered by the sauce.

Arrange the onions on the bottom of a plate, then pour the meat on top of it and sprinkle with the toasted sesame seeds. Serve with steamed rice.

Indonesian Style: King Prawns with Peanuts   Serves 4

  2½ pounds 16–20 count raw shrimp
  4 spring onions, chopped
  1 clove garlic, minced
  1 teaspoon finely chopped ginger
  1 teaspoon sambal
  1 teaspoon ground coriander
  ½ teaspoon ground turmeric
  1 teaspoon finely grated lemon rind
  1 tablespoon lemon juice
  4 ounces chopped, unsalted roasted peanuts
  2 tablespoons peanut oil

Peel and devein the prawns, leaving the tails on.

Combine the spring onions, garlic, ginger, sambal, coriander, turmeric, lemon rind, lemon juice, and roasted peanuts. Cover and refrigerate for 1 hour.

Heat the oil in a wok. Add the prawns and mixture and stir-fry over high heat till the prawns are cooked. Serve with rice.

When you own a restaurant or any other type of business, you always have to come up with new ideas to keep your custumers in suspense so that they will come back and see what's new.

Over the years I had all kinds of crazy ideas, and one of them was a dish I called the COW PATCH. It relates to Switzerland, and when you visit the old country you will see what I am talking about.

We do have cow farmers in Switzerland, since the land is very expensive and the government demands that a certain amount of land be strictly allocated just for farming purposes. People have to eat.

I remember quite well on my last visit to the old country, there used to be a lot of open spaces, but now houses had sprung up all over the landscape. The farmers sold all the land because the money was good, but the folks also had to eat, so new regulations were put in place to prevent that from occurring. Farming is still alive and doing well in Switzerland.

Let's cut to the chase and I will tell you what I came up with. First, I prepared a nice and crispy rösti, and I topped it with beef chasseur, which is a kind of geschnetzeltes but with wild mushrooms and crispy fried onions. It had a demi-glacé sauce and looked just like the real thing. By the way, it sold very well.

Gnocchi Parisienne

These are made with cream puff pastry.

> ½ quart water
> 3½ ounces butter
> ¼ ounce salt
> Dash of nutmeg
> 10 ounces flour
> 9 whole eggs

To prepare the cream puff pastry, bring the water, butter, salt, and nutmeg to a boil. Add the flour and make a smooth dough. Then add the eggs one by one. Blend well in between each egg.

With the help of a pastry bag and ½-inch tube, form marble-sized dumplings into almost boiling salted water. When all the dumplings are floating on top of the water, remove them with a skimmer and place in a buttered au gratin dish. Cover with a thin béchamel sauce, sprinkle with Parmesan cheese, and dribble melted butter over the dumplings. Bake in the oven at 425 degrees for about 30 minutes or till they are lightly brown. Serve at once.

There are also Roman-style Piedmontese and German-style gnocchi, but I think that the French styles are more of a challenge than the others.

This is the story behind the brass bell in the kitchen at the Swiss House.

We had been in business for just about six months. It was hard to get the attention of the wait help; let's just say the girls liked to talk. I could not see myself running after each one of them.

At first I had a little bell like those you might have seen at the post office, but the life span of that bell was rather short lived. The chef abused it, and let's say I was often ignored!

At that time, we had a girl bartender called Louise, and one day out of the blue she showed up with a nice solid brass bell that did the trick. Ever since then even our guests became fond of it and commented when they did not hear the bell ringing during their dinner.

Yes, at times the ringing was done excessively, and Lily would come to the kitchen wondering what was going on. I would tell her that she should make sure our customers got the proper service they deserve and the wait help should pay attention.

The kitchen has a large window through which I could see who was coming through the front door and was also able to see the progress based on how quickly the customers were eating. This gave me a good idea of when I had to start cooking table by table, since I cooked everything to order. It takes practice to do so, and it is difficult to do when the dining room is not paying attention.

I had a rule from day one that there would be no food left under the heating lamp. The bell was my way to communicate with the wait help to let them know when food was ready to pick up so that it would not stay under the heating lamp. Our guests knew that and were very appreciative of that. And I think if you pay for a meal, it should at least be done properly. Many times, customers came into the kitchen to see where the bell was located and even tried to ring it themselves.

I guess every business has some sort of a system to get the job done, and it might even become memorable. It sure was for me, and I decided to keep that bell for a souvenir.

And now for some observations on life.

- If life is a school, did you ever think that you made your grades?
- A copy is never the original.
- Have you ever seen your own achievement, and what was your answer—it could be scary if there was none!
- Did your mother ever teach you to do anything right other than sit on the couch?
- Have you ever thought to do something before you were told?
- It's easy to take a bath when you don't have to wash the top.
- Have you ever thought to find your own niche in life?
- Everybody can follow someone's footsteps, but it is difficult to find your own.
- Dedication requires hard work and persistence, and there is no room for complaints.

- Daydreamers do not even hear the music.
- It is funny to think that there is no room for improvement!
- Don't hang on to others' achievement and glory.
- Learning means you have to adapt to something new with eagerness in order to benefit from it.
- Life is not an easy chair if you want to be recognized.
- Don't criticize the achiever if his shoes look old and worn out.
- Have you ever thought to wear your boss's shoes?

Those are just a few thoughts I wish to put on paper, and I guess many of us have learned over the years to come up with ideas.

Truffle drawing on ham for buffet display Caribe Hilton Puerto Rico

CHAPTER 14

LILY'S ONE HUNDRED PERCENT SUPPORT

It is now over two years since Lily passed away, and I have had a lot of time to reflect on what occurred over the last forty-one years. It gave me time to illustrate what it really took to fulfill a life's dream.

I always had the support of my wife Lily 100 percent, and she was willing to do whatever it took to make my dream possible. It caused a lot of wear and tear because all our energy was directed to fulfilling my dream and to becoming successful.

In many cases where there are husband wife partnership it does not work out. There is too much stress, and you have to sacrifice almost any sort of leisure. At times it consumes as much as seven days a week. Yes, you could write pages and pages of things to do, but you get the drift.

The restaurant business is one of the most demanding kinds of adventures there is, especially if you want to be successful. It takes many years just to become a chef and pastry chef, then to make a career and be recognized as a qualified chef, which requires you to move to different places and countries. You constantly have to adapt to new environments, different styles of cooking, and new languages, and it also makes it hard to settle down anywhere.

Once you get on the train, it will take a long time before you can get off it. It becomes almost addictive, and to become a well-rounded chef means being able to handle all the diversity presented at all those many hotel chains. Not only your cooking is required. You also have to be able to handle the administrative tasks. In a large operation, you do little cooking but you have to teach your help to do the job right.

Labor cost and food cost have to be in line so that your department can be profitable. This includes training employees, upgrading concepts, motivating the kitchen crew, dealing with all surrounding kitchen-related departments, attending all kinds of meetings, writing work schedules, arranging vacation requests, covering sick leave requests, and making sure you do not have any overtime because it would affect your payroll.

If you have to deal with the unions, you do not want any conflicts. They will send the shop steward, and you will waste a lot of time explaining their grievance.

Those things are just a sideline of what's in store for you. When you open your own business and are aware of such issues, you are a step ahead. But you still have to be able to do everything, including all the cleaning and maintenance, paying all the bills, handling payroll, and doing all the purchasing of food and beverages.

You must also hire your employees, train them, set all the standards, set house rules, and make sure there are no loopholes, because one of them will surely take advantage of you and it could get ugly. Do not let them take any shortcuts. Yes, you will be told you are a dictator or even worse. Get used to it, because you are dealing with the human race.

Very often you find some wise guy who thinks that his or her way is better than yours. Think again! Often you get somebody who will work for a short while and then move on, and later you find out that he or she is working for your competition next door.

The turnover in the restaurant business is enormous, and if you cannot do any job at your place yourself, it would be difficult to function when people do not show up for work. It all depends on the mood of your employees; they may even show up to work drunk or having just finished a joint. It is a good thing to have some trustworthy employees. I know that you sometimes have to take a gamble; to reference check your employees nowadays is a difficult task because of all the laws.

Over my many years in business, I challenged myself in many ways in different food competitions. I also cooked for the Chaîne des Rôtisseurs.

My first real chef job was in a five-hundred-room hotel. It was at the Sheraton Hotel in Rochester, New York. The last job I had before I dove into my own business was as the executive chef of a nineteen-hundred-room facility at the Sheraton Waikiki in Honolulu, Hawaii. I was often asked, "Are you sure you can handle it? After all, it is nineteen-hundred rooms with a lot of responsibility." Yes, if you have the confidence and are willing to do so, it will be possible.

Life's dreams can definitely become reality. When I was six years old, that was my dream, to learn to become a konditor and also a chef, then travel around the globe and open my own restaurant. It surely did not come overnight, but if you believe in yourself, then give it a try. You never know!

I never was braggadocious and kept a simple life. The only one I had to prove it to that I could do it was myself. Once you do exactly that, it is mission accomplished.

I do not have any children, which gave me a lot of flexibility. It was not meant to be. There are things in life you do not have any control over. Over our forty-one years of marriage, we had a good life, and we accomplished what many people would just imagine being possible to do.

I have lived in Grass Valley for over thirty-three years and intend to stay here for the duration of my life. If God wills it, I wish to continue to stay occupied as a hobby chef—maybe a private chef on a small scale and whatever comes along. I surely have all the experience, and I do not want to waste it as long as my health is holding up. There is also a possibility of taking a few trips. Australia comes to my mind.

When I look at the new top chefs in Europe and what they are doing, it is completely different, but the basic classical kitchen is still visible.

I had some customers when I came up with the new approach of cooking who asked me if there would be something on the plate to eat. My clientele wanted real meals, even Mr. Pritzker, founder of Hyatt Hotels. One of our guests mentioned that sometimes when Mr. Pritzker goes out to eat the portions are so small that he goes across the street to have a hamburger.

Our customers always knew that our portions were good. Even the so-called doggie bags became in handy. We were well known for having good-quality food and being very consistent. Our customers knew exactly what they would get and were looking for.

Lily always strived for excellent service. She knew all the guest by name and also remembered what they had for a beverage the last time they visited. My barber, Todd Frei, told his clientele that Lily was well known for stiff drinks. We also were well known for a very clean restaurant, including the bathrooms.

Grass Valley is a small town, and most of the people know each other. We had to be sure that we were on the ball—one bad meal and the entire town would get wind of it.

Let's go back to cooking.

Beef Steak Tartare

This dish originally came from Mongolia, which is north of China. The Tartar horsemen kept the meat between the saddle and their mount's back to be pounded and crushed during a fierce ride. Now it is finely chopped by knife.

Beef tenderloin
Finely chopped onions
Raw onion rings
Anchovy fillets
Capers
Tabasco sauce
Worcester sauce
Fresh raw egg in shell
Oil
Brandy
Salt
Freshly ground pepper
Raw egg

All ingredients must be kept cold.

Your chopped fillet is shaped loose like a hamburger and presented on a leaf of lettuce as a doily. The egg is set in the middle in one half of the eggshell, then decorated with the onion rings.

All other items come in a small container on the side and are usually prepared tableside with the help of a fork in a small wooden bowl. You have to incorporate the condiments slowly and based on the person who eats it and will dictate how much seasoning he or she likes.

The tartare is then served with dark rye bread and butter. Today the meat is ground with a meat grinder, but if you do so you will waste some of the meat in the grinder. Therefore, I use a large, sharp knife. The amount of one fillet is 6 to 8 ounces.

⚜   ⚜   ⚜

Braised Leeks Baked with a Mornay Sauce

This is a typical Swiss-French dish that is not often served in the United States.

Leeks can be found in the produce section in most grocery stores. For this dish you usually use most of the white part of the leeks.

First, cut the leeks into 2½-inch sections. Then wash them very thoroughly to make sure you do not have any sand on them.

Then blanch the leeks in lightly salted water. They should be almost be cooked but not overcooked.

Cover the inside of a gratin dish completely with melted butter. Arrange the leeks side by side and top with the Mornay sauce and a generous amount of shredded Gruyère cheese. Bake in the oven at 350 degrees till nice and golden brown.

This dish goes well with smoked sausages or ham hocks. You can use the green parts of the leeks for a vegetable soup. Leeks are expensive, and you do not want to waste anything.

Baked Swiss Chard

Chard is another typical fall European vegetable. And it can be used in two ways—either use just the leaves or combine the leaves and the stems.

The leaves can be just sautéed with butter, garlic, salt, and pepper. Grind the leaves and fix it like creamed spinach.

First, wash the whole leaves two or three times to make sure you get rid of all the sand. Then trim the leaves from the stems. Cut the outer part from the stems because they may be a bit stringy and hard to chew.

Cut the stems into batons about ¼ inch by 3 inches. Blanch in lightly salted water maybe 2 to 3 minutes and set aside.

Take a bunch of leaves and roll them up tightly. Cut it into thin ribbons. Then sauté the leaves in olive oil with some garlic, pepper, salt, and nutmeg.

Brush the inside of an earthenware dish with soft butter. Then lay the bottom with the leaves and arrange the top with the stems; it has to be covered evenly. Generously ladle the béchamel sauce over it.

Sprinkle with Gruyère cheese and Parmesan cheese, then bake in a 400-degree oven for about 25 to 30 minutes or till golden brown.

I recommend that you put the container on a cookie sheet because it may bubble over, and this way I spare you the time you would have to spend cleaning the oven.

Congee   Serves 4–6

Lily always liked to eat congee when we ate out at her famous Chinese restaurant. This is a dish like oatmeal but made with long-grain rice. Do not use Uncle Ben's rice.

> 2 pounds meaty pork bones, cut 2 to 3 inches long
> ¾ cup long-grain rice
> 1 tablespoon oil
> Salt
> 2 inches completely cleaned fresh ginger, sliced lengthwise
> 9 ounces dried scallops (available in Asian markets)
> ½ cup unsalted raw blanched peanuts
> 1 stalk scallion, trimmed and thinly sliced on the bias

Put the pork bones into a large, heavy pot and cover with at least 2 inches of cold water. Bring it to a boil. This is just to blanch the bones, which will give you a clean product. In other words, just a quick boil. Then drain the water and return the bones to the pot.

Wash the rice in cold water till the water is completely clear. Add the washed rice to the bones. Add the oil, salt, ginger, and about 9 cups of water and bring to a boil while stirring now and then.

When it boils, add the scallops and peanuts. Reduce the heat, cover with a lid, and simmer for about 1½ hours, stirring once in a while. Then take it off the heat and let it rest covered for 1 hour.

After it rests, remove the bones but leave the meat in the soup. Take out the ginger. If the congee is too thick, add some hot water. Garnish with scallions.

Here are a few Chinese food cures.

Grapefruit

Indigestion, bad breath, poor appetite. Collect the peels of the grapefruit; cut off only the outer rind. Put the rinds in the sun to dry to make dry grapefruit peels.

Caraway Seeds

Stomachache, abdominal pain. Boil 1 tablespoon of caraway seeds, 1 teaspoon of cinnamon, and 1 teaspoon of dried ginger in 12 ounces of water, and drink it as a soup.

Sweet Basil

Headache from the common cold, indigestion, and stomachache. Use several sweet basil leaves as a seasoning to substitute for parsley or green onions for relief of headache due to the common cold.

Pound Cake

Yields 2 cakes

1 pound sweet butter
1 pound sugar
2 whole eggs
8 egg yolks
1 pound flour
8 egg whites
Rind from 1 lemon; use fine grater

In a stand mixer, cream the butter and sugar thoroughly. Add the whole eggs and the yolks one by one and ½ cup of flour. Mix well. Beat the egg whites till stiff. Add the remaining flour and the grated lemon peel to the creamed mixture. Fold in the beaten egg whites.

If you use loaf pans, line them with parchment paper before filling. Bake loaves for 1 hour at 325 degrees.

Vanilla Waffle

Yields 90 pieces

2 pounds flour
14 ounces butter
1 pound sugar
8 eggs
½ teaspoon salt
1 teaspoon pure vanilla
Grated zest of 1 lemon

Make a well in the flour. Combine all other ingredients and place into the well. Work the flour into the mixture little by little until a smooth dough is formed.

Shape the dough into walnut-sized balls and bake on a French waffle iron until golden brown. You may cut the amount in half.

If you ever consider to do some cooking or baking and use a recipe, before you start make sure you have all the items you need ready to go, including pots, pans, baking sheets, and any other utensils. This is called *mise en place*, or setup. It will make things easier, and you do not have to be stressed out.

I have already given you a recipe for biscotti made with baking powder and hazelnuts. Now I will give you one made with yeast and almonds. The process is similar, but this will make the cookies taste slightly different.

After you bake them and they have cooled, cut them diagonally into ½-inch pieces, then cool on baking racks till completely cold. Then if there are any left, store in an airtight container for a few days. Refuse temptation?

Almond Biscotti   **Yields about 40 pieces**

    2 cups powdered sugar
    2 cups flour
    2 tablespoons ground anise
    2 tablespoons ground cinnamon
    2½ teaspoons active dry yeast
    Grated zest of 1 lemon
    6 medium eggs
    2½ cups toasted almonds

Blend sugar, flour, anise, cinnamon, yeast, and lemon zest in a stand mixer; add paddle to it, then let it run till all the items are well mixed.

Beat 2 eggs and put aside. Blend the remaining eggs one by one into the mixture and bring the speed up to medium when all the eggs are in the mixture so that the eggs are completely worked in.

Dust your table with some flour. Roll the dough on top of it, then also dust your hands with flour. Now you work the almonds into the dough.

Divide the dough into 4 even parts and shape into loaves 3 inches wide and 14 inches long. Place on the sheet pan covered with parchment paper and dust off the extra flour with a dry pastry brush. Make sure you space them about 4 inches apart.

Brush evenly with the set-aside beaten eggs. Bake in a 375-degree oven for about 30 minutes while you spray with a spray bottle over them and also into the oven so that the yeast can work its magic. This is done all through the whole baking process till your baked goods are good and brown.

Remove from the oven and let cool. Then slice diagonally with a serrated knife into ½-inch pieces and place on a cooling rack till completely cold.

Store in an airtight container. They will last a few days. These cookies do not need to be toasted again. Once baked and sliced and cooled, that's it. Good luck.

CHAPTER 15

REMINISCING OVER
MY CAREER

Over the years I moved all over the place, and I got a lot of new ideas for recipes and styles of cooking. It would not be possible to mention all of them.

But what I present to you here is what I did in my own restaurant in Grass Valley at the Swiss House. Most of all I really enjoyed moving to different countries and discovering different concepts of food, and it has kept me interested for many years. When I look back over the years, it is very rewarding and it is fulfilling just to think what can be done with a lot of effort and belief. This is not a job for someone who does not wish to put their nose to the grindstone, but it is worth the effort if you would like to be a real chef.

For me it was like preparing to go to the Olympics. You get one chance in a lifetime, and getting there and then coming out as a winner is very satisfying and also a prestige.

In many ways, today since we have so much fast food it is hard to imagine that fine classical restaurants still exist, and I think they will always be there but in smaller numbers.

I am sure that people still like to eat good food. Some people even have private chefs and entertain in their own homes. The older generation goes for more comfort and does not always want to go out in public; there is more privacy at home, and their home is their castle.

My recipes are accurate, sound, and correct so that even a home-maker with basic cooking knowledge can be proud of the outcome, considering you follow the ingredients and instructions. I do not use confusing terms or off-the-wall items. Today we have all kinds of specialty stores where you can get almost anything you will ever need. There are even food magazines that have a section where you can order items that are hard to find, such as saffron and demi-glacé, online or over the phone. Most of the major cities have Asian and Indian markets, as well as products from France—it is endless.

My brother-in-law Charles recently told me about a website called Blue Apron, among a few others. I was amazed to see what's out there—not only utensils and cookbooks but also prepared food that is ready to heat and eat.

Yes, we have a lot of so-called hobby chefs, and some of them take it really seriously. They cook for their husband or wife on a birthday or other occasion. I am pretty sure some of them do a very good job.

It is OK to go out to eat, no dishes to be washed and no cook-ing—let's say easy street. Give the food industry a little respect. They do depend on you if they want to stay in business.

Let's make some butter cookies.

Butter Cookies   **Yields 50 cookies**

> 1 pound flour
> 14 ounces butter
> 5 ounces powdered sugar
> ¼ teaspoon salt
> 2 teaspoons vanilla extract

Make a well in the flour. Place the soft butter, sugar, salt, and vanilla extract in the well, then mix thoroughly. Work in the flour gradually and knead into a smooth dough.

Refrigerate the dough for 1 hour. Roll the dough to a ¼-inch thickness on a marble slab dusted with flour. Cut into circles and press down with a fork. Bake in the oven at 375 degrees for 8 to 10 minutes.

Macadamia Nut Brittle

2 tablespoons butter
2 cups sugar
1 cup white corn syrup
½ cup water
2 teaspoons baking soda
1½ cups macadamia nuts, chopped

With a teaspoon of butter, grease a baking sheet or marble slab. Combine sugar, corn syrup, and water and cook at 300 degrees till it reaches the hard crack stage. (Test: Syrup forms a brittle thread when dropped in cold water.)

Remove from heat. Stir in remaining butter, baking soda, and nuts. Mix till blended. Pour a thin layer of candy on a greased baking sheet. When candies are cold, break into pieces.

Butter Cream for Pastries and Cakes   Yields about 1 quart
This type of cream is very delicate and has to be handled with respect because it is made mainly with butter.

8 eggs
14 ounces sugar
16 ounces sweet solid butter

Beat the eggs and sugar in a double boiler till it looks like genoise batter (sabayon). Remove from heat and beat the mixture until it is cold.

Whip the butter nice and fluffy and then gradually add it to the egg and sugar mixture, beating constantly.

You can color and flavor it as you wish. Remember, it has a lot of butter and has to be kept in the fridge. Most places use shortening instead of butter. It is less delicate and easier to work with, but there is no comparison—especially when it comes to the taste.

Some people also call it icing.

Pastry Cream

This is a product used for napoleons and cream puffs.

1 quart milk
2½ ounces vanilla cream powder
7¾ ounces sugar
8 egg yolks
1 teaspoon vanilla extract

Heat the milk to the boiling point. Blend the vanilla cream powder and the egg yolks. Slowly pour the hot milk into the sugar and egg mixture.

Bring the mixture to the boiling point. Stir quickly and cook only until the cream is thick and smooth. Then add the vanilla extract.

Praline Mixture   Yields 2½ pounds

1¼ pound sugar
10 ounces hazelnuts
10 ounces almonds

The nuts need to be roasted but not dark; otherwise, they will taste bitter.

Place the sugar in a heavy pan. Stir constantly over low heat until the mixture is golden brown. Then add the roasted nuts and immediately pour onto a slightly oiled marble slab or cookie sheet.

When cold, crush the mixture in the food mill and sift. You can use this mixture on ice cream, pudding, or anything you feel like. Store in an airtight container; if it gets wet, it will stick together. You also can use this in the form of bridles as a dessert garnish.

Beer Batter   Yields 1 quart

This batter is mainly used for seafood (fish and chips).

1 pound sifted flour
¾ pint of beer
10 ounces water
½ cup oil
2 egg yolks
⅓ teaspoon salt
8 egg whites

Place the flour in a bowl. Make a well in the center of the flour. Add the beer, water, egg yolks, and seasoning. Blend well. Beat the egg whites until stiff but not dry. Fold in the egg whites to the flour mixture.

Swiss Woven Egg Bread (Challah) Zopf

Zopf means "braided bread." I usually prepared it for Easter and Christmas.

> 4 pounds bread flour
> 1½ ounces salt
> 3 ounces fresh yeast
> 1 ounce malt
> 4 eggs
> 1 quart milk
> 16 ounces butter (room temperature)

This amount is for a larger number of units and can be reduced to fit your needs—it all depends on how big you intend to make the loaves. I usually use 1 pound of dough per loaf.

In a mixing machine, combine the flour, salt, fresh yeast, malt, eggs, and milk. On low speed, blend it well together, then slowly add the butter, but make sure the butter is just soft enough so that it can be properly added to the dough. Let the mixer run for a few minutes, then take the dough out of the bowl and knead it on a slightly flour-dusted table and work it into a ball.

Put the dough back into the mixing bowl and cover it with a plastic sheet. Let it rise in the fridge overnight.

The dough should be firm. The next day, divide the dough into the desired number of pieces, about 8 ounces each; it takes 2 pieces per loaf. Roll the pieces into cigar-shaped long units, then braid together like long hair.

Cover the baking pan with parchment paper. Arrange the egg bread on the pan. Have enough space between so that when properly raised they will not stick together. Then again cover it with a plastic sheet and let it rise at room temperature till it doubles in size. Egg wash it and bake till golden brown at 350 degrees for about 40 minutes. I like to eat it with fresh sweet butter and honey, hot cocoa, or coffee.

❧   ❧   ❧

Veal Scallopine: Swiss House   Serves 1

This dish was only prepared on special request because it requires special items that are costly.

3 each 2-ounce veal tenderloins, piccata style
1 ounce fresh morels
1 ounce chanterelles
1 ounce cèpes (porcini mushrooms)
Flour to dust
1 ounce Madeira wine
½ ounce brandy
1½ ounce demi-glacé (brown sauce)
¾ ounce heavy cream
Freshly ground black pepper
Salt
½ ounce finely chopped shallots
Some very finely minced garlic
Chopped parsley
1 ounce clarified sweet solid butter

First, season the veal piccatas and dust with flour. In a stainless steel skillet, add clarified butter and quickly brown the veal piccatas, then put them aside.

Sauté the garlic and shallots over low heat. Add the three different mushrooms. Flame with brandy and Madeira wine, then cover and let it reduce to half. Pour in the demi-glacé and heavy cream. Simmer and reduce till you have a light creamy-looking sauce.

Put the meat on top and just heat till the meat has reached the boiling point. Dress it on the service plates, sprinkle with some chopped parsley, and garnish with spaetzli and fresh baby spinach quickly fried in garlic.

Flamed Bananas Swiss House **Serves 1**

1 6-ounce barely ripe banana
¾ ounce sweet butter
1 ounce organic honey
½ ounce brandy
½ ounce Grand Marnier
1 ounce fresh orange juice
A few drops of lemon juice
½ ounce heavy cream
1 scoop vanilla ice cream

Cut the banana in half lengthwise. In a stainless steel shallow frying pan, melt the butter and quickly fry the banana, then put aside.

Pour in the honey and caramelize it a bit, but not dark. Flame with the brandy and liqueur. Add the orange juice and lemon juice, then reduce to half. Add the cream and bring to a boil. Return the banana to the pan and keep warm. Then place on warm dessert plates. Cover with the liquid, and in the middle, arrange the vanilla ice cream. It is delightful and even heavenly.

To make always nice and fluffy baked potatoes, put them on a bed of salt. The salt will get rid of extra moisture.

When you cook a steak, do not salt before you put it on the broiler or frying pan. Then when the steak it is done, let it rest for a few minutes before you serve it. The meat will look nice and evenly cooked as you cut into it, and if you bought good steaks, they will be tender. Try it, you will like it!

That basically goes for any meat, including lamb. When you go to a restaurant and order rare prime rib and you have a hard time cutting it, that means it was not properly handled and did not have enough time to rest, which therefore makes it hard to cut. It could also be that the meat was low grade.

Vegetables cannot be kept in a steam table because they will lose their texture and also color, especially green vegetables. Yes, the older folks probably like their vegetables well done, and they will tell you to do so. If you cook vegetables too long, you will reduce the nutrition and you may as well not even eat it. Yes, I start to sound like your mother, but it is never too late to know the right way.

Vegetables have to be al dente like spaghetti, and if they're over-cooked it is a turnoff. It takes quite a bit of skill to be consistent to do it day in and day out. Unfortunately nowadays, a lot of people do not even know the right way to cook vegetables.

The only thing that seems to matter to people today is the price. We have too many fast-food outlets, and the time folks spend eating is about thirty minutes—and they even eat in the car. This will all have an impact on their health; they may even become grossly over-weight and diabetic. I know you hear it all the time even on TV, but most of us ignore it and think "it will never happen to me." I know food is one of life's simple pleasures, but everything in moderation.

When you go out to different restaurants, in some places you see chefs who are really heavy. This is because they eat all day long because they have to taste the food they serve to their clientele, and it is difficult to discipline themselves—and after a long day they do not feel like going to the gym. In my case I often ended up just having a roll and a piece of cheese. Over the years you get a feel on amounts so that you do not have to taste every dish.

Over all these years, even as a youngster, I remember most places where I was by a certain type of music. I left Switzerland for London in 1964 just when the Beatles came on the scene, and it was crazy with "Let It Be." Then I came to the United States, to Puerto Rico, and it was Al Martino and "Spanish Eyes." He was the entertainer at the Caribe Hilton. Next stop was in St. Croix West Indies, where it was "Yellow Bird," which was performed by a steel band.

When I arrived in Boston, the Beach Boys had a top record there, *Surfer Girl*. Moving on to Washington, DC, Elvis Presley had his comeback with "Muss i denn." As I had my first chef's job in Rochester, New York, Tom Jones was on the radio with "Delilah." Then I arrived in Niagara Falls, Canada, and it was the Anne Murray with "Snowbird."

Moving to Hawaii, it was a variety of Polynesian cocktail. One of them stuck the most in my head; it was the Hawaiian wedding song, because I got married in Honolulu.

Then I ended up in Hong Kong, where I had a young Chinese cook who had one melody in his head, which was "I did my crying in the rain." Obviously, he was listening to a radio station with more than just Chinese music.

After my two-year contract in Hong Kong came to an end, I returned to Hawaii. At that time "Cheryl Moana Marie" was played on the radio station. I had a nice selection of all kinds of records. I still have them and I often listen to it. It enhanced the many miles I traveled. Everything is just like a movie, and it becomes alive and it's real.

In Grass Valley, on our music system we had a potpourri of all kinds of international flair. This is a part of my life besides all the different cultures. Countries, languages, and so much more. It is very fulfilling.

I had my life enhanced with so many wonderful things. Usually I do not talk about it, but as you get older it is a part of reminiscing and a recollection of all the blessings you had, and now you can really enjoy it.

I have a lot of photos from all over the place, also of my trade as a chef from food shows. I try to incorporate some of it into my memoirs so that you can see exactly what I am talking about. Every person's journey is different, and we all have a story to tell.

Yes, we all have our ups and downs, but this makes life exciting. The only thing that matters is how you deal with things. You always try to correct your shortcomings with a better solution and enhance your overall prospects.

Life is like a school without a degree; the learning never ends.

The ups and downs I experienced opening my own restaurant kept things interesting and honest. To achieve such a thing, you need a good foundation and a belief. Then go for it. Know your potential, perfect it, and you will see results.

Not everybody is cut out to be a self-starter. But if you hang out with the right people, you may get the drift.

Find something you really enjoy; but if it is only a job, you will get discouraged. In my case so far it was just a hobby. Yes, there were parts of it I needed to pay more attention to, but overall I flourished, and for that I am thankful.

When I look back over the time I spent in the apprentice program as a pastry cook, it often brings many anecdotes of real hardship. It was like a convent—very strict. But I guess this had its point. You cannot deviate too much in the pastry department and expect good results. If you tried to apply this system today, people would think you were crazy. I guess the labor laws were very weak, and we did not have anyone to come and check on us.

Basically, if you did not like it, you could always do something else. But I know it did the trick. I learned a lot, and it gave me a head start in the second apprentice program to become a chef.

We had breaks, and things were very clean and organized. The kitchen was like a hospital—you could eat off the floor, and everything was cleaned twice a day.

The chefs at that time had respect, and the kitchen was run as a well-oiled machine. It was a seasonal resort place, and during the season we had very few days off, but the camaraderie was great. We ate well and had fun during the season. Most of the kitchen crew moved on to the next seasonal place.

It was OK for me, because this way I had a good idea what was expected of me. It helped build a good foundation for me, and I could count on the folks who were trying to teach me the proper way. I know that there is more than one way to skin a cat, but first you need to know the very basics. Your skills will come eventually with practice.

The people working as chefs in sophisticated organizations work under a lot of stress, and sometimes they do not treat you with kid gloves. We all are often criticized as cold and rude, but by the end of the day when the wait help is counting their tips, everything is OK. In larger places we have food expediters, which takes some of the pressure off the kitchen crew. The dining room has a person in charge of the environment. You need to have complete control over your operation.

The wait help likes to eat good food, and things do disappear; you get the idea. All of a sudden, things are not going to the tables and instead are nowhere to be found. And guess who is going to be blamed? The kitchen.

In the United States we have TV programs that show you how it occurs. Many places hire organizations that set up cameras and infiltrate the wait help as so-called spies. The profit margin is low, and every penny counts.

There are many areas in the food business where you have to keep an eye on things. Safety is a big problem, and honest employees are sometimes hard to come by.

These are just a few of the things I experienced over the years, and believe me, I am not the only one. If you have a bar, it becomes even more so; for example, call brands being served instead of house brands. Many times, when a friend of the bartender comes into the bar, he or she will over pour and the house will lose money.

When my visa in Hong Kong expired, I moved to the United States, to Dearborn, Michigan. At that time Lou Rawls performed at the showroom with his hit "You'll Never Find Another Love like Mine."

After the opening at the Hyatt, I ended up in New Orleans near the Superdome, and of course jazz was the name of the game. At the Hilton, Pete Fountain was the big attraction with his clarinet.

Mardi Gras was a nuthouse, and so was the Super Bowl. And Hyatt's big food and beverage convention was another challenge.

A year later I ended up in Hawaii once again, but this time in Maui at the Royal Lahaina. The music kept on going with the Hawaiian Calls type of arrangements.

I then was offered a job at the Sheraton in Waikiki. At that time there was a band from the Philippines that had a unique sound with some sort of flute.

From there I decided to open my own place in Grass Valley. And that concludes my musical chairs.

I arrived in Grass Valley April 3, 1985, and took over what was then called the Empire House. I was often asked by many of my customers, "What are you doing in Grass Valley with all your credentials?"

I answered them that I had been all over the world and was seeking a place where I could establish myself and finally settle down.

It took me a while to get used to it. It sure was a big change, but at the same time it was my first opportunity to open up my own place. It was just like a newborn child and took all the necessary attention you can imagine, along with the uncertainty of not only being new in town but also being the new kid on the block.

I worked a few months at Scheidels Restaurant, which gave me some idea what was in store for me. The basic business side was no problem. I was well trained in the field, and I was never afraid to roll up my sleeves and put my nose to the grindstone.

First, we had to convince our clientele of the changes we wanted to implement from Mexican seafood and steaks to a classical European style of food. We also upgraded the dining room from white paper coverings to linen with real cloth napkins and nice table lanterns. The complete upgrade of the quality and presentation and even the manner the service was conducted created a challenge for a while, but soon it was well received, and we saw a good number of steady guests.

A lot of different organizations came to check us out. A lot of them just wanted a bargain, and the way we accommodated them with linen and the little extras was overwhelming. At the same time, our regular patrons got less service than they wished to receive. In short, it was sort of a learning curve, and we made the proper adjustments to maintain the standards we had set at the beginning. Of course, every venture has its pains, and regardless of who you are, you will grow out of them.

Our competitors were watching us very closely, and a certain part of the business pie was at stake. The local newspaper gave us a couple of write-ups, and that helped us be in the picture and blend in with our competition in the area.

At the beginning, there were very few recognized restaurants compared to today. And we could not compete with the low prices of the fast-food places. We tailored our business according to our prices. We were different because we served soup and salad, whereas the rest of them gave just soup or salad. Of course, when you look at the price it was lower, but when you add it all up, they could not see the advantage of choosing between one and the other.

Our food was always of the highest standards and always top quality, never convenience food. It was mostly cooked to order, of which I am very proud still to this day.

Yes, I am a perfectionist and have a lot of pride. My steady locals and tourists came to appreciate this over the years. This gave us the longevity we enjoyed and still enjoy today. Even though it has been a couple of years since Lily passed, I still have calls from older guests who fondly remember the Swiss House as their favorite place to eat in Grass Valley. I am often told, "We hope that we will have the pleasure of eating your food and baking items again sometime in the future."

I will keep myself busy other than sitting in a chair and watching television all day long. I still have a few tricks up my sleeves; only the good die young, as the saying goes. If you want to live a full life, you have to stretch it to the limit.

All this is only possible while having good health and a positive outlook on life, and so the beat goes on. Life becomes more meaningful with age and events. The only sad thing is that you cannot transfer the knowledge you have gained over all the years.

And you may think that you know someone you were living with over many years, and then when he or she dies, you find that you really don't know him or her at all. Look back at my own situation and you will see what I am trying to say.

These are just some recollections I have guarded over the years, and they give me poise to take the next step toward the future.

In smaller types of restaurants where the chef does the cooking, his or her personality will come to the forefront, and the place will reflect the chef's personality. In large operations, they work on set recipes, and the kitchen is divided into sections such as sauce station, vegetable soup, cold kitchen, and pastry dessert. Each one has his own specialty chef, and things really depend on the chef's qualifications. If the head chef is not strong to lead his crew, you end up with inconsistency.

I remember the time that Roland Ozbold, a Jewish assistant sauce cook at the Hôtel du Rhône in Geneva, was on his way to Canada. The French executive chef wanted to give him a going away present by fooling him. The chef told him to prepare an order of grilled lentils. He also told him how to do so. It was funny that the chap did not realize that it was a joke.

First, the chef gave him a requisition to issue the lentils out of the storeroom, and then he repeated the way it should be done. Roland started to oil and season the lentils and tried to place them one by one on the very narrow steel rods on the electric grill. For his demise, as soon he was able to place one of them, they would just keep falling off.

The chef told him to use some egg whites so that they would stick and be able to stay on the broiler. We watched as Roland's face started to turn red, and finally the chef called him an idiot. It was a good thing that it was his last day before he traveled to Montreal. There were quite a few incidents over the years, but this one was one of the better ones.

Shrimp Toast (Chinese Style)   **Yields 24 pieces**

This is mainly used as an appetizer.

12 ounces raw, peeled, and deveined shrimp
2 whole eggs

1 clove garlic
3 ounces finely chopped water chestnuts
½ teaspoon sesame seed oil
1 bunch green onion
¼ ounce grated ginger
¼ ounce ground white pepper
¼ ounce salt
3 ounces sesame seeds
Peanut oil to fry
6 slices white sandwich bread

Separate the egg whites and yolks into two different containers. Slightly beat the egg yolks.

In a food processor, place the shrimp meat, egg whites, clove of garlic, water chestnuts, sesame seed oil, green onions, ginger, salt, and pepper. Prepare a smooth mixture like forced meat, about 20 to 30 seconds,

Trim off the crust of the 6 slices of white bread. Brush the top of the bread with the egg yolk. Spread the shrimp mixture evenly over the 6 slices of bread, and sprinkle with the sesame seeds.

In a shallow frying, pan add the peanut oil and fry over moderate heat, meat side down first, till nice and brown on both sides, one or two pieces at a time. Then set each piece of toast on paper towels, and at last cut into triangles. Serve hot.

You may serve peanut sauce with it. This will give you 24 pieces. If you want to make a larger amount, just make as much as you think it would take.

You can prepare the filling ahead of time, but I do not recommend putting it on the bread until you are ready to fry because it will get soggy and hard to handle.

Peanut Sauce

I use creamy peanut butter.

In a blender, add the peanut butter, some white wine, garlic, ginger, Tabasco sauce, curry powder, and soy sauce. If you wish, you could add some chopped roasted peanuts. The sauce should be well balanced not overpowering.

Swiss House Egg Rolls

1 pound lean ground beef
½ ounce garlic
¼ ounce fresh ginger
Chili flakes
5 ounces white sliced onions
6 ounces celery julienne
5 ounces carrots julienne
8 ounces bean sprouts
2 ounces Chinese fungus
3 ounces soy sauce
2 packages rice noodles
Cornstarch diluted in cold water
7 ounces shredded white cabbage

Sauté the ground beef with cottonseed oil. Add the garlic, ginger, chili flakes, and sliced onions. Then add the celery julienne, carrot julienne, bean sprouts, soaked and drained Chinese fungus, soy sauce, rice noodles, and cornstarch. Then add the shredded white cabbage last.

It is important not to overcook the filling. It should be crunchy and fairly dry. If the filling is not dry, then your egg rolls will fall apart in the deep fryer.

The wrappers I use are the very thin ones and sealed with egg wash. You can buy the wrappers from Asian markets. When you roll them, make sure not to make them too thick. The end product should be nice and even.

Fry the egg rolls in peanut oil at 350 degrees till golden brown. Serve with hot Chinese mustard sauce. Some people would ask for sweet sour and sauce.

You can prepare them ahead and then freeze them. I packed them into well-sealed plastic bags.

There is a way to keep the salt in your saltshaker working properly—add some uncooked rice to it. The rice will absorb all the moisture. And you never have to hammer it on the table before you get results.

To clean your copper cookware without chemicals, use a lemon. Cut it in half and rub it around the pot along with some salt. This will do just fine. You have to rub it into the metal, then wash it under running water and towel dry it.

To get good results when cooking beans, first you have to soak them in cold water overnight. The next day boil them, but without salt. For quicker results, you may use a pressure cooker.

To make a fluffy stuffing for your turkey, add some baking powder to it. Do not use too many eggs; this will make it dry. Some people put all kinds of different items in it, such as chestnuts, oysters, apples raisins, bacon, and sage—but not fresh sage, because it will be overpowering. I am sure that a lot of folks have their own favorite recipes for stuffing, and the type of bread you use makes a difference too. The liquid you use is also important, such as chicken stock or milk. But be careful with the seasoning; your gravy may be a bit salty and could offset your taste buds.

Rice Pilaf

To cook rice pilaf rice, I use Uncle Ben's rice. Yes, it is more expensive, but the end result is very consistent.

The ratio of rice to liquid is 1 part rice and 1⅓ parts chicken stock. If you use regular long-grain rice, then your ratio should be 1 to 1. Uncle Ben's rice has been parboiled.

Use some finely chopped onions. First sauté the onions in butter, then add the rice. Let the rice get transparent, then add the boiling liquid. When it returns to a boil, cover with a lid and finish it in the oven at 350 degrees for 30 minutes.

When you take the rice out of the oven, use a fork and loosen it up. Let it rest for a few minutes before you serve it.

To make rizi bizi, add fresh green peas. This is a classical term. Or make some fried rice or anything you like—use your imagination.

Risotto

Risotto is a completely different animal. You use Vioalone or Arborio rice not long grain. You can buy in the supermarket, and it comes in a 1-pound box. I keep the rice in the freezer to be sure the bugs stay out of it.

The risotto should be al dente, and you add the stock little by little while cooking it on the stovetop, constantly stirring—but make sure you do not end up with mush. Then add solid butter and Parmesan cheese and a dash of dry white wine.

In many places, the risotto is made with shrimp or even with saffron and is very delicate. Saffron is very expensive and has to be used sparingly, otherwise it may taste bitter.

Marinade

There are all kinds of marinades you can use to tenderize beef, pork, chicken, scallops, and shrimp. The items to do so include soy sauce, wine, vinegar, curry powder, and olive oil. Some Chinese restaurants even use baking soda, but if you do not know how to handle it, it may taste terrible. You can also use garlic, ground pepper, thyme, red hot pepper flakes, yogurt, and coconut milk—there is a long list based on the style of cooking.

When it comes to quality products, I would stay away from marinade because you would ruin your dish, which does not need any help.

Homemade Noodles   Serves 10

14 ounces flour
3½ ounces semolina (hard wheat)
¼ cup oil
5 eggs
¼ ounce salt
¼ cup milk or water

Combine the flour and semolina and make a well in the middle. Mix the oil, eggs, salt, and milk or water and slowly work this into the flour until you have a smooth dough—it should be firm.

Wrap the dough in a damp towel and let it rest for about 2 hours in a cold place.

Then cut the dough into 5 pieces and roll and reroll each piece till it is paper thin. Lay out the rolled pieces on a table or hang the pieces over a wooden rod to dry without allowing them to become brittle.

Fold the sheets of dough lengthwise into a scroll and cut into strips. Now you have noodles.

The noodles can be boiled while fresh and tossed with butter, or you may also dry them, but first you lay them out and let them dry for about 36 hours in a well-ventilated area. Those noodles can be turned into baked noodles, Alfredo, or even primavera.

With this dough you can also make ravioli, cannelloni, or lasagna.

Frog Legs Swiss House   Serves 5

1½ pounds frog legs, medium size
½ teaspoon salt
¼ teaspoon ground white pepper
1 dash curry powder
¼ cup brandy
1 ounce white wine
2½ ounces butter
1 ounce finely chopped shallots
2 ounces white mushrooms, sliced
1½ ounces heavy cream
Some lemon juice

Split and season the frog legs with brandy, salt, and pepper. Marinate for a couple of hours in a stainless steel dish.

Heat the butter in a sauté pan, add the shallots and mushrooms, and sauté over low heat. Then add the frog legs, curry, and the rest of the seasonings. Sauté for a few minutes. Deglaze with the white wine and the marinade, then add the cream and simmer for another couple of minutes, but make sure you do not overcook. Frog legs are very delicate, and the cooking time is short.

Before you serve them, add the lemon juice and sprinkle the chopped parsley. Rice is usually served with them.

Emmentaler Cheese Toast

This is also called chässchnitte.

1 thick slice white sandwich bread
2 ounces thin-sliced ham
2 ounces sliced Swiss Emmentaler cheese
2 eggs
½ ounce butter
1½ ounces white wine

First, toast the sliced of bread. Lay the toast on a fireproof baking dish, then top it with the ham and cheese. Pour the wine on top and bake it in the oven at 350 degrees till it is well melted.

When the cheese is done, top it with 2 eggs fried in butter. It is a good cold weather dish. Enjoy a nice salad with it.

Rice Pudding   Serves 10

5 ounces rice (do not use long-grain rice)
1 quart milk
1 vanilla bean, or pure vanilla essence
Grated rind of 1 lemon
4½ ounces sugar
2 eggs
2 ounces butter

First, wash the rice thoroughly and drain.

Heat the milk and vanilla bean to the boiling point. Add the lemon rind and rice. Boil for about 35 minutes. If needed, add some more milk.

Remove from heat, then combine the sugar and eggs and fold into the rice and milk mixture. Pour the mixture into a buttered baking dish (Corningware). Top it with a few flakes of butter and bake it in a water bath for about 30 to 40 minutes or till the pudding is nice and yellow.

When done, dust with powdered sugar. You may serve it with stewed fruits. It's a classic.

❖   ❖   ❖

Shrimp and Vegetable Tempura   Serves 4

    20 large shrimp, 15–20 count
    Tempura flour for coating
    2 cups tempura flour
    2 egg yolks
    2 cups ice water
    Oil for deep frying
    1 large zucchini, cut into strips
    1 red bell pepper, cut into strips
    5 ounces green beans (look for whole beans)

Peel and devein the shrimp, but leave the tail intact. Cut incisions under each shrimp, leaving the tail on. Coat with the tempura flour except the tail.

In a bowl, gently mix the tempura flour, egg yolks, and ice water. Do not over mix.

Heat the oil in a wok or deep fryer to a moderate heat, 325 degrees. Working with a few pieces at a time, dip the shrimp into the batter but leave the tail uncoated.

Fry the shrimp briefly in the hot oil till golden brown, then place on paper towels. Repeat the same procedure with the vegetables. Serve immediately with soy sauce.

The tempura flour can be purchased from a specialty Asian store. You can use a variety of vegetables, such as broccoli, cauliflower, carrots, green beans, and bell peppers.

❖   ❖   ❖

Green Noodles with Pesto   Serves 4

   1 pound spinach noodles
   2 cups tightly packed fresh basil leaves
   4 cloves fresh garlic, peeled and chopped

   ½ cup pine nuts
   1½ cups freshly grated Parmesan cheese
   ¾ cup virgin olive oil
   Salt
   Freshly ground black pepper

Cook the noodles al dente, then drain and return to the cooking pot. Be aware that green noodles cook quicker than regular pasta, so be careful—you do not want mush.

Prior to cooking the pasta, in a food processor blend the basil, garlic, and pine nuts till finely ground; add the cheese till well combined. With the motor running, slowly pour in the olive oil, salt, and pepper.

Add enough pesto sauce to the noodles to coat well. Garnish with basil leaves and dry roasted pine nuts.

Pasta dishes go good with spring mix salad and a walnut vinaigrette dressing. If you do not have the time to make your own pesto, it can be purchased in your favorite grocery store. It comes in different combinations.

How sweet it is! Jackie Gleason, I remember too. Miami, Florida.

Swedish Meatballs

I use one-third ground beef, one-third ground pork, one-third ground veal, and white sandwich bread, crusts cut off, that I soak in milk. I also use finely chopped onions, heavy cream, chopped parsley, lingonberries, and clear beef or chicken stock.

Season the meat with salt and ground white pepper, nutmeg, and some fresh eggs. Remember, too many eggs will make it dry.

You can use a food processor to make the meatballs, then combine all the other items except the lingonberries and some of the chicken stock, and only half of the cream. The end product should look like a medium sausage filling. Make the meatballs the size of walnuts and lay them out on a tray covered with wax paper.

In the meantime, in a saucepot bring the chicken stock to a boil. Make sure you use enough stock so that the meatballs are able to float when done. Remove them and keep warm.

In another pan, simmer the onion with a little butter till transparent. Add the cream and the part of the stock in which you poached the meatballs—just enough to be able cover the meatballs. With the help of a little cornstarch diluted with water, thicken the sauce till nice and creamy.

Last, add the berries, then top with the chopped parsley. If you wish to serve them as an entrée, double the size of the meatballs. You may serve it over pasta.

Polenta Swiss Italian Style

The ratio of liquid to cornmeal is 1½ quarts water or milk and 1¼ cups cornmeal and some salt.

Bring the water and salt to a boil, then gradually stir in the cornmeal. Reduce the heat and cook while stirring constantly till a crust begins to form around the edge. It will take about 30 to 40 minutes. Add a few flakes of butter before serving.

It can also be poured into a shallow buttered pan and cooled overnight. Then cut into wedges and serve it panfried.

Roasted Almonds

5 ounces almonds
¾ cup sugar
2 tablespoons water
Oil

Blanch the almonds and peel off the skin. Pat dry with a towel. Place the almonds in a skillet and slightly brown without fat, rotating constantly.

Cook the sugar and 2 tablespoons of water in a separate container until the sugar is dissolved. Add the almonds. Stir for 5 to 10 minutes until the nuts are completely coated. Remove from heat and let cool.

Return to heat until the sugar liquifies again. At that moment, pour the nuts onto a greased cookie sheet. Separate with a fork and let cool.

Keep in an airtight container.

I have often been asked what's the difference between gravy and a sauce. Gravy is derived from roasting a turkey or a pork roast. After you have taken the roasted item from the roasting pan, you will have some liquid remaining in the pan. Add some flour and liquid such as chicken stock or water and you have your gravy, which needs a very short time to cook.

In contrast, sauce starts by roasting bones and meat scraps, then adding a mirepoix, tomato paste, flour, seasonings, and liquid—usually water. The sauce is then simmered for several hours. I do not think that a homemaker has time to do this, and that's the reason why convenience food exists.

The brown sauce is the basis for several different other sauces such as peppercorn sauce for a pepper steak or red wine sauce.

Clam Casino

Littleneck clams
Red and green bell peppers
Butter
Ground white pepper
Curry powder
Salt
Italian bacon

First, dice the red and green peppers into about ¼-inch pieces. Then prepare a compound butter with bell peppers, ground pepper, curry powder, and salt.

Wash the clams in cold water. Then shuck them and cut the clams loose from the shells. Discard one half of the shell. Keep the one shell with the clam in it and top it with the compound butter. Lay a small piece of the bacon on top of each.

Bake in the oven on a bed of salt at 350 degrees for about 15 minutes, till the bacon is crispy. Do not let it burn!

You can make the clams a day ahead if you wish to entertain, but keep them in the freezer because seafood spoils fast. Serve on small plates with cocktail forks.

Strawberry Shortcake

3 each 1-pint boxes fresh ripe strawberries, sliced
¼ cup honey
4 teaspoons lemon juice
2 cups sifted flour
2 tablespoons sugar
3½ teaspoons baking powder

½ teaspoon salt
½ stick sweet butter
1½ ounces vegetable shortening
¼ cup sour cream
3 tablespoons soft butter
2 cups French cream (half whipping cream and half sour cream)
Some milk

Combine strawberries with the honey and lemon juice. Marinate for about 1 hour.

In a bowl, mix all the dry ingredients together. Add the ½ stick of butter and the shortening, then thoroughly blend in the ¼ cup of sour cream with the help a fork. Add just enough milk to make a soft dough.

Then roll out on a floured surface about ¾ of an inch by 7 inches. Spread with the remaining butter, then fold it over. It will be about 1¾ inch thick.

Divide the dough in half. For 4-inch biscuits, roll ¾-inch to 1-inch thick and cut or pat into 4 rounds. Place the biscuits on an ungreased cookie sheet and prick with a fork.

Bake at 350 degrees for about 20 minutes till golden brown. While still hot, split in half. Place on a serving dish.

Drain the berries, reserving juice and about one-third of the berries. Fill the center of one biscuit, then cover with a second biscuit and spoon remaining berries and juice over the top.

Serve warm with the French cream.

For the French cream, combine the heavy cream and sour cream in a saucepan and heat to 110 degrees. Place in a bowl and allow to stand at room temperature until thickened, then refrigerate. This cream will keep for about two weeks when kept in the fridge.

⚜ ⚜ ⚜

Oysters Rockefeller

Use Blue Point oysters.

This is the Chef Karl version. Oysters have to be handled with care—you do not want any food poisoning. Usually when I get them, I prepare them the same day and then freeze what I do not serve the same day.

First, wash and scrub the oysters. Then shuck them and remove the actual oyster from the shell. Keep the deeper part of the shell with the oyster. Then refrigerate till you are ready to assemble.

In the meantime, prepare a béchamel sauce. Blanch the spinach, then cool it off under cold running water. Strain the water off and with the help of a towel squeeze all the water out of the spinach.

Coarsely chop the spinach and fix creamed but not dry spinach. The spinach is first sautéed with butter, shallots, minced garlic, thyme, salt, and white pepper. Add a touch of Pernod, then add the cream. Let it cool off completely before you top the oysters with a good amount of the creamed spinach.

To the remaining béchamel sauce, add egg yolks and grated Parmesan cheese. This is called a glacé. Cover the spinach completely with the glacé and sprinkle with Parmesan cheese.

The oysters are then baked on a bed of rock salt at 350 degrees till nice and brown.

Popover   Yields 12 pieces

Serve with prime rib or roast beef.

1 cup all-purpose flour
¼ teaspoon salt
1 cup liquid nonfat milk
3 large eggs
4 teaspoons shortening, or fat drippings from roast beef

Combine the flour and salt in a medium bowl. Stir in the milk. Beat in the eggs until the batter is completely smooth. Place 1½ teaspoons of melted shortening in a 12-cup jumbo muffin pan. Place in the oven and heat for about 5 minutes until the shortening is melted and hot.

Fill each cup two-thirds full and bake at 375 degrees for about 45 minutes. Do not open the oven before the baking time is expired. They need complete privacy to expand properly.

German Apple Cake   Serves 6–8

> 4 ounces unsalted butter, melted
> 2 eggs
> 1 cup sugar
> 1 cup flour
> 1 teaspoon baking powder
> 1 teaspoon vanilla essence
> 1½ teaspoons cinnamon
> 4–5 tart apples (Granny Smith)

Preheat the oven to 350 degrees. Grease an 8 x 8 inch baking dish.

Combine the butter, eggs, and ½ cup of the sugar in a large mixing bowl and beat thoroughly. Add the flour, baking powder, and vanilla and blend well. Spread evenly into the baking dish.

Combine the cinnamon and remainder of the sugar. Peel the apples, then core and slice them thin. Coat the apple slices well with the sugar and cinnamon. Arrange the slices on top of the batter in overlapping rows, pressing lightly into the batter.

Bake for 1 hour. Cool and cut into squares.

Chocolate Macaroons   Yields 24 pieces

15 ounces sweetened condensed milk
2 each 8-ounce squares unsweetened chocolate
1 cup coarsely chopped almonds
2 cups shredded coconut
1 teaspoon vanilla
1 teaspoon strongly brewed coffee
⅛ teaspoon salt

Preheat the oven to 350 degrees. Oil the baking sheet.

Combine the milk and chocolate on top of a double boiler. Heat on high heat, stirring constantly. Add the nuts, coconut, vanilla, coffee, and salt and heat until mixture thickens, about 5 minutes.

Drop by teaspoonfuls onto a prepared sheet and bake for about 10 minutes or until bottoms are set. Watch carefully, since they can burn easily. Do not overbake: macaroons should have a soft, chewy texture.

When done, transfer to waxed paper liner and let cool completely.

The classical restaurants have given way to too many fast-food places: pizza, hamburgers, fried chicken, tacos, and many more. I guess that the economy has something to do with it, and people living today are not that concerned about what they eat, but it surely shows on their bodies.

I believe that fast food is not very healthy at all. But most of the folks have to make sure that they can feed their families. And people do not have the time or the knowledge to do their own cooking.

All those various nations have given the industry a new twist to come up with a lot of opportunities to branch out, but at the same time a lot of convenience products have showed up to make up for the lack of skilled labor. Today you can find all kinds of items in many stores that quite often you can just heat and eat. The younger generation has a big generation gap. Cooking has not been taught at home, and so all the fast-food operations are benefiting from it.

With all that fast food, people get into health problems. Their diet is completely out of balance and ends up supporting the pharmaceutical industry and even leads to early death. This overeating raises the cost of health care and has many more side effects.

The hotels in Hawaii are considered resort facilities and are mainly occupied by tourists. These hotels had a lot of conventions and needed large facilities to accommodate such service. To cook for a large number of guests is easier than strictly à la cart cooking. The number of attendees was often up to three thousand, and there were only two or maybe three items to prepare and you knew exactly how many of each to make.

It was almost like a factory assembly line. It had to be coordinated very well and was dished out a short while in advance. You also had a steward department to assist you. If you are a well-trained chef and have some pride, this type of cooking has nothing to do with high standards; it loses its personality completely.

Yes, it was a part of becoming a diversified executive chef, and not too many people can handle that type of responsibility and pressure. For me this was a test to see whether I would be able to do so.

When I arrived in Hawaii for the first time, the hotel was under construction. Richard Straus was the person who was chosen to open it, and he introduced me to the Moana Surfrider Sheraton Hotel. Then he became the chef of the Sheraton Waikiki, which was then under construction.

I was very young and also ambitious, and I said to him that I would like to be the chef of the new hotel! He looked at me and said, "You are too young! But I will give you a tour so that you can see what it looks like."

Several years later my dream came true, and I had the task under the general manager, Nord Schreiber, to bring the cost under control. The food cost was 39 percent, and the labor cost was also well over. It took me almost two years to accomplish my task. At one point the food cost was $10,000 and I got it down to 32 percent. I had to calculate the entire menu items and all the waste there was.

I kept the cost for my duration as executive chef at 32 percent, for which I am proud.

Then I decided to do something of my own. I worked in many large hotels, and as a head chef you basically become a number and are a small part of the puzzle to make it work.

Needless to say, it takes a lot of skill and also requires talent. We as European chefs are mainly trained to be excellent chefs and not politicians, and I guess we are not just looking for brownie points. Today they are sent to some seminar and given a CD to do what took us many years to accomplish. Again, they found ways to eliminate expensive chefs—if they could even find any.

I also had apprentices during that time, but it was controlled by the unions and had a lot of restrictions, which at times made it hard to bring out the best in the students. Nevertheless, it was rewarding to be able to help bring new talent into the field.

I worked with Hilton, Sheraton, Western Hotels, Hyatt, and even some privately owned hotels in Hong Kong, and in Maui at the Royal Lahaina. Each one had its own challenges and was unique, and I approached every one with the attention necessary to make it function successfully.

Today I wish I would have started a few years earlier on my own interests, but life will sometimes take you in a different direction, and maybe for the better. Who knows? Over my many years in the trade, I accomplished a high level of success early in my career. I was fortunate to hang out with the right people and was willing to put in the extra effort, which was needed, but it was not always pretty. Every success has a price tag.

Yes, I set goals and made every effort to reach them. I opened several new hotels in Hong Kong; Dearborn, Michigan; and also St. Croix in the Virgin Islands. When I look back it gives me a good idea what you have to endure and how much you really have to sacrifice in order to reach your goals. I basically worked all the holidays and could not just say I am going to join a group of people skiing or whatever.

That basically started when I was about sixteen, and the demand was always there, come rain or shine. I knew what to expect and accepted the concept.

If you choose your destination and you know that it will bring you satisfaction, then it is not a job and has no real hardship attached to it. To me it was like a hobby because I enjoyed it so much.

I was privileged to work under many excellent chefs and had the opportunity to work in many places. This was mostly by referral and was also based on my performance. You have to be attentive, respectful, and do as you are told. If you cause friction, people shy away and you lose out on promotions and success.

There were all kinds of chefs who took the time to teach me things because I exhibited an interest and maybe even some talent.

I mainly worked seasonal places and had a chance to pick up a few new little tricks. This was mainly granted to young chefs who showed interest and were eager to learn. It was often after hours, and the teaching was done on a one-on-one basis.

This gave me an advantage, since the average person was just in for the required time. My trade was more than just a job, it was a hobby and I never lost interest.

The next season I was hired as chef garde manger of the cold kitchen back at the Waldhaus in Sils Maria with the same chef. I prepared myself for the position to make sure I was on top of things.

When I entered the kitchen, looking for the chef, I saw three Middle Eastern guys running around and was wondering, what's going on?

The chef called me into his office and said, "I would like to ask you if you could take on the position as chef saucier rather than the cold kitchen." He then said, "You worked with the chef saucier last season at the Chantarella Hotel, Mr. Zogg, and he would trust you more than our newcomers."

I accepted the position, and I also told him not to interfere with me if not necessary. He said nothing, and I started to get ready for opening day.

The three Arabs had their prayer rugs and also knew how to beat up each other. The oldest one of them was in charge to make sure they stood in line.

I was well aware that the chef had a shortcoming, which was that he had a hard time writing menus and being able to balance the colors on the plates—not everything in white, so that you have a contrast, including soup and dessert. I remember looking at the menu board where he placed the menus for the week so that you would know what he liked to serve the guests each day. I noticed that he had fallen again into the same routine. When I told him, he became unglued, took his menus down, and said, "Why don't you write them!"

I guess I was challenged to do that, and based what he had purchased, I constructed nicely balanced menus. During my lunch break and before dinner, I put several menus together for the next couple of days and gave them to the chef. He looked at them and said nothing. I was proud that he finally accepted my criticism and that it was constructive.

During the season we had a few disagreements. As the season slowly came to an end, I was offered a one-year contract at the

London Hilton as chef de partie. Just a few days before I was ready to fly, I got a letter from the chef in Sils Maria. He wanted me to work for him again! Andre Troxler was his name. I declined and told him that I was going to the London Hilton Hotel.

As I started in London, I had another offer from the same hotel in Sils Maria to take over the chef position. Again, I declined. I stood by my principles and took the job in London. I did not want to be wishy-washy. Loyalty means a lot in life, and people need to know they can count on you. If you say one thing and do another, you become unreliable. You will set yourself a trap.

Starting a new station in a well-organized kitchen will take some time to get used to before you feel comfortable. You cannot afford any type of second-guessing. I was blessed, and very seldom did I disappoint my own judgment. My exposure during all the years learning the trades properly paid off. If you are serious, do not compromise—in other words, don't come up with things that do not make any sense. There is not much leeway in the classical kitchen; things have to be done in a certain way. With experience comes consistency, and consistency will result in success. All that's needed is endurance and respect for the individual who is trying to get into it.

This type of profession has to be considered a labor of love. It will never be a nine-to-five job, unless you work as a cook in a fast-food outlet and then become a line cook, with not much responsibility if any. This may be fine for students who must pay for their tuition or have not yet decided what they want to with their life. To secure a better-paying job, you have to attend a cooking school or work for several places where you can gain the experience. Many times, that has advantages over the expensive schooling. If you invest in anything, you have to make a decision that it will benefit you in the long run and your money will be well spent. That goes for all endeavors in life.

There are a lot people who attended higher education and have degrees but are going nowhere, and they have to pay back the loan for a long time and in the end work for a fast-food outlet. Most people want to get married, raise a family, buy a house, and save up for their kid's education and retirement. Very few ever reach the status of Bill Gates.

You have to decide early in life, and starting over and over again is not the way to go. Often it looks like the sky is the limit, but reality is what counts.

For all the years I worked for so many hotels, I took my assignment seriously and demanded the same from the employees I had under my supervision. The same applied when I had my own business. Many times I was told that I was too strict, but all this came because of my upbringing and being a perfectionist. Yes, at times I had to dial it back a bit, but before you know it I fell right back into my strong beliefs.

Over the long run, it served me well. Still today, I have young chefs who acknowledged that the school of hard knocks served them well and even thanked me for it. They also said that because of it, they got the job by being decisive and could see the value of being well trained and not just following without having a solid base. I never worked for anybody who became successful without solid principles and standards. Cleanliness in the food business is of utmost importance and has to be taken as a religion.

Veal Scallopine with Gruyère Cheese   Serves 4

    4 each 3½-ounce veal scallopine (veal tenderloin), pounded in between
        plastic sheets
    Salt
    Ground white pepper

Flour for dusting
2 ounces butter
4 slices Cure 81 ham
2 ounces Gruyère cheese
½ ounce dry white wine
¾ cup dry white wine

Season the meat on both sides and dust with flour. Then sauté the scallopine in butter till they are golden brown. Grease an oven-proof glass platter, then arrange the meat side by side, leaving just a small space in between. Place the ham on top and cover with the cheese. Drizzle with the ½ ounce of wine and bake at 380 degrees for about 10 minutes, till the cheese is completely melted.

Deglaze the pan in which you browned the meat with the ¾ cup of wine. Slightly reduce, then pour over the scallopine and serve with angel hair pasta.

The chef is an artist. Michelangelo did not paint the ceiling at the Vatican in one night, so be patient. It will be worth your wait, I promise you.

Yes, as you may see, what I am trying to tell you is that in today's society, people have become very unpainted. Quite often many of them cannot even find time to enjoy a good meal. Quite often when you go out to eat, you see couples communicate by cell phone and it makes you wonder where we are going next.

I know time is money, but in my opinion, this is well over the top.

We had some guests call in their order over the phone who requested that the onion soup be waiting at their table by the time they arrived. They did not want to waste any time at all. I guess if you have to go to a concert or a movie and would rather have a quick meal, then just have popcorn and a Coke—that's OK with me.

Then there are some honeymooners who come in late and do not wish to be rushed. We often took their circumstances into consideration and gave them a break.

Sometimes we had small groups, and we knew they were not in rush to leave the place. We offered them some after-dinner drinks, coffee, and maybe even desserts. Yes, you had to have the lights on, and to cover your expenses you do anything to compensate both sides of the fence. Many times, they preferred to have a nightcap in the bar and were quite happy doing just that.

Our bar was in a location where you were comfortable and secure. We seldom had real rowdy folks, and even then, it is a bit out of town, and nobody was looking through the windows or reported you to the authorities. I believe a freestanding location has its advantages.

I know convenience counts, and some people prefer privacy. Take your pick. Parking was never a problem. Yes, there were every now and then some out-of-towners and so-called freeloaders taking up some of the parking spaces without asking, and they were reminded via a little note on the windshield of the posted parking rights.

It also happened that the parking lot was a garbage dump. The chef then also became a police officer or even a son of a bitch and surely got an earful by looking out for my rights.

I guess this goes with the territory—the good, the bad, and the ugly. People respected us for the standards we had and mentioned it every now and then.

I remember when I grew up and was working for all kinds of different places, I noticed the decisive way business was conducted. It was strict and right to the point, no ifs or buts, and if you run your own business, you will understand their viewpoint. It will definitely take discipline and pride, and not just for one day. It has to become second nature.

This is just a brief memory and a reflection of what it took over the years to become successful. If you are once in this frame of mine, it is difficult to get out of it. It will definitely build character. It looks like being in boot camp, and if you can handle it, you are on the right track.

If you structure your life properly and make it interesting, you will never get tired of what you are doing. Explore whatever you do, seek whatever is interesting to you, stay away from mediocre standards; then every day becomes a new challenge and also drives you to better yourself.

Look it at this way: if you eat the same thing every day, you will get tired of it and will never want to see that type of food ever again.

If you are able to fix and repair things when broken—in other words, become a handyman—it will have value in any business. It will help you curb your cost and let you stay away from a panic situation. On some occasions, when I had a cook's helper with heavy hands who poured too much butter or oil into the frying pan and was not watching and it caught fire, the panic started to creep in. It needed a cool head to correct the situation without burning down the place.

If the broiler is overloaded with meat that has extra fat in it, like lamb, and you do not pay any attention, it could surprise you and catch you off guard. The answer is, use some soda water to extinguish the shooting flame, but first you have to remove the meat from the broiler. You have to be able to think straight. That comes with experience. And if your Ansul system goes off and the fire department shows up, you are out of luck; being listed in the next day's newspaper is no joke.

It never happened to me over my time at the Swiss House. But having a fire like that just goes to show you what you are up to, not to mention your insurance going up and maybe much more.

Twice a year the inspector will check that you are up on all requirements and the fire protections are met, and all you have to have is a very clean environment. Every now and then you read in the newspaper about restaurants being destroyed because of grease fires. You really have to be mindful and check every section, including the deep fat fryer, before the kitchen is closed for the day.

It's like parking your car, getting out of it, and leaving the engine running overnight. Surprise, surprise! Yes, you would think it's just common sense, but think again.

For some of our loyal customers, we prepared the classical Chinese fondue called shabu shabu. This type of a meal requires a lot of different items. It is cooked in a broth and has several dipping sauces, and each person mixes their own combination based on what they like. It has a lot of vegetables, including Chinese cabbage, onions, green onions, carrots, pea pods, Chinese mushrooms, and bean sprouts. The meats are sliced very thin and include shrimp, lamb, beef, and chicken. It also uses tofu, raw eggs, long-grain rice, soy sauce, sesame seed oil, sesame paste, and Chinese rice wine.

This was always for a very special occasion. The chef did not stay behind the stove because every person did his or her own cooking. On top of that, it is eaten with chopsticks. Some people had a hard time and after a while were asking for forks.

Many times, we were asked to accommodate them on various occasions, but we wanted to show our appreciation to our loyal guests. We also complimented our frequent patriots with a free meal, a bottle of wine, dessert, or after-dinner drinks. When we had birthday celebrations, we gave chef's choice free desserts.

At one time Lily mentioned that she would like to have a dogwood tree for the front of the house. Lo and behold, the next day someone dropped a nice tree near the back door of the restaurant, and still to this day we do not know whom we have to thank for it. The tree is doing very well in the front of the house and looking good.

Quite often we got fresh vegetables from customers who had grown more than they could eat themselves. These surely were utilized properly and came in handy.

Lily worked very hard in the bar and dining room to accommodate all requests. Often when someone showed up with a little baby, she babysat so that they could enjoy their meal, and many times she came to the kitchen to show off the baby. She did it proudly and was aware of the good deed she offered.

I remember one time Lily cut her finger at the walk-in cooler door and came to get me from my break and said that she needed a Band-Aid. I looked at it and said, "You need to go and get stitches." So she called a friend of ours to take her to the Yubadocs office. This happened just as the restaurant was about to open the door for dinner.

In the bar we had several folks who realized my dilemma and started to tend the bar and serve drinks. The person who jumped in had experience doing so. While I tried to serve the food, I asked these helpful patrons to assist me, and I told them where and what to bring to different tables. I told them to write the orders on a piece paper and then I would transfer it to the proper food checks. It was a nightmare. Then, to my surprise, the back door of the kitchen opened and Lily and her friend showed up, and Lily took over.

You see we really had people who cared. Originally, they had planned to have dinner that night and were waiting for almost two hours but did not mind doing so.

My first exposure to get involved in ice carving and sculptures was at the London Hilton Hotel. The more or less artistically inclined chefs did it. It fascinated me anyway. At that time the chef garde manger was Franz Kuene, and he was the one who carved the ice sculptures and had the talent.

I remember one time, one of the three-hundred-pound ice blocks broke in half. I was wondering what they would do with it, so I asked the executive chef, Mr. Bazani, if I could practice on that piece of ice and see if it would look like something you could recognize. The chef explained to me that the ice cost several British pounds and there was no time to just play with ice.

I took it upon myself, came in on my own time, and got the OK to do so. Prior to that, now and then I snuck in where the ice was carved. First, I outlined what I thought I could carve out of a half a block and knew I would be able to accomplish. It was a fish. Several fellow employees came by and thought that it was OK. And several days later, it was used for a cocktail party.

I worked at night one day a week from 10:00 p.m. to 6:00 a.m., and usually the night shift was somehow spotty. This gave me some time to see what kind of sculpture work I could get involved in.

There were several wire structures mounted on wooden boards, and a pan of firm tallow mixture was available, so I decided to see what I could do with just that. I came up with a horse with wings, then I put it on the top shelves over the worktable in the cold kitchen. My shift was over, and I left for the day. When I came back the next day and was waiting for my assignment, I made my round in the main kitchen. The chef entremetier (vegetable chef) asked me who made the horse figurine in the cold kitchen and said that it looked good.

It was near the end of my contract when the head chef called me into his office and told me that this was the last month I could choose the place to finish my obligation toward my contract. I chose the cold kitchen. Shortly after that, I arrived in Puerto Rico and had the chance to really get into artistic cold kitchen work. I believed in myself and did whatever I could to practice, and I gained confidence in mastering ice carving and tallow sculptures. It got to the point that I thought I could see how I would measure up with some of the recognized chefs in the field, and the only way to do so was in competition.

I did well locally, but it was not what I was looking for. So in 1972, while working at the Ilikai Hotel in Hawaii, there was an international Culinary Olympics in Frankfurt, Germany, held every four years. In order to qualify, they had a competition in Seattle, Washington, and I sculptured the emperor of China life size. It was copied from an ivy carving I had to purchase from a jewelry store for seven hundred dollars and was reimbursed by the time I was done with the project.

I tried to ship the sculpture to Seattle, Washington, but it was too big. At that time only a 747 plane was big enough to take it without laying it down, so I missed out and decided to fly it directly to Germany, not knowing what I was doing. I took a chance and spent almost a thousand dollars just to do so. The person in Germany, Otto Denkinger, was told prior to me doing so what was in store for him. I told him that the sculpture would have insurance for ten thousand dollars on it and I would be covered if something went wrong. It was a lot of insurance, but the sculpture was a piece of art. I would have lost everything if it was destroyed.

The crate I sent it in was covered with Hawaiian posters, and people fought over it just to get one in Frankfurt. When my shipment arrived, Denkinger had a hard time getting it out of the customs office because of the heavy insurance, but at the end he was successful and was able to display my artwork. It won me a gold medallion.

Later on I donated it to a hotel owner in Frankfurt. It was displayed in the lobby, and he offered me a free stay at his place whenever I visited.

Denkinger presented me with the gold medallion in Hawaii. That was the year that Nixon opened trade with China, and I got married to my wife, Lily Pai. It was rewarding both ways; all the effort paid off.

Yes, there are many books written on ice carving and sculpturing, and all of them can get you started, but it is up to you. Only you can get it done. It may also require some talent; you never know what's in you. Try it—you may like it.

You may wonder what ice carvings have to do with food. Ice carvings were used to keep insects away from the food, especially on buffet lines with seafood, roast beef, salmon, and any other items that could attract flies. Long before all the refrigeration was available, most of the perishable items had to be iced so that they were safe to eat.

Many times, in the winter the ice was cut out of frozen lakes. Then came the ice houses, where ice was produced in steel containers in uniform three-hundred-pound blocks. Sometimes the ice was colored, and on some occasions fruit was frozen into the blocks.

In some winter resorts, massive structures of ice sculptures were done, especially during the holiday season. There was even competition among college students to see who could do the best work.

At the beginning, ice was carved with chisels and a small saw. Classes were given on how to prepare the ice prior to carving it. If the ice is too cold and you hit it with a chisel, it could break very easily. Today ice is carved professionally and even with chain saws. In some bigger cities, you may even find ice carvers in the phone book or on the internet. Some professionals can make a good living, but you have to have a talent for it. Often, the ice is carved in a cooler and done in several pieces at a time and then kept in the freezer.

All this fancy work gives fine restaurants a high-class prestige and separates them from the average eatery. This is an art form, seen less and less and mostly at special events. There is an extra cost involved.

One thing that comes to my mind is at weddings, lovebirds or wedding bells. This type of artistry is part of the first-class qualification of a top-notch chef, which is a slowly dying breed.

In some places like Las Vegas, sometimes they have a person who just does ice carvings and may work for different hotels. But today's chefs in large hotels are mainly administrators and are seldom seen in the kitchen using knives.

Cold roasted turkey display at the
Hong Kong Plaza Hotel

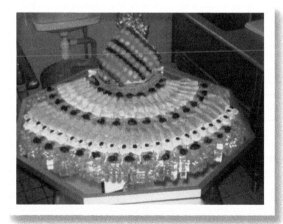

Cold ham display Sunday brunch
Plaza Hotel Hong Kong

CHAPTER 16

COOKING DEMONSTRATION

Egli Fillets with Almonds (Perch)   **Serves 3**

> 21 ounces boneless, skinless perch fillets (7 ounces per person)
> Salt
> White pepper
> Lemon juice
> Worcestershire sauce
> Flour to dust
> 5 teaspoons butter
> 3 teaspoons sliced white almonds

Marinate the fish fillets in salt, pepper, lemon juice, and Worcestershire sauce. Let stand for about 10 minutes.

Melt half the butter in a shallow frying pan. Dust the fish fillets with flour, then sauté the fish on both sides till golden brown.

Place the fish on a service platter and keep warm. Then use the second half of the butter in a separate pan and toast the almonds nice and golden brown. Pour these over the fish and sprinkle with some chopped parsley. Serve with boiled potatoes.

✣ ✣ ✣

Ladyfingers (Biscuits)   Yields 100 pieces

3 eggs
2 egg yolks
6 ounces sugar
6 ounces flour
Lemon rind from half a lemon

Whip the eggs and egg yolks with the sugar in a double boiler to a soft peak till it draws a ribbon. Remove from heat and continue to whip until cold. Fold in the flour and lemon rind. Place in a pastry bag with a straight tube, then dress the batter finger size on parchment paper.

Bake in the oven at 390 degrees for about 15 to 20 minutes. When cold, remove with a pastry knife and lay out flat so that your biscuits will stay straight. It is difficult to make just 10 pieces.

Empire Toast

At the time that we were serving lunch and dinner, it was then called the Empire House. One item on the menu was called Empire Toast and was very popular. It was served on an English muffin.

3 ounces pulled chicken thigh
Seasoning salt
Flour to dust
½ ounce cottonseed oil
1½ ounces freshly sliced mushrooms
½ ounce white wine
2 ounces demi-glacé
½ ounce heavy cream
1 ounce freshly diced tomato
1 ounce crispy fried onion
½ toasted English muffin

Some chopped parsley
¼ ounce butter

Cut the raw chicken meat into julienne (small strips) and season with the seasoning salt. Flour dust and panfry it in oil. Remove the chicken.

Sauté the sliced mushrooms. Deglaze with the white wine, then pour in the demi-glacé and cream. Reduce the sauce so that it is velvety looking.

Return the chicken fillets and bring to a quick boil. Then place on half a toasted English muffin and arrange the diced tomatoes and fried onions on top. Sprinkle with chopped parsley.

The diced tomato should be quickly sautéed in butter before placing in the middle of the dish. The fried onions are done in the deep fryer and can be prepared in advance. Keep them on paper towels so that they do not look greasy.

Peppercorn-Spiked Chopped Sirloin

This was also on the lunch menu.

In most places, hamburgers are a very common item. They come with a bun, and often costumers do not eat the bun at all. So I made a chopped sirloin. We ground our own meat, and I shaped 7 ounces of chopped sirloin into a football shape. Then I pressed a good amount of cracked black peppercorn into it. I panfried it and topped it with a creamy black peppercorn sauce. As a garnish, I dressed it up with fried onions and chopped parsley.

We also had a small food menu for the bar, which was quite popular. But at times it was difficult to handle, especially during dinner service. So we discontinued it during dinner service. The people who were serious diners knew about it and had a full dinner in the dining room.

We also conducted cooking classes in conjunction with Sierra College. The classes were conducted right out of the kitchen at the Swiss House, usually with ten to twelve people. I first told them what I would demonstrate, then explained the time it would take and also what can be substituted when you do not have everything available or there are hard-to-find items. Then I demonstrated setting up the so-called *mis en place* (setups) before you start to cook so that you do not have to run around going crazy.

Cooking can be challenging, and I explained in detail what is important in order to get good results every time. It is also of importance that you have all the items you will serve at the same time. That means you have the soup, salad, potatoes, and vegetables all ready to go by the time the main dish is completed. I showed every step that needed to be taken in order to do so. Some of the dishes were hands-on. Question-and-answer sessions added to the instruction, and copies of the recipes were handed out.

At the end of the classes, we served what was demonstrated, and they enjoyed it with a glass of complimentary wine. The last item the students had to do was turn in a comment card that was sent to the college so that they could see what grade the instructor would get, in order for me to teach future classes.

I remember one of the first lessons. I was making fresh home-made raviolis. When I was ready to roll out the dough, one of the attendees thought this would be too difficult but surely enjoyed eating the ravioli later on.

As I recall, we taught them to make osso buco, Hungarian goulash, European-style pot roast, and chicken in red wine. At times

I also went to Channel 3, a television station in Sacramento, and on one occasion I remembered it was General Yeager's birthday. I mentioned it during my few minutes' cooking demonstration, in which I made a dish the general used to eat at the Swiss House—jaegerschnitzel.

To do a cooking demonstration on TV, you had to be well organized because sometimes there was important news, and all of a sudden you were told to cut it short so that there was enough time for the news segment to fit in. Most of the time, after the news program was over the TV anchors enjoyed my cooking, and every time I visited for another demo, they asked me to make sure they could sample my food. In order to appear on Channel 3, you had to ask for a spot because so many restaurants were looking to promote their facility. Many times, the traffic was very heavy coming from Grass Valley, and you had to be on time, then go through the security system, set up your spot, and then stand by till you were told, "Ready, go!"

It promoted our business, and I got experience with an almost shotgun performance. While working in Hong Kong, I did it several times, with the difference being that I did not know what they were saying. Nevertheless, it helped the Plaza Hotel.

I also was involved in teaching apprentices in Dearborn, Michigan, and Honolulu, Hawaii. And I talked to students at the community college interested in the culinary field. To me it is vital to hand over some of my knowledge to other future chefs so that they may benefit from it. Once you are gone, it is too late, and it is a shame to let all the experience be gone with the wind. It takes years to get it. I also know that thing change all the time, and quite often things become outdated, but a good reference is priceless.

People will always need to eat, and changes have to be made. All we can hope for is that food will be always available. Now everybody is talking about organic food, and sometimes it could also be misleading, meaning not honest: who is doing the judging? What do you think of GMO?

Look at all the trash floating around. I wish people would become aware of their surroundings. You cannot ignore Mother Nature without consequences, and since convenience has come along, a lot of trash is lying around. Many things do not matter anymore; the basics are lost and no longer count. We all have a responsibility.

Whatever is taught in society has not yet been recognized. I only hope that eating a hamburger is not all it takes. Who knows?

I guess having a little garden at home and knowing what it takes could help. Creating so much waste and all the chemicals and what else will eliminate so much needed fertile space, which is wasted. Sooner or later society will have to wake up and face reality. It could get expensive.

I also believe that the United States could let the farmers grow much more food and use it in part to offset our trade deficit. At the same time, it would help feed all the nation's hungriest people. Sometimes common sense gets in the way or does not even exist.

Look at all the food that is wasted. People have become too picky, and if an apple has a spot on it, it's thrown out. I know when I was growing up, we could not even think of doing that, because during the war it was difficult to feed your family. When we had just a few extra homemade items, we were very happy and appreciative.

I think parents should teach their children what the world is like and what it could be. There are far too many folks out there who think everything should be free. There is no free lunch. Someone has to pay for it, period.

In some cases, people have too much pride, and doing something by themselves feels cruel and like others have no compassion for them. To them, self-reliance is a foreign country, and they think, "I deserve it," or "It is my right!" I think they all should go and see the

Third World countries and see what hardship those folks live under, then maybe they would change their mind.

People in general are living the good life and take everything for granted. It's not how many PlayStations you have but how can you live life with fewer material possessions and still be happy.

Yes, I know some of the parents who have seen the world a bit took notice and serve as examples. I wish there were more like them who could testify to the facts, but in today's environment you have to beware of what you are saying or they might put a label on you.

When I look at the situation globally, everywhere you look there is chaos and nobody seems to care. I think if it keeps on going this way, it will hit a state of global emergency and the so-called leaders (politicians) seem to have their heads in the sand. Everyone wants to please everybody instead of finding solutions. Christmas comes but once a year. Now folks think everything is just fine and dandy and we have a never-ending abundance of whatever people wish for.

Every time there is a crisis and the answer is we need more money, compromises are never in the cards. On the other hand, so much waste and fraud are right in front of their faces. Needless to say, we are told that we do not know what we are talking about or we have no idea.

So often when there is a problem, people think they can just put a Band-Aid on it and it will be OK. At the same time, things become more expensive and cheap fixes never last. People think, just raise the taxes—it's the easy way out. Many times, very few experts are consulted who would know what kind of solutions are needed to solve the problem.

I am sure you know what I am talking about. Just read the newspaper or watch television, that will give you some answers, and then you get shocked and wonder what's next.

Yes, we have a lot of honest folks out there who would be able to help out but do not want to be dragged through the mud and would rather mind their own business in order to keep their sanity. We do have a lot of rekindled situations, and proper measures have been taken in some parts of the world, but it seems to be too drastic and politically incorrect and we will ignore what the end result is going to be. It's devastating. It also will divide society, and leaders will blame each other, and so go the musical chairs.

I surely hope that there will soon be someone who will step up to the plate and has a proper vision to take the bull by the horns. Of course, I still would like it to be in harmony, but it has to be done with respect and consideration for the fellow man, without being reckless, and everyone has a stake in it to make it work. We do not have any sound solutions, and it limits what is feasible; just accuse the next guy of having no common sense or no compassion.

I know times have changed, but there are only one hundred pennies in a dollar no matter how you slice it, period.

This may sound like an old fogey, but talk to the older folks and I am sure this sounds like an echo to them, and they have a hard time coping with the situation we are in.

I hope to God people will come to their consciences before it is too late. Illegal immigrants need to be restricted. Now they get a lot for free, and in many ways they are better off than us citizens. Free this, free that. Get the proper papers. Someone has to pay for it—there is no free lunch. Yes, we do have still citizens and are well aware; just look at your taxes. You have to fork up and get basically nothing out of it.

Take the labor situation and look at the unemployment picture if you are looking for help today. More benefits are handed out, and there is no incentive for many out there to look for jobs because the government is handing out a better deal with benefits so that it is easier just to wait at home for the welfare check to arrive. Together with the free money and the drugs, it's no wonder crime is taking over, and new funds have to be allocated to take care of the new-found class of freeloaders. We are also overtaxed, and the middle class is shrinking.

I am asking myself what comes next. Do you? If this reflects the new society, then we definitely will face a very hard time. There are some sound solutions: teach people how to fish rather than just give them all money. Some self-reliance and respect would help. Educate them and let them know that having children is a responsibility.

I now have had sufficient time to reflect on my past, and when you look from the outside what went on over all these years, it is mind-boggling that it is even possible to get into such a trade, knowing what's at stake. Look how many restaurants fail in a very short time, thinking it is just open the doors and you have it made. Wait till you turn on the lights and the stove and any other business-related things, then come the end of the month when the mailman delivers the bills, what a shock and even worse if you are not familiar what else is in store for you!

Building a business is based on your perceptions, knowledge, and how much time and effort you are willing to put into it. You also have to have the intelligence to make quick decisions and even the foresight to avoid pitfalls before they hit you.

The profit margins are really slim, and you definitely need a plan or even a road map to stay clear of blunders and surprises. Yes, it may sound scary, but if you are not willing to accept this type of challenge, then stay away from it.

You need a basic team you can trust. In my case, it was Lily. It has to be someone who knows the trade inside out; there is no time to second-guess. Proper procedures and maybe even standard recipes are recommended.

I had the luxury, since I was properly trained, of having one part of the most expensive sections of the payroll be covered by myself as chef and owner—even though not too many employees want to work for a chef and owner, because everything is closely watched and every penny counts. The kitchen staff was always fed well, and the dishwasher was content.

It is easier to find wait help than a steady dishwasher. In our place the dishwasher was also utilized as a prep cook. This gave the person something a little more interesting to do than just hang out around the dishwashing machine.

I was usually the last one in the kitchen to close and made sure that everything was taken care of properly. The make or break of the business lies in the details. Proper utilization of every imaginable item counts, and the proper handling of food is the most important issue to make sure you do not have guests coming by the next day saying, "I got sick in your place last time we dined in your establishment."

Your dishes, glasses, flatware, and everything else have to be of good standards, and cold food has to be served on cold plates, hot food on hot plates, and no lipstick on your glasses. On this subject I could write many pages, but that would be boring.

One thing that gets you going is when you see that your effort is appreciated and the business is flourishing; after all, that is the goal you must accomplish in order to stay in business. This may sound like a home owner's how-to manual, but to me it was important and will be for any future restaurant owner.

Cleanliness is the next thing to godliness. That applies to the whole idea of any food operation, even the washrooms, kitchen floor, and around the building and parking lot. We had linen on the tables and cloth napkins, and dinners came with soup and salad.

Most of today's restaurants serve either soup or salad, and in many cases everything is à la carte. It may look like that is a better deal, but when you get your bill, look again. It's just a matter of how you set up your concept.

When I left Europe, the restaurants served complete menus,

including bread and butter. I know people watch their weight and many times just have a salad with a glass of wine, and if there is still some space that needed to be filled maybe a dessert.

Our clientele was middle-age folks who did not want to drive at night. It was known as a place where they still could have a conversation without shouting, which they appreciated. During the week the bar was patronized mainly by locals, and on the weekends it had steady once-a-week guests, and most of them had dinner with us.

My life's path definitely was colorful and never a dull moment, but then again, I took a path of my choice and got a lot of satisfaction out of it. Remember, success has a price tag on it. In many cases you have to put your nose to the grindstone as they say, and challenges come in all different ways. Just don't be afraid; you will get past the challenges.

I collected a lot of menus and souvenirs and also have a good collection of photos, and most of the places I worked gave you recommendation letters, but if you are not serious that does not mean a thing. There were a few places after I left that wondered how I did all that work and found out that I was constantly short-staffed. The only good thing was that I could handle it.

When a food and beverage manager sits behind the desk and talks to his girlfriend, that does not mean he knows what's going on in his department. To make sure everything works, when things get dicey then they have to find someone to blame. They will find the chef, and the food and beverage manger will get off the hook. Yes, I had exceptional food and beverage managers, and under those types even the chef looks good.

Managers sometimes are like politicians. They give you little or no credit over your capabilities and think you are in over your head. It is OK for them to think big, because when you strive toward something that gives you a challenge. Working in a place for several years, it becomes monotonous. I always believed when you reach that stage, it is time to cut the umbilical cord and start something of your own.

I know it is risky, but you never know! If you do not give it a try, you cannot succeed. The sweet smell of success is priceless, and the proof is in the pudding. You also have the freedom to do what you want without being told what you should and should not do, but first you have to gain the confidence to do so.

A pizza place does not take too much skill, but if you wish to do better then I guess you have to be trained for what you wish to accomplish. There are no shortcuts. There is also science in the kitchen, which has a lot of meaning if you want to have good results.

Look at the knives alone. Each one has a different shape and size and makes your task easier; you do not want to peel garlic with a cleaver.

When cooking baked potatoes, look for Idaho potatoes. Pierce them prior to baking them on a bed of salt in order to get the moisture out of them. They will be nice and fluffy.

How can you tell an old egg from a fresh one? Put the egg in cold water. If it goes to the bottom and lays flat, that means it is fresh, but if it stands halfway up it is old but can still be used in baking.

Why should a roast be allowed to rest for about fifteen to twenty minutes prior to carving? The outside has less juice than the inside, and when you let it rest, it gives the center juices time to be better distributed. Letting it rest will also release the muscle and allow it to relax, and therefore the roast will seem to be more tender.

Your roast should never be cooked on high heat; it will burn the outside and make it dry. Start searing the roast on high heat, then reduce the heat and finish in the oven at a medium temperature,

300 degrees. Do not cook the meat well done; this causes cancer. Use a temperature gauge to be sure your meat is medium or, better, medium rare.

The cooking time depends on the size of your roast. When you grill steaks, do not put salt on the meat in advance. Let them stand at room temperature, then season them and put them on the broiler; otherwise your expensive meat will be tough.

Usually, meats should be at room temperature before cooking, even roasts. The meat will cook more evenly. Frozen meat is just wasted because it is very difficult to judge its doneness.

How can I remove a glued-on label from a new metal pot thoroughly and easily? Apply a little rubbing alcohol, paint thinner, or lighter fluid rather than water. Or if the label is on the outside of the pot, fill the pot with boiling water and let it stand for a few minutes. In most cases the heat will loosen the glue that holds on to the metal.

Why do I add liquid to scrambled eggs? Your cooked scrambled eggs will be fluffier and more tender if you beat into the raw eggs approximately one or two teaspoons of water per egg. This liquid produces steams as your egg mixture cooks, giving the scrambled eggs a lighter texture. Milk produces the same effect and has the extra advantage of enriching your product. I use heavy cream—it makes a big difference.

To make peeling boiled eggs easier, as soon your eggs are boiled, place them in ice water and let them cool off completely before you start peeling.

How can I tell if a wrapped piece of meat sitting in the butcher's display case at the supermarket has been frozen? A large pool of juice (blood) in the package container is probably a result of the rupturing of cell walls, caused by freezing.

An ancient Chinese philosopher once advised his assembled followers, give a man a fish, and you feed him for a day. Teach a man to fish, and you feed him for a lifetime. There is a parallel in cooking. Teach yourself the science of cooking and you can cook creatively for a lifetime.

What does the color of beef fat reveal? Yellow-tinged fat indicates that the steer was grass-fed. White fat suggests that the animal was fed (at least during its final month) corn or other cereal grain. Consequently, a steak surrounded by a white layer of fat should be more tender but will likely cost you more.

Is meat still safe to eat if you forget to cut off the government grade or inspection stamp? Yes! The ink used is harmless vegetable dye.

There are many terms and names in gastronomy. All of them came from famous people and sometimes countries or even chefs, such as Escoffier, who was the father of the classical French kitchen. In Germany it was Walterspiel. Then came the modern approach, and one of them was Bocuse.

It spread all over the globe. The latest fad is fusion cooking, and Asian and European items are combined in almost endless possibilities; you name the countries and you see where it will end.

There is also a competition around the globe to see who is the most prestigious chef, who is awarded with stars. It is very difficult to achieve and is judged by highly qualified chefs, not the newspapers or food snobs.

Mornay sauce was created by Philippe de Mornay, a political and gastronomical crony of King Henry IV of France.

Gioachino Antonio Rossini was an Italian who lived for a long time in Paris. He was a world-famous opera composer. He is the person for whom tournedos Rossini are named. This is what he ate in the then famous French restaurants.

There is a long history of prestigious folks during the Napoleonic era, and most people do not know the history behind all of the classical terms and where they originated. But all those items became the basics of most of today's modern style.

Certain principles have to be followed in classical kitchen science. In today's food concepts, a lot has gone by the wayside. Fast food has taken over, and high-class or fancy restaurants are few and between.

Maître d'hôtel butter takes its name from the headwaiter and is a compound butter used on steaks, chicken, and even fish. If you are a person who is fascinated with cooking and cookbooks, there is a treasure of ideas out there—it is endless. We have a lot of imitators within the profession, and unfortunately a lot of the real deals are lost by using so-called shortcuts or changing the ingredients, substituting or even coming up with a completely different dish, or compromising the quality altogether.

Bread is bread, and an apple is an apple. There is no denying that.

In today's global market, you can get anything you will ever need. Just use the internet.

Today's top chefs have a real bond among each other and stand by the traditional basic concepts. They get irritated over what is done in the industry and even have their own organization that has certain qualifications in order to be a member. It is altogether a different breed of cats, and young upcoming chefs try to become understudies, quite often with little or no pay.

If you have the desire to follow in the footsteps of a great chef, you have to be willing to do what it takes. And if you are one of the lucky ones, be appreciative. You have to already have a good foundation so that you do not irritate others in your environment with your naiveté.

Those most successful understudies are most of the time very private and not braggers. They have a lot of respect for the field and will get their life's goal accomplished. You really have to be dedicated 100 percent. Not one day working in construction and next day working for a roofer. If you happen to look through some of the fancy food magazines, you will see it is done very clean and looks like artwork. I believe that the person who is presenting the dish almost has to be a perfectionist, and he or she will not go for second best.

Chefs of such stature are very rare and work for themselves. There is no mass production whatsoever. They have a certain concept in which they are very comfortable, and they never work with convenience food. The skills required will set them apart. Chefs work under a tremendous amount of pressure and are seldom understood. It is hard enough just to produce consistently high-quality food and present it in a picture-perfect way, not to mention dealing with people with little or no appreciation for what it took to get there.

This is to say that in the places where high standards are the norm, employees are very carefully selected and are aware of what is expected of them. They have a lot of pride in their efforts to contribute to the establishment's success. They have top-notch backgrounds before they are even considered for work in such places.

The chef is the king, and he or she makes the rules, period. Yes, it sounds cocky, but look into the background of all the top chefs in France alone and you will see what I am talking about.

It is serious business and also very respectful. I cannot stress it too much, and it will make all the difference. During my apprentice program in the kitchen in Switzerland, a French chef trained me, and I can vouch for it.

I am sure that in today's circumstances things have changed somewhat, but a lot of things stay the same. The goal is to arrive at high standards. The complexity in the field is enormous, and it takes many years to perfect and then maintain such high standards.

I chose Grass Valley because I wanted to get away from big cities, but nevertheless I had the training and experience just the same.

⚜ ⚜ ⚜

Fillet de Sole Prince Murat

Use Dover sole.

Fillet the fish, then cut it into strips and season it with salt, pepper, Lea & Perrins sauce, and a few drops of lemon juice.

Roll the strips in flour to create so-called goujons, which look like sticks. Deep-fry till golden brown. Cut small cooked artichoke bottoms into wedges. Prepare château potatoes and roast in the oven. Sauté the artichokes and potatoes in butter. Add the fish with some meat glaze, lemon juice, and very little au jus just to make it glacé.

Serve with a nice Bibb lettuce salad with vinaigrette dressing.

Cornettes D'oeufs Grand-Mère (Grandmother)

This is elbow macaroni in a rich béchamel sauce with lots of Swiss and Gruyère cheese, baked in the oven and topped with golden brown white bread crumbs sautéed in butter. It's delicious. In the United States you call it macaroni and cheese, but make sure your sauce is thin because the baking process will firm it up, and it will get dry.

Pommes Walterspiel (Baked Apples)

This is a dish created by the German chef Walterspiel.

Use any type of apple that does not get mushy when you poach it. First, peel the apples and leave one strip of peel around the middle of the fruit. Then core the apples and fill with almond paste and yellow raisins.

Poach the apples in white wine, butter, sugar, and a bit of water.

Cover with parchment paper so that the apples do not dry up during the poaching. Poach for 30 minutes at 350 degrees.

When the apples are done, let them cool off. Cut a round of sponge cake, place an apple on top, cover with half-whipped cream, and decorate with chocolate rolls.

Chocolate Sauce

Use dark Swiss chocolate and dissolve it in heated heavy cream, but don't let it burn. The quality of the sauce depends on the quality of chocolate you use.

Pommes Elisabeth

These are potato croquettes with spinach worked into the mixture, breaded then deep-fried. They should look like a pear. Place a short piece of raw spaghetti for the stem before frying.

Toast Woodcock

This is scrambled eggs on toast topped with fillet of anchovies and some chopped parsley.

Risotto Verbena

This is a risotto with cepe mushrooms cooked al dente, and then topped with julienne-cut and sautéed calf liver, tomato concasse, and chopped parsley.

Macaroni Pasticciata

This is macaroni baked in cocottes. Fill each cocotte halfway with macaroni, then cover with rich meat sauce, macaroni again, and finally top with béchamel sauce, tomato concasse, and Parmesan cheese. Then bake them at 350 degrees for 40 minutes. The macaroni needs to be cooked before you assemble the dish.

Hollandaise Sauce

This is a very delicate butter sauce that is kept warm and needs to be handled properly. It is made with egg yolks and melted clarified butter.

First, make sabayon, then add the melted butter and season with salt, cayenne pepper, lemon juice, tarragon vinegar, and Worcestershire sauce. In the old country, you make a reduction for the seasoning.

If it gets too rich during the process, add some warm water to it. A footnote: hollandaise sauce uses a double boiler to make the sabayon and 6 egg yolks per pound of clarified butter. Do not make scrambled eggs.

Croute des Gourmets

On top of a slice of white toast, arrange some Parma ham and creamed mushrooms. Then place a few white asparagus tips on top and glacé with hollandaise sauce.

Pâte à Frire (Beer Batter)

½ pound flour
1 ounce oil
2 egg yolks
2 egg whites
¾ pint beer
Salt
Nutmeg

Make a batter with the four, oil, egg yolks, beer, salt, and nutmeg. Be sure you have no lumps in it. Beat the 2 egg whites to snow, then slowly fold the egg whites under it.

Escalope de Veal Holstein   Serves 1

6-ounce veal scallopine
Salt
White pepper
White bread crumbs
Clarified butter

Slightly pound the veal like a Wiener schnitzel. Then season with salt and white pepper and bread with white bread crumbs.

Panfry it in clarified butter golden brown on both sides, then top it with a fried egg and anchovy fillets. Look for good quality veal, maybe even milk fed.

Fillet de Sole Ostende Cleopatra

Use real Dover sole fillets

Flatten the fillets so that you have nice and even pieces. Season with salt, pepper, lemon juice, and Lea & Perrins sauce. Flour dust and panfry in oil.

Place on a serving dish, then top with sautéed peeled and deveined 30-count prawns, brown butter, a small amount of rich beef au jus, and chopped parsley.

Toast William

Dilute some Roquefort cheese with milk, but not watery, so that you are able to spread it on top of a slice of toasted bread. Then cut half a Williams pear into a fan and place on top of the bread. Bake in the oven at 350 degrees for 10 minutes.

Stuffed Bell Peppers Indian Style

Cut the bell peppers in half, then remove the seeds.

Prepare a stuffing consisting of cooked long-grain rice; red, green, and yellow diced peppers; sultanines (yellow raisins); cooked chicken liver; diced cooked lamb meat; and diced fresh peeled tomatoes. Sauté the stuffing quickly in olive oil and season with salt and pepper and some chicken stock.

Cover your baking pan with soft butter, then fill pepper halves with the filling. Pour some chicken stock in the bottom of the pan. The chicken stock will produce steam. Slowly cook in the oven at 350 degrees for about 30 minutes. Do not over cook; remember, the stuffing is already precooked. Serve with brown sauce.

Crêpes Bergere

10 ounces flour
6 medium eggs
2 tablespoons water
Salt
Pepper

Prepare a thin batter like pancake mix with the flour, eggs, salt, pepper, and water. Do not use milk because they will stick on the pan. Use a nonstick pan.

Make a rich creamed mushroom sauce. Add cooked diced chicken meat to the sauce and let it cool overnight. Then fill the crêpes with the filling, place in gratin dishes, and top with béchamel sauce and Parmesan cheese. Bake in the oven at 350 degrees for about 30 minutes, till nice and brown. Serve with salad or vegetables.

Sauce Remoulade

Use mayonnaise for the base (recipe below).

First, chop capers, gherkins, parsley, onions, tarragon, and chervil. Blend with anchovy paste and mayonnaise. Add some cayenne pepper and French mustard. The sauce should be firm, not watery.

Mayonnaise

5 egg yolks
1 ounce Dijon mustard
1½ ounces white vinegar
1 teaspoon white salt
½ teaspoon ground white pepper

20 ounces cottonseed oil
Pinch of cayenne pepper
Juice of ½ small lemon
1 tablespoon Lea & Perrins sauce

The quantity of ingredients depends on how much sauce you wish to make. Make sure every ingredient is at room temperature.

If you have a stand mixer, use it but run it on medium speed. Mix the egg yolks, mustard, vinegar, salt, and pepper in the bowl. Whip them with a wire whip as you slowly pour in the oil, lemon juice, and Lea & Perrins. If it gets too thick, add some cold water.

When you have the amount of sauce you wish to make, check for seasoning. Then put it in a plastic container and store in the fridge. You can use the mayonnaise for all kinds of salad dressings or use it on sandwiches. It is a versatile product and can be stored for a couple of weeks. Tartar sauce, mustard mayonnaise, Thousand Island dressing, and blue cheese dressing are a few items you can make with the mayonnaise.

Tripe in Tomato Sauce

Blanch the tripe. Rinse in cold water, then slice into medium-size julienne.

Finely chop some onion, mince some garlic, then sauté in oil. Add caraway seeds and tomato paste. Dust the tripe with flour and fill the pot with clear beef stock. Season with bay leaf, thyme, salt, and pepper. Then bring to a boil, reduce the heat, and let it simmer till done, about 1 hour.

Make sure you purchase tripe from young animals because it will take less time to cook.

I recommend doing it in a pressure cooker or Crock-Pot because it will shorten the cooking time.

Tripe is not often used in US restaurants, but some Mexican restaurants serve it under the name menudo.

The tripe has to be cleaned properly, and diners need to know what they are eating.

Ham Hocks with Sauerkraut

This dish requires good-sized smoked ham hocks with meat on them, not just bones.

First you need fresh sauerkraut. Rinse half the amount under cold water. Slice white onions, mince some garlic, and simmer till the onions are transparent in oil. Pour in white wine and water. Do not let it turn brown. Then tear the kraut apart with the help of a fork and add applesauce.

Make a spice bag consisting of caraway seeds, marjoram leaves, juniper berries, thyme, cracked white peppercorn, salt, bay leaf, and garlic. Tie with string and place under the kraut, then put the hocks on top. Cover with parchment paper and a lid, then slowly braise till the hocks are done. Make sure to use low heat. Do not let it burn.

To bind the sauerkraut, use finely shredded raw potato. Mix in some white wine and stir it into the kraut while still hot before serving.

Here you also could use a pressure cooker. Cooking time is about 1 hour. Boil some potatoes on the side and enjoy. Good eating.

Bread Pudding   Yields 10 servings

Use a 9-inch round cake mold 1½ inches deep.

8 French dinner rolls
4½ ounces sugar
5 eggs
½ ounce pure vanilla extract
¼ ounce ground cinnamon
1 quart milk
2 ounces raisins
6 ounces sliced apples (canned in water)
8 ounces sweet solid butter

Lay out the mold with parchment paper. Use some Pam to hold the paper in place.

Slice enough of the French rolls to cover the mold inside. Dice the rest of the rolls into ¾-inch cubes.

In a mixing bowl, get the sugar, eggs, vanilla, and cinnamon nice and creamy with the help of a wire whisk. Then pour in boiling milk, stirring constantly.

When everything is well blended, add the bread cubes, raisins, and apples. Let it soak up some of the moisture, then pour it into the mold. Top with the still firm butter flakes and bake in the oven at 350 degrees for approximately 1 hour.

When baked enough, let it cool completely. To remove easily, quickly heat the mold over a gas flame or hot plate on top of the stove for a few seconds. Turn it upside down on a plate. Remove the paper and slice as you wish. You may reheat it in the microwave oven or regular oven till warm. Serve with a custard sauce.

I remember one time while demonstrating cooking on Channel 3 that I had a situation where I was questioned on the calorie count for a dish I was preparing. The anchor at that time was Beth Ruyak.

My answer was, "If it is too much, you always can eat an apple." That night we had customers who were watching the news while eating dinner at the Empire House and got a good laugh out of it.

In Nevada County there are quite a few hunters and a variety of wildlife during the hunting season. People came in and asked me how I would prepare venison meat. A lot of them made venison jerky. Other folks just gave it away because they had a whole full freezer of it at home.

Medallion of Venison

About 1 pound well-trimmed venison cutlets
7 ounces chanterelles
1 medium onion
2 teaspoons flour
2 teaspoons butter
Salt
White pepper
3 ounces white wine
1 ounce brandy
½ cup whipping cream
1 teaspoon chopped parsley

Wash and clean the mushrooms and cut into halves or quarters, depending on their size.

Finely chop the onion. Season the meat with salt and pepper, flour dust, then sauté both sides in butter over medium heat. Put aside and keep warm.

Melt the remaining butter and sauté the onion and mushrooms. Pour in the white wine and brandy. Season to taste, then finish with the whipping cream and chopped parsley. Pour over the meat and enjoy. I serve lingonberries on the side.

Côtes D'agneau Vert-Pré (Lamb Chops Broiled or Panfried)

I purchase USDA Choice rack of lamb. Then I trim and cut six chops (3 ounces each) out of it. You may ask the butcher at your favorite supermarket to do that for you.

Marinate the chops in thyme and ground black pepper. The meat will then be sautéed in a cast iron pan to medium rare.

Let it rest. In the meantime, fix your Lyonnaise potatoes and Provençal tomatoes, then garnish with watercress. Lyonnaise potatoes are home fries with sliced onion cooked together over low heat.

Provençal Tomatoes

Sauté bread crumbs, finely chopped garlic, parsley, and thyme in butter, then arrange on top of tomato halves. Bake in the oven at 350 degrees for 15 minutes. Tomatoes get mushy quickly, so beware not to overcook. Serve hot pepper jelly with it (see recipe earlier in the book).

Baked Brie Cheese in Puff Pastry Served with Horseradish Sauce

Brie cheese is available in most supermarkets. This is an elegant appetizer, and if you are not up to making your own dough, you also can buy it at the local supermarket.

Cut the cheese into approximately 5-ounce wedges. Then take a thin sheet of puff dough and wrap the cheese in it. Egg wash twice, then bake in the oven at 350 degrees till golden brown. Be sure the dough is not too thick, otherwise the cheese will melt out before the crust is done.

The horseradish sauce is made either with whipped cream or sour cream. Just blend the horseradish together with either the whipped cream or sour cream.

This dish can be prepared a day ahead of time and kept in the fridge overnight, but you have to bring it up to room temperature before baking it to get good results. If you prepare the item a day ahead, do not egg wash it because it will get soggy and will not bake properly.

Cover the cheese with clear wrap if you fix it a day ahead because it might get moist, especially if the fridge is opened too many times.

Crawfish Etouffee

We served this dish at the Hyatt in New Orleans. The seasoning salt is important and usually made ahead of time.

Seasoning

Ground white pepper
Dry English mustard
White salt
Cayenne pepper or any red pepper
Black pepper
Dried sweet basilicum
Dried thyme

Blend the seasonings together and use as needed.

Main Dish

Butter
Green onions
Tabasco sauce
Chopped garlic

Seafood stock or clam juice
Chopped onions
Chopped celery
Chopped green and red bell peppers
Flour
Vegetable oil
Peeled crawfish, tails only
Long-grain rice

In a cast iron pan, make a dark roux with the oil and the flour but do not let it burn. Remove from stove. Add the vegetables and some of the seasoning. Stir till cold

In a saucepan, bring the stock to a boil, then add the Tabasco sauce and vegetable roux mixture to it and slowly bring back to a boil. Simmer for about 5 minutes, constantly stirring with a wire whisk till completely smooth.

In another saucepan, melt butter and with a shaking motion cook the crawfish. Add some more butter, stock, and seasoning as needed.

Place a portion of cooked rice in the middle of the serving dish and arrange the crawfish combined with the etouffee sauce around it. The dish should be a bit spicy. We used Uncle Ben's rice and added the typical local ingredients: carrots, celery, onion, bell pepper, garlic, and chicken stock.

Oyster Stew

At the Sheraton Boston, we served oysters on the half shell and sometime had orders for oyster stew. New England is well known for good seafood, especially lobsters.

For oyster stew, use fresh Blue Point oysters, chopped shallots, a pinch of garlic, white wine, heavy cream, salt, white pepper, and chopped parsley.

First, wash the oysters and make sure there is no sand to be found. Set the liquid aside for later.

Sauté the shallots and garlic in butter. Add the white wine, pour in the heavy cream, season with salt and pepper, and add the oysters and juice. Then reduce till you have a creamy sauce. We had a small steam kettle, and it worked very well for making stew.

When the oysters are done, pour in a serving dish and top with the chopped parsley. Do not overcook the oysters—we do not want rubber duckies.

Swiss Apple Tart with Custard Topping

Lay out a 9-inch pie shell with pâte brisée. The dough recipe can be found earlier in the book. Pierce the dough with a fork so that the dough will lie flat when you bake it. Avoid air bubbles.

Sprinkle the dough with grated hazelnuts and arrange the apples in thin wedges side by side all around till the whole pan is covered. The apples should be of a proper type to make pies. Do not use Granny Smith (too hard); use Gravenstein. Bake in the oven at 350 degrees till the crust starts to get brown, then add the custard mix. The crust has to be baked before you add the custard mix; otherwise, the dough will not bake properly—it would still be raw.

Custard Topping

> 2 cups coffee creamer
> 2 ounces sugar
> 1 teaspoon vanilla extract
> Pinch of ground cinnamon
> 2 small eggs

Beat all the ingredients together, then pour on top of the apples, making sure they are evenly covered. Continue baking till the custard is completely done and properly firm (set). Remove from the oven and let it cool.

Total amount of custard is 8 ounces. If you wish, you can top it with whipped cream.

Make sure you bake the tart properly so that the bottom of the tart is also baked, not like a half-baked pizza. You may have to bake it on the bottom rack of the oven for a few minutes to achieve the proper result.

Flamed Veal Kidneys Armagnac   Serves 2

2 veal kidneys
1 ounce butter
2 ounces diced peeled tomato (concasse)
3 ounces white wine
1 ounce demi-glacé or meat glaze
2 ounces beef au jus
1½ ounces Armagnac
2 ounces heavy cream
1 teaspoon chopped parsley

Prepare the kidneys but leave some fat on them. Slice into medallions.

In a sauté pan, quickly sear the kidneys in butter on both sides, then place on a plate and set aside. Add the concasse. Deglaze with the wine and add the meat glaze and beef au jus. Season with salt and pepper. Slightly reduce to about half, then tilt the pan and flame it with Armagnac. Return the kidneys. Pour in the cream and bring to a quick simmer. Before you serve the kidneys, sprinkle with chopped parsley. Serve with rice pilaf.

This is a typical European dish. It is difficult to find kidneys with the fat on because of FDA rules, and especially veal kidneys. Maybe some French restaurant carries this dish on the menu.

Whitefish Provençal   Serves 6

2¼ pounds halibut or striped bass fillets
1 ounce olive oil
3 ounces finely chopped white onion
15 ounces diced tomatoes, drained
¾ cup pitted black and green olives, cut into lengthwise quarters
2 ounces white wine
1 teaspoon fresh organic basil leaves
1 teaspoon finely minced fresh garlic
1 teaspoon fresh organic thyme leaves

Cut the fish fillets into six portions. Season with salt and white pepper. Then bake in a 350-degree oven halfway though, about 5 minutes.

In a saucepan, heat the olive oil and sauté the onions till transparent. Then add the remainder of the ingredients and simmer for about 3 minutes. Spoon over the fish and complete the cooking process in the oven for about another 5 minutes. It should lightly glaze the fish.

Dress the fish on top of roasted Brussels sprouts or any favorite veggies.

Irish Soda Bread

4 cups all-purpose flour
¼ cup white sugar
3 teaspoons baking powder

1 teaspoon salt
1 teaspoon baking soda
½ stick butter
2 cups red currants
1 large egg, beaten
1¾ cups buttermilk
2 teaspoons caraway seeds

First, grease two 8-inch cake pans.

Combine all dry ingredients in a large bowl. Add the butter and mix till it looks like crumbs. Then add the currants, beaten egg, buttermilk, and caraway seeds. Knead into a dough till it is smooth. You may need some more flour.

Divide dough in half and form two round balls. Place in the square cake molds and press down. Cross cut about ½ inch deep. Bake at 350 degrees for 35 to 40 minutes.

Irish Stew   Yields 10 servings

3–4 pounds cubed lean boneless lamb meat from the breast or shoulder
1 pound sliced onion
7 ounces leeks
10 ounces carrots
4 ounces turnips
7 ounces celery
10 ounces potatoes
1 clove garlic, minced
10 ounces white cabbage
Salt
Ground white pepper
Bay leaf
Thyme
Marjoram
Worcestershire sauce

Blanch the meat quickly, then return to the saucepot. Add the sliced vegetables, potatoes, salt, pepper, and all other spices in a spice bag. Cover with water. Top with the cabbage leaves and simmer for about 1 hour.

Serve in deep dishes and garnish with some Irish potatoes.

Lavash (Middle Eastern Sesame Cracker Bread)   Yields 12–15 pieces

   5 cups unbleached all-purpose flour
   1 envelope dry yeast
   2¼ teaspoons salt
   ¾ teaspoon sugar
   ½ stick butter, melted
   1½ cups warm water (120 degrees)
   ¾ cup sesame seeds

Grease a large bowl and set aside.

Combine first four ingredients in a mixing bowl. Blend soft butter with 1 cup of warm water and add gradually to dry ingredients, beating continuously. If the dough seems to be dry, add more water as needed. Knead until the dough is smooth and elastic.

Place in the greased bowl, turning to coat the entire surface. Cover with plastic wrap and a hot damp towel and let rise in a warm place until doubled in bulk, about 1 to 2 hours.

Remove oven rack and preheat the oven to 350 degrees. Place the oven rack in the lowest part of the oven, then place a baking sheet on the rack. Divide the dough into pieces about the size of a tennis ball. Spread sesame seeds on the dough and roll one piece at a time on a large breadboard or countertop as thin as possible without tearing the dough.

Bake lavash one piece at a time on the baking sheet until golden brown with darker highlights. Cool on a cooling rack. Lavash will keep for up to a month if wrapped in plastic or tinfoil and stored in a dry place.

Busecca: Ticino Tripe Soup from the Swiss Italian Region

1 medium onion
2 cloves garlic
3 ounces diced bacon
½ ounce olive oil
3 potatoes
3 medium carrots
½ celery root
3 tomatoes
2 leek sticks
12 ounces precooked tripe
Salt
Pepper
1 dash saffron
Marjoram
Thyme
Basil
Rosemary
2 ounces tomato paste
1¼ quarts beef bouillon
3 ounces grated Parmesan cheese

Chop the onion and mince the garlic. Sauté in hot oil with the bacon. Dice the potatoes, carrots, celery, and tomatoes. Cut the leeks into little wheels. Cut the tripe into strips and sauté with the vegetables.

Season with all the spices. Add the tomato paste and steam for a couple of minutes. Then pour in the bouillon and bring to a boil. Reduce the heat and simmer gently for about 30 to 40 minutes. Serve with the grated Parmesan cheese.

Zurich-Style Tripe

    1 pound 5 ounces cooked tripe
    2 onions, chopped
    1 leek stick
    1 medium carrot
    2 ounces butter
    1 cup dry white wine
    2 cups beef bouillon
    Salt
    Pepper
    ½ teaspoon caraway seeds
    1 bay leaf
    2 ounces flour

Cut the tripe into 1½-inch squares. Slice the onion and leek into rings. Peel the carrot.

Sauté the onion, leek, and carrot in butter. Dust with flour and pour in the wine. Add the tripe, followed by the bouillon. Season with salt, pepper, caraway seeds, and bay leaf. Cover and simmer for 1 hour. Before serving, remove the carrot and bay leaf. Serve with small boiled potatoes.

Braised Rabbit

    2.2 pounds fresh rabbit
    2 ounces butter
    4 ounces lean diced bacon
    1 medium carrot
    1 medium onion
    2 cloves garlic, minced
    Salt

Pepper
2 bay leaves
2 cloves
2 cups red wine
2 cups beef bouillon

Cut the rabbit into pieces, hind and front legs and saddle. All should be of the same size. Sauté the pieces of meat on all sides together with the bacon.

Add the sliced carrot, onion, and minced garlic. Season with salt, pepper, and bay leaves, then pour in the wine and bouillon.

Cover and simmer over low heat for about 1 hour. Rotate the meat from time to time. Add more bouillon as needed. If you wish to have extra sauce, add more bouillon and bind it with a brown roux. For the homemaker, use some brown sauce mix.

The sauce is especially tasty if you add a few dried mushrooms presoaked in water. Serve with mashed potatoes and green beans almondine.

⚜   ⚜   ⚜

Rösti Jura Style

This dish is from the French part of Switzerland.

2½ pounds potatoes boiled the previous day
3½ teaspoons butter
1 onion finely chopped
Salt
Pepper
5 ounces lean sliced bacon
9 ounces Gruyère cheese, sliced

Peel and grate the potatoes. In a skillet, heat the butter and sauté the onion. Add the potatoes and season with salt and pepper.

Grease an ovenproof baking dish and fill evenly with the potatoes.

Cover with the bacon slices and cheese. Place in a preheated 350-degree oven. Bake until the cheese has melted and the bacon is crisp.

Liver Kebabs

This is a special dish from Zurich.

1 pound calf liver
3½ ounces very lean bacon (4 slices)
12 fresh sage leaves
1½ ounces butter
Salt
Pepper
¾ cup beef bouillon

Slice the liver into ½-inch thick slices, then cut the slices into 1½-inch squares. Cut each slice of bacon into 3 pieces. Alternate the liver, bacon, and sage leaves on skewers.

Panfry the kebabs on all sides in hot butter until brown and crisp. Remove from pan and season with salt and pepper. Cover and set aside to keep warm.

Add the bouillon to the drippings, let it reduce, and pour over the kebabs as a final touch. Serve over a bed of green beans and bacon. Make sure the liver is completely peeled; if you get it from the supermarket, let the butcher do it for you.

Pork Roast

1½ pounds pork loin, trimmed of excess fat
Salt
Pepper

4 tablespoons Dijon mustard
2½ ounces butter
2½ cups white wine
1½ cups chicken bouillon
3 medium carrots
1 large onion
2 pounds small new potatoes
2 ounces butter

Sprinkle the meat with salt and pepper, then brush generously with mustard. Place in an ovenproof casserole pan. Heat the 2½ ounces of butter until very hot, then pour over the meat.

Roast in a 390-degree oven. After 10 minutes, add the white wine and some bouillon and continue to roast, basting frequently. If necessary, add some more bouillon to it.

Chop the carrots and onion. After 1 hour, arrange the vegetables around the roast. Leave in for 30 minutes.

Boil the unpeeled, scrubbed potatoes in a small amount of salt till semi-tender. Drain. Sauté in the remaining 2 ounces of butter until lightly brown. Add to the meat 5 minutes before serving and cover with the sauce.

Roasted Veal Short Ribs

2 pounds deboned veal short ribs
Pepper
Nutmeg
Sage
Rosemary
Salt
3 teaspoons butter
1 large onion

1 bay leaf
1 clove
2 carrots
2 cups dry white wine
1½ quarts clear beef stock

Season the meat on all sides with pepper, nutmeg, sage, and rosemary. Heat the butter in a Dutch oven. Add the meat and sear on all sides. Place in a preheated 465-degree oven and bake for 20 minutes. Salt the meat and bake for another 15 minutes.

Reduce the heat to 365 degrees. Spike the onion with the bay leaf and spice clove. Then peel the carrots, cut them in half, and add to the meat.

Heat the wine in a small saucepan and baste the meat with it from time to time. Occasionally turn the meat. Leave the oven door ajar for the steam to escape. It is important that the meat be juicy and tender, but with a crispy crust on the outside.

After a total baking time of 1½ hours, remove the meat from the oven. Deglaze with the wine. Add some hot beef stock and bring to a boil. Season to taste and reduce slightly. Slice the meat ⅓ of an inch thick. Serve with mashed potatoes and the sauce on the side.

Gluewein (Mulled Wine)   Serves 1

6 ounces red wine
½ ounce dark brown sugar
1 small cinnamon stick
1 spice clove
2 pieces cardamom
1 thin orange slice
1 thin lemon slice

In a small pan, bring the wine and all other ingredient to a boil. Pour into a coffee mug and drink it as hot as you can stand it. You will start to perspire. Drink before you go to sleep. It is a good remedy to cure a cold. Quite often it is also consumed during Christmas season.

Banana Nut Bread

   1¾ cups all-purpose flour
   ¾ teaspoon baking soda
   ¼ teaspoon salt
   2 ounces sugar
   2 eggs
   ⅔ ounce vegetable oil
   3 tablespoons milk
   2 large ripe bananas, mashed
   ½ cup chopped walnuts

Mix together the flour, baking soda, salt, and sugar. Blend in the eggs, oil, and milk. Stir in the banana and nuts.

Pour batter into a greased 8½ x 4½ x 2½ inch pan. Bake at 350 degrees for approximately 1 hour or until done. Check for doneness by inserting a toothpick into the center of the loaf; when it comes out clean, it is done.

Curry Flavored Peanut Soup

The soup quantities depend on how much you wish to make. I will just list the items that will go into the soup.

   Flour
   Butter

Creamy peanut butter
Chicken broth
Curry powder
Salt
Sugar
Ground cardamom
Cayenne pepper
Coconut milk

First, make a blonde roux. This is flour and butter blended together, then heated in a saucepot with a thick bottom till golden brown.

Add the peanut butter and blend well together with a wire whisk. Heat the chicken broth and slowly pour it to the roux and peanut mixture. Use your whisk and work it till it is lump free.

Season with curry powder, salt, sugar, cardamom, cayenne pepper, and the coconut milk. Let it simmer over low heat about 20 minutes.

Veal Medallion Mediterranean

3 each 2-ounce veal scallopine from the tenderloin
Flour to dust
Salt
Pepper
3 ounces butter
½ white onion, sliced
1 ounce sliced white mushroom
4 pieces 16–20 count shrimp, peeled and deveined, tail on
½ firm avocado, cut into cubes
1 cup white wine
½ cup heavy cream
1 teaspoon lemon juice

½ cup demi-glacé
1 small red pimento
1 teaspoon chopped parsley

Dust the veal scallopine with flour and season with salt and pepper. Panfry in clarified butter. Put aside, keep warm.

Sauté the onion and mushroom in the same skillet. Add the shrimp and deglaze with the wine. When the shrimp are done, remove and keep on the side.

Add the demi-glacé, heavy cream, salt, pepper, and a few drops of lemon juice to the skillet. Bring to a soft boil and at last combine all the items in the sauce. Arrange it nicely over the veal medallions and garnish with the pimento and chopped parsley. Sprinkle the avocado cubes on top of each serving. Serve rice pilaf with it.

Caraway's Radiatore Pasta with Mushrooms and Cream

1 pound radiatore pasta
2½ pounds assorted domestic and wild mushrooms
3 medium shallots
2 teaspoons butter
1 ounce sweet sherry wine
2 cups heavy cream
Salt
Pepper
2 teaspoons chopped chives

Bring 6 quarts water and 1 teaspoon salt to a boil, then cook the pasta and drain. Place in a service bowl and keep warm.

Cut the mushrooms into ¼-inch-thick slices and set aside. Peel and thinly slice the shallots.

Heat butter in a large skillet; add shallots and sauté over medium heat until soft. Add mushrooms and sauté, stirring occasionally, until most of the liquid has evaporated.

Stir in 2 ounces sweet sherry wine and the heavy cream, and reduce till you have a creamy sauce. Season the mushroom sauce to taste with salt and pepper and add the chives. Pour over hot pasta and serve pronto.

Poached Scallops Contessa

 6 large raw scallops, cut in half (looks like two wheels)
 2 ounces green apples (Granny Smith), cut into ½-inch julienne
 2 ounces white onion, julienne
 1 ounce curry powder
 2 ounces ¼-inch banana slices
 1 ounce diced red pimentos
 2 ounces sweet white wine
 2 ounces heavy cream
 Seasoning salt
 Butter flakes
 Chopped parsley

Poach the scallops in the wine quickly over medium heat. Remove and keep warm. In a second skillet, sauté the apples and onion with the butter flakes over medium heat, then dust with curry powder. Add the cream and the liquid from the scallop poaching.

Reduce the sauce by half, then add the apples, onion, bananas, and scallops and bring to a quick boil. Dish out on a serving plate and garnish with pimentos and chopped parsley. Serve the dish with couscous.

Creamy Yellow Squash Soup

Yellow squash
Root celery
Carrots
Onion
Lean sliced bacon
Butter
Chicken stock
Peanut butter (unsweetened)
Flour
Salt
Ground white pepper
Curry powder

Peel and seed the squash and cut into 2-inch cubes. Dice the celery, carrots, onion, and bacon.

Sauté all in butter, Pour in the chicken stock and some peanut butter. Season with salt, pepper, and some curry powder.

Bring to a boil and then fix a white roux (butter and flour) to thicken the soup very lightly. Simmer till all the vegetables are tender.

Then with the help of a blender, purée the soup nice and creamy. You can add some heavy cream to it to make it very special. When you use the blender, be careful so that you do not get burned. Fill only half full, and put the lid on top.

Yokohama Soup

This is a Japanese soup we served at the Moana Surfrider Sheraton Hotel in Honolulu, Hawaii.

2 teaspoons butter
1 teaspoon finely chopped shallots
1 teaspoon flour

2 cups fish bouillon
2 cups clam juice
½ cup heavy cream
1 teaspoon cooked chopped spinach
Salt
Pepper
1 cup unsweetened whipped cream

Melt the butter, then add the shallots and sauté for a minute. Pour in the flour and stir for a few minutes or so, then add the two stocks and remaining ingredients, except for the whipped cream.

Bring to a boil and season to taste. Pour in a soup cup, then top with whipped cream and glaze under a salamander or cheese melter.

Scampi in Champagne

2 ounces clarified butter
20 each U-15 shrimp, peeled and deveined
2½ ounces finely chopped shallots
2 cups dry champagne
1 cup heavy cream
Salt
Freshly ground white pepper
1 teaspoon freshly chopped basil
Chopped parsley

Heat the clarified butter in a large stainless steel skillet until it sizzles. Add the scampi or shrimp and sauté till they turn pink. Remove and keep warm.

Next, sauté the shallots; make sure you do not burn them. Deglaze with the champagne. Reduce to half, add cream, and reduce to half again. Season with salt and freshly ground white pepper and the fresh basil.

Bring back the shrimp for a minute, then place on a serving plate and top with the reduction. Sprinkle the parsley over the final dish as a garnish. Serve at once with rice. Scampi are a cross between lobster and shrimp.

White Onion Soup with White Cheddar Cheese

> 2 pounds white onions, thinly sliced
> 6 ounces unsalted butter
> 1½ cups dry white wine
> 1½ quarts chicken stock (chicken broth)
> Pinch of ground caraway seeds
> Pinch of ground thyme
> 1 bay leaf
> Salt
> Ground white pepper
> ½ pound sharp white cheddar cheese

In a stainless steel saucepot, sauté the onions in butter over low heat, stirring frequently, till they are transparent but not brown. Add the wine and seasonings. Pour in the chicken stock and simmer for 15 minutes.

Use onion soup bowls and top with croutons and sliced or grated cheddar cheese. Bake under a cheese melter until nice and brown.

Watercress Cream Soup   Serves 12–14

> 1 ounce cottonseed oil
> 2 ounces sweet butter
> 3½ medium onions, sliced
> 5 ounces celery, sliced

6 medium potatoes, diced
9 cups chicken bouillon
Salt
White pepper
3 cups half and half
5 bunches watercress leaves

Heat oil and butter in a saucepan. Add onion and celery and simmer until soft. Add the diced potatoes and the bouillon, then boil till the potatoes are soft.

Add the watercress and cook for another 5 minutes. Remove from heat and purée the soup in a food processor. Season with salt and pepper and chill.

Before serving the soup, add the cream, adjust the seasoning, and garnish with a few raw watercress leaves. Serve hot or cold.

Vichyssoise   Serves 10

This is an American specialty. The procedure is similar to watercress cream soup, but with leeks and potatoes.

1¾ ounces butter
1¼ pounds leeks, finely chopped
2½ quarts clear chicken stock
1 spice clove
1 bay leaf
1 large onion, studded with the clove and bay leaf
2½ pounds potatoes, diced
2 cups heavy cream
5 ounces butter-toasted croutons
1 bunch chives

Melt the butter in a saucepot and sauté the leeks. Pour in the chicken stock. Add the studded onion and the potatoes. Cook till the potatoes are soft. Purée in a blender with the cream and adjust seasoning.

When serving, garnish with chopped chives and serve the butter-toasted croutons on the side. Can also be served hot or cold.

Butter-Toasted Croutons

Use sliced white sandwich bread. Cut off the crusts and then cut into ¼-inch dice.

In a shallow frying pan, melt some butter till it starts to foam. Add the diced bread and with a shaking motion let the croutons get nice and brown. Pour into a strainer, then lay out on a paper towel to cool.

The leftover butter can be used for any other type of cooking. Never waste.

Ham buffet display Sheraton Boston Hotel

CHAPTER 17

HOME MADE SAUSAGES

Let's make some homemade sausages. Sausage making is a completely different subject and needs its fullest attention. You have to keep everything very clean while you work; otherwise, you could end up with a product that's not fit for human consumption. The ingredients have to be of top quality and absolutely fresh. Also, you need to work in a cool place to prevent spoilage. Most of the sausages you buy in the store contain preservatives. The recipes I list here do not have any preservatives and therefore have a short life span. First, we will make curried bratwurst.

Curried Bratwurst   **Yields about 4 pounds**

   3 pounds boneless pork shoulder (it will contain about 1 pound of fat),
      cut into small pieces
   ½ pound boneless lean beef, cut into small pieces
   1 teaspoon salt
   3 teaspoons curry powder
   1½ teaspoons ground coriander
   1½ teaspoons ground white pepper

1 teaspoon English mustard
½ teaspoon ground ginger
¼ cup cold water
3 yards prepared hog casing

Grind meat and salt together using a fine blade.

Stir spices into cold water. Pour over meat and mix thoroughly, using your hands to knead the mixture.

Fill casing loosely, twisting into 5-inch links. Immediately refrigerate sausage. Use within two days and freeze the remainder.

To broil or grill, place sausages into boiling water and simmer for about 15 minutes. Broil about 3 inches from the heat. Turn and broil till nice and brown.

⚜   ⚜   ⚜

Chorizos

3 pounds lean pork, cut into small pieces
½ pound skinless fresh pork fatback, cut into small pieces
4 pounds lean beef from the shoulder
1 medium onion, finely chopped
4 cloves garlic, crushed
1 teaspoon paprika
1 teaspoon oregano
1 teaspoon brown sugar
3 teaspoons chili powder
1 teaspoon ground pepper
¼ teaspoon coriander
½ teaspoon cumin
1 teaspoon salt
⅓ cup red wine vinegar
3½ yards prepared hog casing

Grind together pork, fatback, beef, onion, and garlic medium fine.

Mix together the spices, sugar, and wine vinegar. Pour over the meat and knead by hand till all the liquid is completely absorbed.

Chill overnight in the refrigerator before stuffing into casing. Stuff into 6-inch links and tie with butcher string.

Any remaining meat you did not use in the sausages can be frozen and later used as part of a meatloaf.

To cook, place links in a skillet, add some water, and cook till the water has evaporated. Continue cooking until brown on all sides.

Kielbasa

> 1½ pounds pork butt, cut into small pieces
> ½ pound lean beef, cut into small pieces
> 1 teaspoon salt
> ½ teaspoon pepper
> 3 cloves garlic, crushed
> 1 teaspoon marjoram
> 1 teaspoon caraway seeds
> ¼ teaspoon nutmeg
> 3 teaspoons cold water
> 2½ yards prepared hog casing

Grind the meat twice with a medium blade.

Mix all spices with the cold water and pour over the meat. Knead the mixture until thoroughly blended.

Chill the mixture overnight and then stuff into the casing, making links the desired length (kielbasas are generally about 2 feet long with the ends tied together to form a circle). Refrigerate for up to 3 days.

To cook, place sausage in a large skillet, prick with a fork or large needle, cover with water, and simmer for about 45 minutes. Remove from water and cut into rounds. Brown in a small amount of vegetable oil and serve with sauerkraut and boiled potatoes.

Breakfast Sausages

> 3 pounds fresh lean boneless pork
> 2 teaspoons ground sage
> 2 teaspoons marjoram
> ½ teaspoon nutmeg
> 2 teaspoons salt
> 1 teaspoon freshly ground black pepper
> ⅓ cup warm water
> 4 yards prepared lamb casing

Grind the meat twice, using a fine blade.

Stir seasonings into water and pour over ground meat. Knead well till thoroughly blended. Refrigerate mixture overnight.

Stuff into casing and turn into 3-inch links. You also can make patties or freeze in bulk. It can also be used for poultry stuffing.

To fry, place a link in a pan with a small amount of water. Pierce links on all sides. Cook over medium heat until all the water evaporates. Continue cooking until browned on all sides.

Veal Puna

This is a Hawaiian specialty.

> Cottage cheese
> Pineapple juice
> Mango chutney
> Curry powder

Salt
Ground white pepper
Tabasco sauce
3 each 2-ounce veal medallions from the veal tenderloin (milk fed)
¼ wedge papaya
½ banana, cut into oblong slices
2 strawberries

Combine cottage cheese, pineapple juice, mango chutney, curry powder, salt, pepper, and Tabasco sauce in a blender. Sauté the veal medallions in butter but do not flour dust.

Place on a dinner plate and top with the blender sauce, then garnish with the fruit sections.

Broiled Beef Tenderloin with Brie or Blue Cheese   Serves 1

Use a 7-ounce well-trimmed beef tenderloin. Season it with salt and freshly ground black pepper to taste. Broil it to order and then top with 3 ounces of brie. Melt under the cheese melter or salamander. Serve with a baked potato and asparagus.

To make it with the blue cheese topping, add some soft butter to the blue cheese and make a paste. Top the meat, then let it melt so that it just covers the top nicely. Serve with the same garnish.

Gypsy Brochette

This was an item we had on the menu as light fare without soup or salad.

I used tender tips to produce the brochette. It had red and green bell peppers, onions, and mushroom caps and came on a metal skewer on a bed of Spanish rice, topped with garlic-laced demi-glacé.

The meat was marinated with thyme, black pepper, curry powder, broken bay leaves, and olive oil. It was done on the broiler.

Glazed Carrots

Slice medium-size carrots into ⅛-inch-thick wheels. Caramelize butter and sugar till lightly brown. Add Perrier water and clear chicken stock. Season with salt.

Reduce the sugar, butter, water, and chicken stock to a light syrup. Add the sliced carrots and simmer, covered with parchment paper, for about 10 to 15 minutes until the remaining liquid glazes the carrots. Sprinkle with chopped parsley.

Meat Loaf Swiss House

¼ ground pork
¼ lean ground veal
¼ ground beef (ground round)
¼ milk-soaked white sandwich bread
Chopped onion
Chopped parsley
Minced garlic
Ground pepper
Nutmeg
Milk
White wine
Seasoning salt

Mix all ingredients together, then bake in a cake pan at 350 degrees till the liquid on the side of the mold shows clear. Serve with a mushroom-laced demi-glacé and mashed potatoes.

⚜ ⚜ ⚜

Swiss Onion Soup

Salad oil
All-purpose flour
Finely sliced white onions
Chicken or clear beef stock
1 whole onion, spiked with clove and bay leaf

The homemaker could use beef or chicken base without MSG and seasoning salt.

Make a blonde roux (lightly brown) with the salad oil and the flour. It should be soft, meaning somewhat liquid. Then add the sliced onions to the hot roux. Stir well till the onions are tender.

Remove the pot from the heat and slowly pour the boiling chicken stock or clear beef stock into the hot roux, stirring constantly with the aid of a wire whip till everything is lump-free. Bring it back to the stove. Season with salt as needed. Then add the spiked onion and simmer for about 1 hour or so. Skim off the excess oil and check for seasoning.

During Mardi Gras, we have a special flour soup in the Canton Basel-Stadt in Switzerland whose name translates into "burned flour soup" and also "hangover soup." It is similar to the white onion soup, but the flour is roasted dry and fairly dark but not burned. Then you add the hot clear beef bouillon. Make sure you let the roasted flour cool off before you add the stock to it because you could get burned. It is very hot.

Season with several spiked onions and fortify with the necessary seasonings and maybe some beef base. The soup should be cooked over low heat for a couple of hours to reduce the flour taste. When the soup is served, add a shot of red wine and some Parmesan cheese to it.

My last day in the kitchen at the Swiss house

RECIPE INDEX

Osso Buco	98
Gremolata	100
Blue Cheese Dressing	100
Brandy Cocktail Sauce	101
Spaetzli	101
Meat Sauce	102
Caramel Custard	103
Polenta	105
Saltimbocca Romana with Chicken	105
Jaegerschnitzel	106
Pâte Brisée	107
Chocolate Mousse	108
Curried Noodles	109
Cucumber, Swiss Cheese, and Onion Salad	109
Kartoffelpuffer	110
Geschnetzeltes Nach Zücher Art	112
Rösti Potatoes	113
Veal Sweetbreads	113
Frozen Lemon Soufflé	114
Béchamel Sauce	115
Crêpes Suzette	115
Syrup	116
Semmelknoedel	117
Fillet Goulash Stroganoff	117
English Sherry Brandy Trifle	118
Custard Sauce	119
Hot Chocolate Soufflé	120
Shrimp Lil	121
Portuguese Bean Soup	122
Chinese Omelet	122

Tournedos Flambé Swiss House   123
Steak Diane   124
Onion Soup with Three Types of Onion   125
Green Goddess Dressing   126
Hungarian Goulash   127
Vegetable Soup   127
Garlic Butter   128
Roasted Honey Glazed Duck   129
Coq au Vin   130
Gazpacho Soup   131
Thousand Island Dressing   132
Ceviche   133
Pork Chow Mein   133
Beef Tips with Oyster Sauce   134
Steak au Poivre   135
Chicken Cordon Blue   136
Hot Pepper Jelly   138
Fried Shrimp with Walnuts   139
Chicken in Lemon Sauce   142
Fried Mixed Vegetables   143
Walnut Vinaigrette Dressing   144
Tartar Sauce   144
Pork Stew with Lentil and Dill   145
Poached Alaskan Salmon in Romaine Lettuce   146
Satés   147
    Saté Sauce   148

Pork Chops Crusted with Sage and Fennel Crust   148
Poached Chilean Sea Bass Swiss House   149
Shrimp Fajitas with Sabor   150
Poitrine de Volaille Princesse   150
    Creamed Mushrooms   151

Chicken Normandy with Walnut Sauce   152

Beef Shish Kebab ... 153
German Potato Salad ... 153
Ratatouille Provençal ... 154
Chefs Karl's Fried Rice ... 155
Scampi Amoureuse ... 156
Stuffed Cabbage Rolls ... 157
Ravioli Dough ... 157
   Ravioli Stuffing ... 158

Hasenpfeffer ... 159
Sweet and Sour Pork ... 160
Pork Adobo with Spinach ... 161
Red Cabbage ... 162
Roast Duck in a Melon ... 163
Saffron Risotto with Prawns, Fresh Shiitake, and White Mushrooms ... 164
Braised Lamb Shanks (Chef Karl's way) ... 164
Bouillabaisse Marseillaise ... 165
Moules Marinière ... 167
Three Fillets Musketeers ... 168
Tomato Concasse ... 168
Paella Valenciana ... 168
Swiss Cheese Fondue ... 170
Wine Braised Beef ... 170
Bircher Muesli ... 172
Mini Pizza Florentine ... 174
Lecco Poulet ... 174
Sauerbraten ... 175
Pork Barbeque Spare Ribs ... 176
   Barbeque Sauce ... 177

Baked Beans ... 178
Beef Rouladen ... 178
Basler Zwiebelsuppe ... 179

German Beer Soup 180

Peanut Soup 181

Chicken with Peanuts 181

Swiss Meringues 182

Hawaiian Stuffed Prawns 184

Goulash Soup 184

Mulligatawny Soup 185

Dungeness Crab Bisque 186

Crème Fraîche 187

Mee Goreng 187

Shortcake Biscuits 188

Baked Apples with Custard Sauce 189

Chinese Bamboo-Steamed Vegetables 189

Cheese and Mushroom Pies 190

Lasagna Bolognese 191

Cannelloni Al Sugo 192
   Dough 192
   Stuffing 193

Braised Veal Short Ribs Pizzaiola 193

Fudge Brownies 195

Orange Hazelnut Biscotti 195

Fruitcake 196

Baked Noodles Printaniere (Springtime) 197

Linguine with Shrimp, Asparagus Tips, and Basil 199

King Crab Cioppino 199

Jambalaya Louisiana Style 200

Veal Steak with Fresh Morel Sauce (Swiss Style) 201

Butter Confect (Piped Butter Cookies) 202

Arroz con Pollo (Chicken with Rice) 203

Grilled Lobster Tail with Cumin, Lime Butter, and 204
   Avocado Pico de Gallo
   Lobster 204
   Pico de Gallo 204

Tandoori Style Chicken with Mango Jasmine Rice   205
Chicken in Red Wine   206
Cream of Brie Cheese and Leek Soup   208
Blackened Red Snapper   208
  Seasoning   209

Mongolian Lamb   210
Indonesian Style: King Prawns with Peanuts   211
Gnocchi Parisienne   212
Beef Steak Tartare   220
Braised Leeks Baked with a Mornay Sauce   221
Baked Swiss Chard   221
Congee   222
Grapefruit   223
Caraway Seeds   223
Sweet Basil   223
Pound Cake   224
Vanilla Waffle   224
Almond Biscotti   225
Butter Cookies   228
Macadamia Nut Brittle   229
Butter Cream for Pastries and Cakes   229
Pastry Cream   230
Praline Mixture   231
Beer Batter   231
Swiss Woven Egg Bread (Challah) Zopf   232
Veal Scallopine: Swiss House   233
Flamed Bananas Swiss House   234
Shrimp Toast (Chinese Style)   242
  Peanut Sauce   243

Swiss House Egg Rolls   244
Rice Pilaf   246
Risotto   246

Marinade   247

Homemade Noodles   247

Frog Legs Swiss House   248

Emmentaler Cheese Toast   249

Rice Pudding   249

Shrimp and Vegetable Tempura   250

Green Noodles with Pesto   251

Swedish Meatballs   251

Polenta Swiss Italian Style   252

Roasted Almonds   253

Clam Casino   254

Strawberry Shortcake   254

Oysters Rockefeller   256

Popover   256

German Apple Cake   257

Chocolate Macaroons   258

Veal Scallopine with Gruyère Cheese   264

Egli Fillets with Almonds (Perch)   274

Ladyfingers (Biscuits)   275

Empire Toast   275

Peppercorn-Spiked Chopped Sirloin   276

Fillet de Sole Prince Murat   290

Cornettes D'oeufs Grand-Mère (Grandmother)   290

Pommes Walterspiel (Baked Apples)   290

Chocolate Sauce   291

Pommes Elisabeth   291

Toast Woodcock   291

Risotto Verbena   291

Macaroni Pasticciata   292

Hollandaise Sauce   292

Croute des Gourmets   292

Pâte à Frire (Beer Batter)   293

Escalope de Veal Holstein   293
Fillet de Sole Ostende Cleopatra   293
Toast William   294
Stuffed Bell Peppers Indian Style   294
Crêpes Bergere   295
Sauce Remoulade   295
Mayonnaise   295
Tripe in Tomato Sauce   296
Ham Hocks with Sauerkraut   297
Bread Pudding   297
Medallion of Venison   299
Côtes D'agneau Vert-Pré (Lamb Chops Broiled   300
   or Panfried)
Provençal Tomatoes   300
Baked Brie Cheese in Puff Pastry Served with   300
   Horseradish Sauce
Crawfish Etouffee   301
   Seasoning   301
   Main Dish   301

Oyster Stew   302
Swiss Apple Tart with Custard Topping   303
   Custard Topping   303

Flamed Veal Kidneys Armagnac   304
Whitefish Provençal   305
Irish Soda Bread   305
Irish Stew   306
Lavash (Middle Eastern Sesame Cracker Bread)   307
Busecca: Ticino Tripe Soup from the Swiss Italian Region   308
Zurich-Style Tripe   309
Braised Rabbit   309
Rösti Jura Style   310
Liver Kebabs   311

Pork Roast   311
Roasted Veal Short Ribs   312
Gluewein (Mulled Wine)   313
Banana Nut Bread   314
Curry Flavored Peanut Soup   314
Veal Medallion Mediterranean   315
Caraway's Radiatore Pasta with Mushrooms and Cream   316
Poached Scallops Contessa   317
Creamy Yellow Squash Soup   318
Yokohama Soup   318
Scampi in Champagne   319
White Onion Soup with White Cheddar Cheese   320
Watercress Cream Soup   320
Vichyssoise   321
Butter-Toasted Croutons   322
Curried Bratwurst   323
Chorizos   324
Kielbasa   325
Breakfast Sausages   326
Veal Puna   326
Broiled Beef Tenderloin with Brie or Blue Cheese   327
Gypsy Brochette   327
Glazed Carrots   328
Meat Loaf Swiss House   328
Swiss Onion Soup   329

CPSIA information can be obtained
at www.ICGtesting.com
Printed in the USA
BVHW021605190522
637508BV00020BA/658